SAVED BY THE BILLIONAIRE

ERIN SWANN

BECAUSE YOU DON'T ALWAYS HAVE TO BE A LADY.

Cover image licensed from Shutterstock.com

Cover design by Swann Publications

Edited by Jessica Royer Ocken

Proofreaders: Donna Hokanson, Tamara Mataya, Rosa Sharon

Typo Hunters: Michelle Bonner, Renee Williams

ISBN-13: 978-1790324989

The following story is intended for mature readers. It contains mature themes, strong language, and sexual situations. All characters are 18+ years of age, and all sexual acts are consensual.

If you would like to hear about Erin's new releases and sales, join the newsletter. We only email about sales or new releases, and we never share your information.

If you enjoy this book, please leave a review.

Find out more about the author and upcoming books online at:

WWW.ERINSWANN.COM

ALSO BY ERIN SWANN

The Billionaire's Trust - Available on Amazon, also in AUDIOBOOK

(Bill and Lauren's story) He needed to save the company. He needed her. He couldn't have both. The wedding proposal in front of hundreds was like a fairy tale come true—Until she uncovered his darkest secret.

The Youngest Billionaire - Available on Amazon

(Steven and Emma's story) The youngest of the Covington clan, he avoided the family business to become a rarity, an honest lawyer. He didn't suspect that pursuing her could destroy his career. She didn't know what trusting him could cost her.

The Secret Billionaire – Available on Amazon, also in AUDIOBOOK

(Patrick and Elizabeth's story) Women naturally circled the flame of wealth and power, and his is brighter than most. Does she love him? Does she not? There's no way to know. When he stopped to help her, Liz mistook him for a carpenter. Maybe this time he'd know. Everything was perfect. Until the day she left.

The Billionaire's Hope - Available on Amazon

(Nick and Katie's story) They came from different worlds. She hadn't seen him since the day he broke her brother's nose. Her family retaliated by destroying his life. She never suspected where accepting a ride from him today would take her. They said they could do casual. They lied.

Previously titled: Protecting the Billionaire

Picked by the Billionaire – Available on Amazon

(Liam and Amy's story) A night she wouldn't forget. An offer she couldn't refuse. He alone could save her, and she held the key to his survival. If only they could pass the test together.

Caught by the Billionaire – Available on Amazon

(Vincent and Ashley's story) Her undercover assignment was simple enough: nail the crooked billionaire. The surprise came when she opened the folder, and the target was her one-time high school sweetheart. What will happen when an unknown foe makes a move to checkmate?

The Driven Billionaire – Available on Amazon

(Zachary and Brittney's story) Rule number one: hands off your best friend's sister. With nowhere to turn when she returns from upstate, she accepts his offer of a room. Mutual attraction quickly blurs the rules. When she comes under attack, pulling her closer is the only way to keep her safe. But, the truth of why she left town in the first place will threaten to destroy them both.

Join Erin's mailing list and be notified when new books are available.

CHAPTER 1

NATALIE

I STOOD IN LINE AT THE COFFEE SHOP. *Finally a moment of anonymity, a moment of peace.* The clientele at this Peet's was more businessmen and fewer neurotic housewives than the one I'd been frequenting near home. And, nobody here recognized me——at least so far. No one gave me dirty looks, yelled at me, or spit on me. Not yet.

The fireman at the counter rattled off his mega-order at the poor barista, who marked up one cup after another.

"But Lucy, I don't know if I have time for that… But I can't… Okay, okay, okay, you win." The whiny male voice came from behind me.

I glanced back at the lengthening line, held up by the guy ordering for a dozen buddies. Mr. Whiny on the phone to Lucy was the short, bald guy directly behind me.

The broad-shouldered man ahead of me moved up to the counter after Mr. Infinite-List finished reading his litany of assorted concoctions. Ninety-seven dollars and change was a lot of coffee.

I closed my eyes and listened to Broad Shoulders order. I couldn't see his face, but the deep, seductive voice with a hint of gravel predicted a chiseled jawline and stubble——a high-octane man, a real man, unlike the whiny wimp jabbering on his cell phone behind me. The sound of Broad Shoulders's words had me visualizing a deep, dark chocolate pudding, something I could lick all day long.

He ordered a medium caffè mocha, my drink of choice as well.

"Ryan," he said when the barista asked his name.

A very lick-worthy name.

I gulped, realizing how inappropriate my daydreams had become just four months after the divorce. I knew it was four months because the final decree had arrived yesterday. I was finally free of Damien Winterbourne.

When I opened my eyes, Broad Shoulders had paid and moved aside, making room for me to order. I'd been right about him being a high-octane man. The deep blue eyes, the chiseled jawline——everything except the stubble, but that could be cured quickly. Tall and imposing, he tugged at his collar, apparently ill at ease in the expensive suit and tie he wore.

"Miss?" the barista said, pulling me back to reality.

I advanced to the counter. "I'll have the same."

She rang me up and smiled. "And your name?"

I slid my AmEx card into the reader. "Natalie."

The card machine beeped twice, and the little screen read *declined.*

The barista shot me a questioning glance. "Try it again. Sometimes it acts up."

I removed the card and shoved it back in.

The reader complained loudly again.

"Perhaps another card?" the girl behind the counter offered with a sigh.

2

I located my Visa card and tried that with the same embarrassing result. The group in line behind me was restless, and their muttering increased. Nothing nice, no doubt.

"Get a clue, lady" was the only thing I picked out of the mumbling.

Not my day.

I cringed as I pulled back the second card. "Something must be wrong. I'll have to call and get this straightened out." I only had enough cash in my purse to tip the cat groomers.

I left the counter, looking at the floor to avoid the stares of the crowd, and shuffled off to the corner of the store.

The notice on the screen announced a low battery level. I ignored the warning and dialed the number on the back of my Visa. When the annoying mechanical voice asked for it, I keyed in my card number. Instead of giving me my balance information, I was told to wait for the next available agent. I settled into a seat for the wait while the annoying telephone hold music played.

"Caffè mocha, right?" that same one-hundred-octane male voice asked.

I looked up to see Mr. Broad Shoulders, Ryan, holding two cups, with an iPad tucked under one arm.

He held a cup out for me. The full-on sight of this man froze me in place, now that I got a good look at him. His bottomless blue eyes captured me and wouldn't let go.

"Here, take it; I can't drink two." The voice was even deeper and more chocolaty than it had been at the counter.

"You shouldn't have," I offered feebly, reaching for my purse.

His brow knit, and he thrust the cup forward. "Here, I can't miss my quota."

I accepted the cup with my free hand. "Quota?"

His smile returned. "When I was ten, I promised my mother to do at least one good deed a week."

My grin nearly broke my face. "Really?"

A man who kept a promise to his mother couldn't be all bad. Or else it was the most off-the-wall pickup line I'd ever heard.

He turned and walked toward the door.

Not a pick-up line evidently.

"Thank you," I called after him, watching his tight ass like the pervert I was. Hell, it had been a long time, after all. I deserved to watch if I wanted.

My phone buzzed with an incoming text. I removed the phone from my ear and checked the screen.

BROSNAHAND: Call me - we need to talk

Another chat with Mason Brosnahand, my ex-husband's lawyer, was not going to rise to the top of my list today, and probably not even tomorrow. Whatever information Damien's lawyer had to pass on was unlikely to brighten my outlook. Even after agreeing to the divorce, Damien still wanted to talk to me, but the feeling wasn't mutual.

Becoming Damien Winterbourne's wife had been the worst mistake of my life. He'd fooled me, along with all the people who now regretted ever having done business with him. To every one of my previous so-called friends, sharing his last name now meant sharing his guilt. The Winterbourne name was radioactive in Boston, at least until the memories faded.

As soon as I sold the house, I'd get as far away from here as I could, as fast as I could.

Damien was cooling his heels in jail awaiting trial, a good place for him to be. The judge had been perceptive enough to see him as a flight risk.

I ended the call with the credit card company. Waiting on terminal hold would be more comfortable at home. The phone went back in my purse.

I collected my free mocha, my purse, and added a packet of sweetener to my cup before heading out. Coffee wasn't the purpose of my trip to this part of town. Cartier Jewelers next door was about to open.

Turning right out of Peet's, I stopped in my tracks. I stifled my laugh.

With his coffee in one hand and his iPad in the other, Ryan was using his chin to scroll the text on the tablet. He read a page and chin-scrolled down to read some more.

I ventured closer, stretching my smirk to a smile. "Thank you for the coffee, Ryan."

He glanced in my direction. "You already said that." He went back to his reading.

Somebody has a stick up his ass.

Thankfully I didn't mouth the words.

"You're welcome, Natalie," he added after another chin-scroll.

He'd noticed my name, a point in his favor.

I found myself glancing at his profile in the morning sun more than once, a lot more. I decided the face was one a Roman sculptor would have chosen.

After a few minutes of silence between us, Jonas Gisler, the store manager, came to unlock the door.

As I entered behind Ryan, the wall clock read ten exactly. Herr Gisler was Swiss and proudly precise, I'd learned.

Ryan went directly to the counter reserved for the ruby jewelry.

I waited.

"Mrs. Winterbourne, what may I help you with today?" Gisler asked with his Teutonic smile.

Surprise filled Ryan's face. "I was here first," he announced loudly.

Gisler was unmoved as he continued to watch for my response to his question. My status as a repeat customer seemed to trump Ryan's position in line.

I pointed toward Ryan. "It's Spencer now, Mr. Gisler, and he's right; he was first."

Gisler's smile broke down to a mild grin. "As you wish." He moved to the ruby counter. "What may I help you with today, sir?"

Ryan pointed through the glass. "I'd like to see that one, please."

I shuffled closer, pretending to scan the cases for a purchase.

The female sales associate emerged from the back room. She smiled at me politely, but stayed away.

She knew I only dealt directly with Mr. Gisler.

Gisler pulled out a ruby necklace with a huge heart-shaped stone set in a circle of diamonds, and laid it on a velvet mat.

Ryan looked at it, perplexed. "No, that won't do." He didn't bother to check the price tag, as any normal person would have. "Let's see the next one over."

Gisler complied, bringing up another gorgeous necklace.

Ryan shook his head.

"Perhaps if you were to tell me your parameters, I might recommend a few pieces," Gisler offered.

Ryan ignored him and pointed to another necklace and then two more. None of them pleased him.

Gisler sighed. "Perhaps a feminine perspective might help? Mrs. Spencer here has exquisite taste."

I blushed at the compliment.

"Sure," Ryan said, casting a glance my way.

I moved next to him, but avoided eye contact, lest I freeze up. "I'll try, and it's Miss."

"I don't have a lot of time," Ryan said. "I'm due in court soon." His body heat became perceptible as he shifted closer.

"A lawyer, huh?"

He tugged at his collar. "No," he said curtly, my hint to shut up.

The answer explained why he seemed uncomfortable in his expensive suit. A lawyer also would have used a page worth of words instead of one.

A quick peek at the price tags on the necklaces he'd chosen

showed prices from forty to seventy thousand. This was one lucky woman.

"Special occasion?" I asked.

"Her birthday," he replied, choosing more than a single word answer this time.

I'd checked his left hand earlier and found no wedding ring, which most likely meant special girlfriend gift.

"How about this one on the front row, the second from the end," I told the store owner. It was a beautiful, heart-shaped, blood red ruby paired with a smaller heart-shaped diamond. I'd never seen something so lovely.

Gisler brought out the pendant and placed it on the cloth.

"That's too small," Ryan said.

It looked perfect to me. "If I got that for my birthday, I'd be over the moon."

He frowned. "Too small."

If he went too big now, he'd have a hard time topping it with the engagement ring. But that was *his* problem.

"Mr. Gisler, those three in the back, please." I pointed out three more modest stones than he had originally chosen——a little less ostentatious, more ruby and less diamond surround.

"She must be very special to you. Wife? Girlfriend?"

He shook his head. "Sister."

"Right," I said, letting too much disbelief color my voice.

He turned toward me. "Yes, sister." Annoyance tinged his words.

"Then we want to avoid these heart-shaped stones." I pointed out the first several he'd selected. "Mr. Gisler, the third from the end please."

The jeweler pulled out a beautiful cushion-cut solitaire ruby on a white-gold chain without a diamond surround. It was way too large for any normal person to give his sister, but the smile on Ryan's face said we'd found the one.

The price tag was face down, and he didn't bother to turn it over. Instead, he handed his AmEx card to Gisler. "I'd like it gift wrapped and overnighted to this address in California," he said, pulling a piece of paper from his wallet.

"I can take care of that for you, sir." Gisler took the card and the paper to his register.

I moved back to a more respectful distance. "What'd you do wrong?"

He cocked his head. "Pardon?"

"That's an awfully expensive birthday gift." I couldn't believe he didn't see how absurd it was.

His eyes flicked downward. "I forgot her birthday last year."

If I'd forgotten my sister's birthday, she'd be getting a scarf at best. "And you think she's expecting something like this?" The man would rate as totally clueless if he agreed with my question.

"I think she'll complain like crazy actually, but that's just tough. She'll have to take it."

He didn't seem to understand the difference between expecting something this extravagant and accepting such a beautiful gift. If I opened something like this on my birthday, you wouldn't be able to pry it away from me with dynamite.

Gisler returned with the credit card and charge slip.

I couldn't resist peeking. Fifty-eight thousand dollars. If I had a brother, I would want one like Ryan, although right now my hormones were casting him for a different role than brother. Way different.

He replaced the card in his wallet. "You can get it there tomorrow?"

Gisler stiffened as if it was an insult. "You can rely on me, sir."

I shocked myself by reaching over to touch Ryan briefly on the arm.

He didn't recoil. Instead, a warm smile tugged at his lips.

"Ryan," I said. "You know, flowers and a phone call go a long way as well."

He nodded. "Appreciate the advice, Miss Spencer."

"Natalie," I corrected him.

He checked his watch and quickly collected his receipt. "Thank you again," he said, reaching the door in a few rapid strides. "Natalie," he added before the door closed behind him.

Gisler took a loud breath. "Now, Miss Spencer, how may I help you?"

I opened my purse and pulled the red velvet pouch out of the side zipper-pocket. "I'd like to get these cleaned, if I could." I handed him the pouch. "And the post on one of them needs some looking after."

He gently opened the bag and slid out the earrings, my pride and joy. "My. They look more lovely every time I see them."

"Thank you." They were the best pair of diamond earrings I would ever own, eight total carats of beautiful brilliance. Damien and I had bought them here.

He held them up for a closer inspection. "Yes, I see. I can have these ready for you after lunch, if that's acceptable." He filled out the yellow receipt for the jewelry as he always did and slid it across to me.

I nodded. "Perfect. I'll be by around one." That would give me time to pick up Ralph and get to the gym before returning. I folded the yellow cleaning receipt neatly and placed it in the same pocket of my purse that had held the earrings. I carefully zipped it shut before leaving.

The long scratch on my arm still stung.

I'd been told some cats liked car rides. Ralph was not among them, as this morning's scratch proved. Once I'd gotten him to the groomer's, though, his mood had changed, as it always did. He loved the attention. Now I just needed a Star Trek transporter to get him there without having to load him into the car.

I bid Mr. Gisler goodbye and sucked down half my mocha on the way back to the car.

Starting the engine, the radio came alive with Frank Sinatra singing "That's Life." His tune could be my theme song, a reminder to never give up, regardless of the obstacles.

First, there had been Damien's arrest, followed by the ridicule and shame, and then the divorce. Now, I finally had my name back. Once I sold the house and left this city, I could reclaim my future, in a place where the Winterbourne stigma wouldn't follow me. Natalie Winterbourne's life was over, but Natalie Spencer's was ahead of me. I could feel it.

Like a sign, the road bent left, and the sun beat in through the windshield, lifting my spirits. I turned the music up high.

The drive home went quickly in light mid-day traffic, with fewer than normal crazies on the road.

I turned the corner onto my street, and there they were. Two police cars and three black SUVs in front of my house.

I pulled up to the garage and climbed out of the car with my battle face on. I'd had enough of these searches already. They'd been here only last week, for Christ's sake.

But this time was different. Some of the windbreakers had US MARSHAL in bold yellow lettering on the back, in addition to the usual FBI jerks.

The uniformed cop held up his hand as I reached the walk. "Hold it, ma'am. You can't go in."

I started past him. "The hell I can't, this is my house," I said loudly.

He grabbed my arm. "Agent White," he called.

I wrested my arm loose, but stopped where I was. The last thing I needed was some stupid cop tasering me in the back, on my own property.

One of the agents from last week trotted over. He flipped open his badge momentarily, as they all did. They could be dime-store replicas for all the time they *didn't* give me to inspect them.

"Special Agent White," he announced like it should mean something to me. "Mrs. Winterbourne, I'll need your car keys."

This had happened each time. They wanted to search the car as well as the house.

The key fob was still in my hand. I hadn't stashed it in my purse yet. I handed him the fob with a huff. "It's Spencer now, and how long is this going to take? I have to go pick up my cat."

A beefy agent was pulling up the for sale sign on the lawn.

"Hey, cut that out," I yelled in his direction.

Agent White pocketed my key fob. "Mrs. Winterbourne," he said, intentionally trying to piss me off for sure. "This house and automobile, and all the contents, are being seized as products of a criminal enterprise."

"That can't be right," I gasped.

"For any questions about this forfeiture, you may contact the AUSA." He offered me a business card.

I had no idea what that meant, and it must have shown on my face.

"Assistant United States Attorney Willey," he said.

I couldn't be hearing this right.

He forced the card at me again. "You need to talk to him about this."

I took it. *Kirk Willey, Assistant United States Attorney*, it read.

The agent pointed toward the street. "You need to step off the property now, Mrs. Winterbourne."

With my legs shaking, and my breakfast threatening to come up, tears clouded my eyes. "But, this is my house."

"Not any longer," Agent White said coldly. He moved his hand to the butt of his gun.

CHAPTER 2

Ryan

My watch said a quarter of ten. I was running late as I parked across the street from the courthouse. Picking out a necklace for my sister, Alyssa, had taken longer than I'd expected. Without the pretty blonde's help, it would've been even longer. Hopeless didn't begin to describe how I'd felt trying to choose. They all looked so similar.

When Natalie had picked out a piece, I knew I had to go with it. The woman had class; that much was obvious. I sensed that anything she picked would be a winner with my sister.

Tomorrow was Alyssa's birthday. If it hadn't been for the two reminders I'd put on my phone, I would have missed it again this year. And I'd have been up shit creek. I had pi memorized to twenty-five places, but somehow the simple things in life slipped by me.

Jogging across the street, I tugged at my collar for the umpteenth time. I was losing this fucking tie as soon as I got out of court, but I'd been warned: court was all about appearances.

Just inside the glass doors, I took my place in the security line marked *visitors*. It was backed up——not as far as an airport line, but it moved even slower. Every time a person went through the metal detector, the beeping sounded and they were forced back through a second or a third time by the guards.

There was a second metal detector labeled *employees*. Naturally that one had no line. It might be turned off for all I could tell. It hadn't squawked once as a few dozen suits passed through, all without removing their belts the way we were being forced to do.

I checked my watch. Court had started five minutes ago.

The woman in front of me tried and failed with a loud beep. After removing her earrings, she was successful.

Even though I'd emptied my pockets and taken off my watch and belt, I failed the first time through the detector. A quick recheck of my pockets netted a dime I'd missed. After I put it in the little bowl, the machine decided it was done with me and would torture the next in line.

The marshal at the x-ray machine motioned to his tall buddy. They didn't like the picture of my tray of miscellaneous items.

The taller one extracted my lucky knife from the tray before sliding it in my direction. "Sir, no knives allowed in the building. You can pick this up on your way out."

I carried that little red knife with me everywhere. These guys were as bad as the TSA. "It's just a Swiss Army knife," I complained.

Big mistake.

"Step over here, sir," the taller marshal said. "Arms out to your side." He picked up a hand wand to scan me again. "No knife of any kind in the building."

I stood still for the extra scan, the pat down, and the slow-motion examination of my shoes. Clearly I was being taught a lesson about questioning the wisdom of the bureaucracy. To them, a knife was a knife, and I should have kept my mouth shut.

"You're late. You're first on the witness list this morning," our lawyer's assistant informed me when I made it upstairs to the courtroom. "The judge is not happy."

I entered through the double doors.

"So nice of you to join us, Dr. Westerly," the judge said into the microphone in front of him, visibly checking his watch. The amplified displeasure in his voice reverberated off the walls.

～

NATALIE

I SHUFFLED TO THE SIDEWALK.

Not my house any longer?

How could they do this? This was America. They couldn't just up and take my house. I hadn't done anything. I hadn't been arrested. I hadn't been tried. I hadn't been convicted. I was the victim here. Damien had taken from me too——two years of my life, and worse than that, my good name.

A small crowd was gathering across the street.

I blinked back the tears. Theresa, Stephanie, Marci, Ellie, Jana ——not one of my previous *friends* would take a call from me. I couldn't go to the coffee shop or the grocery store without getting stares, sneers, and whispered comments.

In school, *The Scarlet Letter* had been assigned reading. I hadn't understood the character's shame until now. In my neighborhood, it was as if I had *crook* tattooed on my forehead. The Peet's Coffee by the jewelry store had been welcome relief and underscored how important it was to get out of my neighborhood to somewhere I could blend in.

The crowd was growing, and staring at me, the freak.

I shouldered my purse and headed east. I gave the crowd the finger. *Fuck 'em.*

The card in my hand said *Federal Courthouse, One Court-*

house Way. I was going to give Mr. Willey a piece of my mind and get my house back. I pulled up the Uber app on my phone to call a ride.

The app balked and asked me to update my payment information. The credit card company was fucking up my day big time. I turned the corner and pulled out my AmEx. I stopped to dial the 800 number on the back. After punching in my card number, I started walking again to put some distance between me and my unfriendly neighborhood while I pissed away time on hold.

I made it a half-dozen blocks before an agent answered. "Can I have your card number and the name on the card please?"

"I just put in my number."

"It didn't come up on my screen. You'll need to read it to me."

I did, and then verified my address and social. "I need to get my card unblocked or whatever."

"Just one moment, Ms. Winterbourne."

I didn't object because I hadn't gotten around to jumping through all the hoops to change my name everywhere yet.

"I'm sorry, Ms. Winterbourne. There's a freeze on your account, and there's nothing I can do for you from here."

"What do you mean a freeze?"

"A law enforcement freeze is the only information I have. There's a phone number and case number noted on the file if you would like to call them."

How much more fucked up can my day get?

I huffed. "Just a moment. Let me get a pen." I pulled a pen and a receipt from my purse and put it up against a shop window to write on the back. "Go ahead."

He gave me the information, and I hung up. The number sounded strangely familiar.

I checked the business card Agent White had given me: Kirk Willey, Assistant US Attorney. That asshole was behind this as well.

Great. Fucking great.

At least I was headed to the right person. My head had started to hurt. Fishing a bottle of Advil from my purse, I popped two in my mouth. I almost gagged trying to swallow them without water. I seriously had to get myself some chewable tablets. I dialed Willey's number while I walked. Another walker gave me the evil, I-know-what-you-did look. I had to get out of Brookline——or out of this damned state was more like it.

"Mrs. Winterbourne, I was expecting your call," Willey answered with a hint of snark.

"It's Spencer now, and there seems to be some mix-up at my house," I started. "They suggested I call you." Poking the bear didn't seem like my best starting strategy.

"No mix-up, Mrs. Winterbourne. You're an unindicted co-conspirator with your husband——"

"Ex-husband," I corrected him.

"No matter. Ex-husband. And, all the marital assets you received are proceeds of his criminal activities and subject to forfeiture."

Tears threatened again. "But I didn't do anything. I didn't know anything about what Damien was doing."

"That's not how the grand jury saw it."

My legs felt weak. I leaned against the side of the building. "But you're not leaving me anything."

"I'm more concerned about all the families you and your husband defrauded. I'm trying to recover a small percentage of what you stole from them. They're the ones who don't deserve this."

"But..." I didn't have any more words.

Willey sighed into the phone. "I can make time for you in a week or so to discuss a resolution to this."

Finally a spark of hope. "What kind of resolution?"

"If you turn over the remaining one hundred and twenty-four million your husband hid, perhaps I can arrange to return your house."

"I don't know anything about hidden money," I told him.
"Have it your way. We'll be watching you. That money is also subject to forfeiture. But frankly, if that's your attitude, I don't see the value in continuing this conversation. Goodbye, Mrs. Winterbourne."

He hung up before I could even object about the name again.

Tears wet my cheeks. This was so unfair.

CHAPTER 3

*R*YAN

THE JUDGE SCOWLED AS I CAME FORWARD.

The jury was to my right as I approached the witness stand. The effect of the judge's admonishment of me showed in their faces.

I couldn't figure out why lawyers insisted on calling this a witness stand, when you sat on a chair behind a low partition. I took the seat after being sworn in and plastered on my version of an amiable smile.

The company had hired presumably the best patent lawyer in Boston, a fellow named Dillard. A better name for him would have been Dullard. He had all the personality of a cardboard box, but that was probably par for the course with patent lawyers.

Dillard ran me through a recitation of my credentials with methodical precision.

One of the juror's heads bobbed as I mentioned graduating from Stanford. A good sign? I had no idea.

I'd been told by Dillard to make eye contact with the jury while testifying, and I did my best to look from one person to the next. My gaze stopped at the pretty young blonde second from the left in the back.

She smiled at me.

My grin increased as I smiled back.

She winked.

"Dr. Westerly, you are the lead researcher at Chameleon Therapeutics, are you not?"

We had rehearsed these lines last week. "Yes, I'm the founder of the company and the lead researcher."

Dillard led me through an hour of testimony on my work on CTX-13, the compound in question in this court case.

Many of the jurors were about to nod off, but not Pretty Young Blonde in the second row. I shot her another smile.

"Are you familiar with the patent application filed by Valestum at issue in this case, Dr. Westerly?" Dillard asked, setting me up for the important question.

"Yes, sir, I am."

Dillard handed me a printout. "And are you familiar with this document?"

"Yes, these are my experimental notes from last May seventeenth."

"And when you reviewed the Valestum patent in question, what struck you as odd?"

I turned to the third page, where the incriminating evidence of their theft was printed. "Here on page three, they refer to percentages of sucrose uptake after seven different time intervals, but the percentages add up to more than one hundred percent."

"And why is that important?"

This was it. "We had been concerned for several months that our experimental data was being stolen——"

Their attorney objected, just as I had been warned he was likely to do.

I waited as the two attorneys approached the judge and argued their points in whispered tones.

The judge instructed me to continue.

"As I said, we had been concerned, so..." I opened up the experimental notes Dillard had handed me. "I inserted false data in my notes here, with the seven percentages adding up to one-hundred-three-point-seven percent. Those exact numbers, in the same order and with the same erroneous result, appear in Valestrum's patent application."

The jurors were now all awake.

"And that proved to you that Valestum was stealing your data?" Dillard asked.

The question drew an immediate objection, but the jurors' faces showed the point had gotten across.

Valestum had stolen our experimental results. We were sure of it. And now they'd been caught.

I smiled at Pretty Young Blonde again.

She returned the favor.

∼

NATALIE

BROSNAHAND'S MESSAGE THIS MORNING HAD PROBABLY BEEN about the shitstorm I had walked into at home. Maybe he could help. Wiping back tears, I opened my contact list to call him back, but the low-battery alert came up on the screen. Seven percent battery.

Fuck.

The phone went back in my purse. My charger was behind the armed guards at my house, and I needed to save what little battery I had left.

I'd just passed a Starbucks. Retracing my steps, I opened the door and took a seat near the door. I rested my head and closed my eyes. I was divorced from Damien Winterbourne and still couldn't escape him. Hidden money? Where was it now that I needed it? I didn't have a fucking thing to my name anymore.

Behind closed eyelids I tried to recall a conversation where Damien might have mentioned stashing money away——a safety deposit box, or a hiding place of some sort. My search came up as empty as my now-growling stomach.

After a few minutes, I worked up the courage to take inventory. When I'd stopped by last night, the ATM nearest my house had been out of service, and my cash situation was pathetic. My wallet contained two worthless credit cards, a driver's license that still read Natalie Winterbourne, a single ten-dollar bill I had planned to use to tip the groomers when I picked up Ralph, and one dollar twenty-seven in change.

I was sure I could stay at my sister's place in Cambridge. She had moved in with Corbin in LA two weeks ago, but had kept her apartment here——ever the cautious girl, my sister Jasmin. I had a key, but first I had to get there.

We had talked last Saturday, but when I tried to remember her schedule for today, I drew a blank. As a flight attendant, she could be anywhere.

When I looked up, the guy behind the counter was staring over with an unwelcoming look. I was using one of his tables but hadn't bought anything. I needed to get moving, and Ralph needed to be picked up.

I turned right out of the coffee shop. Ralph's groomers were on Boylston, a decent walk from here. Good thing I had chosen yoga pants and running shoes instead of a skirt and heels this morning.

Less than an hour later, I mounted the steps to Beantown's Perfect Pet Spa. The girls here only knew me as Natalie. As a result, they had always been nice, and Ralph enjoyed his sessions, once the trip was over.

They brought Ralph out with his little harness on. I'd tried to get him into a carrier before, and that had cost a pint of blood.

"Allison," I told the young groomer. "I'm having trouble with my credit cards this morning. Can you hold the bill and I'll pay it when I bring him by next week?"

Her response was immediate. "Sure, no problem. He's such a good boy." She scratched Ralph behind the ear, and the cat leaned into it, his purr-motor turned up high. "Do you need any help loading him in the car?"

"No, I can handle it. But one more thing, Allison. My phone is almost dead. Could I borrow yours for a moment to make a quick call to my sister?"

"Sure. I forget to charge mine all the time." She offered me the phone out of her apron pocket with a smile.

I thanked her and dialed my sister's number, one of the few I knew by heart. It went to voicemail, and I left a quick message for her to call me back. I mentally crossed my fingers, hoping she wasn't in the air.

Thanking Allison again, I hefted Ralph, with a firm grip on his harness. I left to start the trek to my sister's place in Cambridge, the only refuge in this God-forsaken town I could think of. I felt guilty about not tipping her, but I could tip her twenty the next time Ralph got groomed.

The cat's purring stopped when we reached the door.

Boylston was a busy street. Ralph fought against me with almost every passing car. Getting to Jasmin's place like this wasn't going to be possible. If Ralph struggled free, he'd instantly be missing or road kill.

I waved down a passing cab, and after managing to close the door without losing my grip on Ralph, I told the driver, "Central Square, Cambridge."

The meter started at two-sixty, and clicked higher rapidly. Ralph had calmed down, but the meter wasn't cooperating.

"I only have ten dollars. Will that get me there?"

An annoyed glance in the rearview mirror forewarned me. "No way, lady. You'll be lucky to make the bridge."

I started the tear faucet for real and bawled my head off.

He ignored me.

The meter clicked over to nine-eighty before we reached the Boston University Bridge.

The driver turned off the meter with a huff. "Lady, I'll take you across the bridge, but that's as far as I go. If I get caught carrying ya with my meter off, I could lose my job."

I thanked him profusely. It was my first break of the day. Well, my second if I counted the free coffee.

He nicely let me out just past Memorial Drive. I surrendered my only paper money and made my way along a tree-lined residential street leading to my sister's neighborhood.

It was hard to walk straight, my legs were so jittery. But the lack of traffic calmed Ralph, and I made it to Jasmin's apartment and inside without any further scratches and only two stumbles.

Once inside, I let the angry kitty loose. My phone went on the charger Jasmin kept in the kitchen. The screen woke, with the little apple telling me it had died of battery hunger on the walk over. I laid down on the couch to rest, and just as my eyes closed, the phone rang.

I jerked up so fast I felt slightly faint walking to the counter.

It was Brosnahand, not my sister. I couldn't avoid him forever. How much worse could my day get anyway?

"Natalie, I tried to reach you earlier," he said, "to warn you."

"I know," I mumbled.

He cleared his throat. "I understand you've been to the house."

Tears clouded my eyes again. "They were mean."

"I'm sorry, Natalie. I didn't have any warning this was going to happen. I've already started to do what I can."

"So I can get my house back?"

"I hope so, but these things take time to resolve in court. I'm afraid there's no magic wand. In seizure cases, it's up to us to prove you *deserve* to get the assets back."

"What happened to innocent until proven guilty?"

"These cases are different. I'll do what I can, but it won't be quick."

"But…but they took everything. They even froze my credit cards," I sobbed.

"And your bank accounts as well, I'm afraid. Do you have a place to stay? A friend, perhaps?" he asked.

My legs trembled. "I'm at my sister's, in Cambridge."

"This must be hard for you."

He had no concept. Hard was having a flat tire at night, or an upset stomach from bad seafood. You woke up the next day and those things were just a memory.

I didn't reply. What good would it do? Closing my eyes, I leaned against the counter. I had less than two dollars in change, no food——or litter——for Ralph, and no one to turn to.

"I can loan you some cash to live on if you tell me where I can meet you."

Finally, a piece of news that wasn't worse than the last. My heart raced with anticipation. I gave him Jasmin's address.

"I'll be over in half an hour," he said. "There is one other thing."

I dreaded his next words.

"Damien would like to speak with you."

"No," I said firmly. "I have nothing to say to him." More accurately, I wanted to tell him I looked forward to his sentencing. I certainly had nothing I wanted to hear from him.

"I see." After a pause he added. "I'll be right over, Natalie. I know you've had a hard day. And please call me Mason."

A half hour later, Mason was downstairs handing me five fresh hundred-dollar bills for spending money.

I decided he wasn't half bad after all. He must have just drawn the short straw having to defend Damien.

Back upstairs, Ralph rubbed against my leg as I closed the door.

I pulled a plastic tub from the closet shelf, the one we had used as a temporary box for Ralph last time I'd boarded him with Jasmin for the weekend. If I didn't find something to fill it, I was going to have one pissed-off kitty. A bag of cornmeal in the cupboard looked close enough and would have to do for tonight. And a can of tuna I'd found would suffice for Ralph's rations.

My search had also uncovered a bottle of chardonnay in the fridge. After a second glass, my jitters started dissipating, and I lay down on the couch to rest.

My life officially sucked, but with money in my wallet, the day was ending better than it had started. In a few minutes I'd try Jasmin again. She had to land sooner or later.

∾

RYAN

I'D LOOKED FORWARD TO THIS MORNING IN COURT EVEN LESS THAN a visit to the dentist. But so far it had been worth it. We'd gotten out into the open how Valestum had stolen our work, *my* work. That had been the entire objective of today's session.

Valestum's lawyer rose slowly to begin my cross-examination. He obviously knew he couldn't erase what the jurors had heard.

"Dr. Westerly, do you think it's ethical to submit a patent application on work you didn't yourself do?"

I hesitated. His question didn't make sense. That was exactly why we'd brought suit against Valestum. "No, that's why we're here today."

Dillard shook his head, an admonition that I was saying too much.

I'd been coached to volunteer as little as possible in response to whatever was asked, and I'd already messed up.

"Dr. Westerly, do you consider yourself to be an ethical person?"

The question wasn't one we had prepared for.

"Certainly. Very much so."

It was an insult to consider that I might be anything else.

"Chameleon is your second start-up, is that correct?"

"Yes, sir."

"Your previous company was Luxxamin Biopharma, is that correct?"

I nodded. "Yes."

"I have here a copy of your Chameleon Therapeutics biography. It says you were the founder of Luxxamin, and the inventor of its drug, Luxxastat. Is that correct?"

I smiled. I was proud of my accomplishments there. "Yes, sir, that is correct, and it has been very well received by the medical community."

Dillard's expression was souring for some reason.

I should have stuck to yes or no.

Their attorney moved closer and handed me a lab notebook. "This is the laboratory notebook of Dr. Borsheim of Valestum. Would you turn to page seventy-eight, please."

I accepted the notebook and started leafing through it. I'd interviewed Leonard Borsheim when he'd applied for a job at Chameleon early on. I hadn't been impressed. I stopped on page seventy-eight.

"Do you see the list of percentages of sucrose uptake?"

I did, and I knew the numbers by heart now. "Yes." They were my fake numbers. The ones they had stolen.

"Take your time, Dr. Westerly. What do those numbers add up to?"

I redid the math in my head to avoid being trapped here.

"Do you need a calculator?"

"No," I said. "The total is one hundred and three point seven percent."

The lawyer smiled. "How many patents did you file while at Luxxamin?"

I took in a breath. "None."

"And yet you claim to be the inventor of Luxxastat. And how many patents have you filed while at Chameleon?"

I shifted in my chair. "None."

"And did you file any preliminary patent applications while at either firm?"

I shook my head.

"Yes or no, Dr. Westerly."

"No, but——"

He cut me off. "Just yes or no, and I think you already answered." He paused and faced the jury. "Dr. Westerly, you previously testified that your experimental notes with the incorrect percentage totals were written May seventeenth last year. Will you please read the date at the top of the page in that notebook you are holding."

My mouth went dry.

"Dr. Westerly, the date at the top of the page, please."

"April twenty-first."

Several jurors gasped.

"You told us you were an ethical person, and it wouldn't be ethical to submit a patent based on somebody else's work. Is that why you didn't submit anything on your work, because you had actually stolen it from Valestum?"

Dillard objected vociferously, but the damage had been done.

∼

NATALIE

. . .

THE RINGING OF MY PHONE WOKE ME THAT EVENING.

The empty wine bottle in front of me came into view first. Life sucked, so I hadn't stopped at two glasses.

I struggled up and located the source of the noise on Jasmin's counter, where I'd left the phone. Flicking on the kitchen light, I blinked a few times at the screen and my vision cleared. *Amy Quigley*, the caller ID said.

"Hello?" I unplugged the charging cable.

"Hi, Nat. Hope I didn't catch you at a bad time," she said. Amy had been my freshman- and sophomore-year roommate at Brown. She'd gotten me some part-time work with her boyfriend, Liam Quigley, a few months back. They were married now. Lucky girl.

It was dark out, and the clock on the microwave read eight-twenty.

I hadn't talked to her since Damien's arrest. Damien and her husband, Liam, had been mortal enemies in business. I'd worried it would be awkward talking to either of them.

"No, not at all," I lied. "How have you been? Sorry I missed the wedding. Some things came up with my sister," I lied again.

I'd been too ashamed to go, even though Amy and Liam had kindly invited me. I couldn't bear the stares and whispered comments I knew I would attract.

"You okay? You sound like you're coming down with a cold."

I was still snuffly from the crying. "Allergies is all."

"If it's not too much, I——we, need your help," she said.

"I'm not sure I have the time right now to be of much help to anyone." All my focus and energy had to go to climbing out of the shitter and getting my life back.

"I know it must be hard after everything with Damien."

She didn't know the half of it. She'd found a wonderful life and had a great husband handed to her on a platter.

I'd gotten stuck with Damien, who was ten steps, at least, below dog shit.

"I'm getting by."

"I thought of you, because Liam has a problem at his new company where he really needs some legal help right now, and we need somebody we can trust."

Had I heard her right? Somebody they could trust, and she thought of me? The ex-wife of her husband's arch-enemy?

"Amy, I'm not a lawyer. You know that."

She continued in her cheery voice, which slowly lifted my mood off the floor. "I should have said legal-like, or paralegal. It's not courtroom or anything. The only problem is…"

I waited for the inevitable problem——like, they needed somebody for free, or the work was in their satellite facility in New York or something else that wouldn't work.

"He needs somebody right now, and full-time too. He can afford to pay well, if you can manage the hours."

Her idea of a problem was suddenly my definition of an opportunity. I'd been so focused on the downside of my shitty situation today, I hadn't even gotten around to how I could dig myself out of this hole Damien had put me in. A job had to be number one on that list.

Josh Fulton, who took over for Liam after he moved over to Chameleon Therapeutics, had been okay, but my name was poisonous to some of the others at Quigley-Fulton. I'd stopped my part-time assignment with them a little while after Damien's arrest, and I hadn't had time to find anything else.

I put my happy voice on. "Sounds like it might be a good opportunity. Would this be from home like last time?" If it was, I was screwed, because I no longer had my laptop. It was in the house the FBI now occupied.

"I don't know. You'd have to ask Liam about that. Can I tell him you're interested?"

Duh.

My stomach grumbled. "Sure. I'll wait for his call. Thanks."

We hung up.

I hadn't eaten since breakfast, and that had only consisted of yogurt and toast. A lunch of nothing but wine didn't count. I checked Jasmin's refrigerator and found an orange that looked edible, but the rest was cans of hard apple cider and soda pop. The real stash was in the freezer: Microwave dinners and cans of frozen grape juice. Unlike me, Jasmin preferred microwaved over real food.

It was my only choice, so a frozen meal went in the microwave, and I started to slice the orange to serve as dessert. No house, no car, no money, and now microwaved meals.

My phone rang again.

It had only been ten minutes, and Liam's name showed on the screen.

"Natalie. Amy tells me you might be available again."

"Depends. What can I help you with?" I desperately needed this, but like a moron, I couldn't shake the habit of being non-committal.

"Come down to my office at Chameleon Therapeutics, and I'll show you. We're just off Mass Ave. in Cambridge, not far from MIT."

I'd looked up the location when Liam had transferred there from Quigley-Fulton, shortly before Damien's arrest.

"I know where it is." The building was walking distance from where I sat now.

We agreed on eight the next morning.

I turned on Jasmin's TV and sat down to my dinner. I found a *Friends* rerun I hadn't seen. Damien hadn't been a fan, but he no longer ran my life.

I turned it up loud, hoping the jokes would sink in and improve my mood.

Ralph joined me on the couch, demanding to be petted and eying my dinner.

CHAPTER 4

NATALIE

I woke up early the next morning. A quick trip to the closest 7-11 yielded a can of cat food and a miniature bag of litter for Ralph. I'd get provisions for myself later. With the limited money in my wallet, I wasn't getting any more than the bare minimum at their exorbitant prices.

Working for Liam Quigley here in town wasn't my first choice, but if I could hack it until I got enough money together to move to a different city, it would do. Getting to a place that had never heard of Damien Winterbourne was still my goal.

I walked down the sidewalk, following the little map on my phone. Chameleon Therapeutics was supposed to be on this block, but I didn't see a sign anywhere. I reached mid-block, and the number above the glass door read 1039, but had no company name. I felt like an idiot. I should have double-checked the address I'd gotten.

Opening the door and mentally crossing my fingers, I approached the receptionist behind the counter.

"I think I'm lost. Do you know where Chameleon Therapeutics is located?"

The woman's badge read *Judy*.

"You found us," she announced cheerily. "Do you have an appointment?"

I double-checked my phone to make sure I was on time. "Yeah, I'm supposed to see Liam Quigley."

She looked at me expectantly.

"Sorry, I'm Natalie Spencer."

"Certainly. Please sign in, and I'll need to see some ID."

I opened my purse and pulled out my wallet. "I just got divorced, and I haven't gotten my license changed yet." I handed her the card.

She read the name and took it down, not reacting with disgust as most did. She must not read the papers much. She scanned it under a blacklight flashlight and handed it back.

She picked up the phone. "A Ms. Spencer is here to see you, but her ID doesn't match. It's for Natalie Winterbourne... Sure thing."

Judy smiled and pointed to the couch as she dialed the phone again. "If you'll have a seat, I'll get somebody to escort you."

A minute later, a short guard with a black-and-yellow plastic gun on her hip came to escort me. Her nametag read *Wanda*.

After confiscating my phone, Judy buzzed us through the door.

We turned left and soon reached the office with Liam's name on it.

He and I exchanged greetings as Wanda departed, and he quickly got down to business. He leaned forward in his chair.

"Natalie, how much do you know about patent applications?"

This wasn't the direction I'd expected the conversation to go. "Actually quite a bit more than the average law student. I took two courses on patent law at Columbia, and I was intending to add a third in my last year, but didn't get to it."

Patent law had been one of the two areas I'd considered specializing in. "Did you know my father was a patent lawyer?"

Liam smiled. "Yes."

Of course he did. Liam was very detail oriented. And Amy knew since we'd been roommates at Brown. She'd even met Dad before the heart attack.

"Talking to Dad when he was working at home is what originally got me interested in going to law school," I explained. "He taught me all about how to read and analyze patent claims, which is the key to any patent——that and the proper research and disclosure of prior art, of course."

"What about the filing procedures?" he asked.

"Things have changed over the years. It used to be that the important date——the priority date——was based on discovery, but now, the *filing* date is the most important date, so speed and accuracy of the initial filing are what count most."

I'd heard over and over from Dad how critical the claim wording could be. I waited for a response from Liam.

"Natalie, what we need is a full-court press on patent filings. Is that something you'd be willing to help with?"

"Sure, I could help with that. Who are your patent attorneys, or do you have one in house?"

He took a deep breath. "That's the problem. We don't have one."

"Dad spoke highly of Schacter, Lawson and Bryce. I could probably help prepare things for them."

Liam shook his head. "That won't do. This has to be done in-house, and none of the documents can leave the facility."

Liam's company seemed a little over-paranoid about security. Confiscating my phone at reception had been a severe step.

"You want me to do the whole thing?"

Liam nodded. "I can't think of anybody better than Maurice Spencer's daughter."

His confidence warmed me. "Are you sure you don't want to have a real patent attorney do the filings?"

"Does the patent office require that?" Judging by his grin, he knew the answer already.

"No, anybody can file the application."

"How soon can you start? As I said, timing is paramount."

I fidgeted in my chair. We hadn't discussed salary yet, and I wasn't sure how to bring it up.

"And, I'll pay ten K per application on top of the hourly rate I was paying you before."

I nodded. "Today, if that works for you."

For that kind of money, I could stomach staying in town a little longer. With my lack of work history, finding anything one tenth as lucrative was out of the question.

Liam rose to shake my hand with a warm smile. "Welcome to Chameleon. After I introduce you to the man with all the ideas, Gwen will get you set up."

I smiled. Today was a far sight better than yesterday.

~

R YAN

I SETTLED IN AT MY DESK TO CHECK THE MORNING RESEARCH-PAPER downloads. Spending all day yesterday at the courthouse had been a complete waste of time. Lawyers were such windbags. Word-stretchers of the first order, taking minutes to make a simple point that could have been condensed to ten words. If yesterday had taught me anything, it was that I was lucky not to have to work with any.

I couldn't identify a single minute that had been useful, or had moved our search for a cure along. They wouldn't even allow me to bring my laptop so I could get some work done while the blowhards droned on——something about courtroom protocol. Just a means for them to look down on those of us who worked for a living, in my opinion.

As I finished my coffee and dumped the Peet's cup in the trash can, Natalie's face came to mind again. I regretted not asking for her number. Women didn't often catch my interest——I didn't have the time——but she'd been an exception. Not only had she been helpful, but she looked good——better than good. She was a bit different than the college coeds I usually selected for my romps.

I avoided women her age as too clingy, too demanding. The younger girls weren't focused on settling down. Spotting the ones open to a casual encounter wasn't hard if you knew where to look. And with thirty-odd colleges in the Boston area, there were plenty of candidates available.

The literature was quite clear on the subject. Regular ejaculation was good for the prostate and warded off the advent of cancer. I didn't intend to die young. All I needed now was research telling women that daily sex prevented cervical cancer, and my searches would be easier.

This morning I'd done two loops of my normal run around the Charles River Basin from the River Street Bridge down the Cambridge side to the Longfellow Bridge, and back on the south side. The exercise kept me focused. Good blood flow was the key to concentration, and I needed it today.

I hadn't been able to get Natalie's face out of my mind during my run, either. Meeting that girl at Peet's and again at the jewelers had been the high point of yesterday. She'd been a ten in those tight yoga pants.

Nonetheless, every day lost was a crime. I had to catch up on the work I hadn't gotten to yesterday, and the memory of her was interfering.

I didn't bother to acknowledge the knock at the door. I recognized it as Liam Quigley's distinctive double rap right before he barged in.

Nobody else dared enter without an invitation. I'd founded Chameleon Therapeutics, but he'd bought a controlling interest in the company almost six months ago. He was a significant improvement from the previous CEO. I was grateful for that, and for the latitude the additional capital gave us. The bulk of the proceeds from selling my last company were still tied up in untradeable preferred stock——not that it would have been wise to fund the whole company myself, even if I could have.

"Ryan?" Liam asked.

I looked up. He was also the only one in the company I allowed to call me by my first name. He was my boss, but more than that, he'd invested because he understood the importance of our mission here and supported my research. He was the first boss I'd had who understood what I did.

"Yes?"

Liam hefted the pile of papers I kept in the visitor's chair opposite my desk and moved them to the floor——the boss's prerogative.

"We've added a paralegal to help with patents."

"A what?"

"A patent assistant, like we talked about yesterday."

I scowled. "I don't need one." They only got in the way.

"We talked about this," he continued. "Patent filings need to become a priority. Yesterday was an example."

I didn't answer. Yesterday in court had been an example all right——an example of why to avoid the courts. We wouldn't know the outcome for a while, but our lawyer's prognosis wasn't good. He'd hid his pessimism behind a lot of useless verbiage, but the undercurrent had been clear enough.

"Not necessary and not wanted," I repeated.

I went back to my screen. I thought I'd made my opinion clear yesterday, but Liam could be persistent beyond reason.

He got up from the chair and wandered back to the door.

I'd won this round——another bullet dodged. Out of the corner of my eye I saw him open the door to leave. I ignored him and kept reading the synopsis of a paper from yesterday's *New England Journal of Medicine*. It was second on the list on my screen, and so far it sounded intriguing. I hit print, and the laser printer in the corner came to life. The paper would go on pile seven.

"Come in, I'd like you to meet Dr. Westerly," Liam said as he opened the door again.

Shit.

I scrolled down the screen, still reading the article that was printing.

"Hi," I said without looking up.

"Good morning, Dr. Westerly," someone said from the doorway. The voice was familiar.

Looking up, I found the woman from the jewelry store walking past the piles of papers to my desk——the face that had mesmerized me yesterday and interfered with my concentration this morning. The last thing I needed in my office was a woman as distracting as she was.

"This is Natalie Spencer. She can get started this morning," Liam said. "Isn't that great?"

She reached out her hand.

I rose to take it, and we shook quickly. "Good morning."

Her grip was warm, strong, and confident.

My cock stiffened as I imagined her gripping my cock, her hand warm and strong. I sat back down quickly and returned to reading my screen.

"Come along, Natalie. He's always grumpy in the morning," Liam said.

I didn't go for the bait; I ignored him. I could be as grumpy as I wanted. It was a founder's prerogative.

"Good to meet you, Dr. Westerly," Natalie said as she retreated with the boss.

I raised my hand while continuing to read from the computer screen.

With Anton, the previous CEO, I would have thrown a fit——
or maybe even something more substantial, like a book, or hell, my
chair, to fend off having to deal with an assistant of any sort, for
any reason. All they ever did was slow me down.

Anton, and Jerry before him, had tried multiple times to give
me *help*, and I'd successfully run them all off. They'd thought
another pair of hands would help. They were wrong.

The door closed, and I was alone again, but reading the paper
on my computer didn't get easier. I had to back up a paragraph or
two. Her face kept appearing on the screen.

I should have done three laps instead of two this morning.
Blood flow, I needed better blood flow.

When I finished the paper, I had to wonder if Liam had a point.
I'd tried not to let on, but yesterday's court session had bothered
me as much as it had him. Patents were going to be an issue going
forward. Clearly.

I gathered the pages from the printer, wrote seven in the upper
right-hand corner of the first one, circled it, and put it with the
other un-filed papers on my credenza behind me.

A fucking assistant was the last thing I needed; I needed more
time to work. An eighth day in the week would be more helpful.

I chuckled to myself, thinking an assistant for fucking wouldn't
be half bad. Her badge could read *Natalie, assistant fuck-bunny*.

But an office entanglement wasn't a good idea. In fact, it was a
monumentally bad one. I'd tried that once at my previous
company, and it'd led to yelling, scratching, and a blackmail
demand when it ended. I winced, recalling that a window at my
previous apartment had gotten a rock through it——not that I
could prove it was her.

No, patent assistant or whatever was better. It would only take
a week or three to get rid of her and have things back to the way
they needed to be.

I circled the day on my blotter. Three weeks out——that's all it
should take to make her quit.

CHAPTER 5

Natalie

Ryan the coffee god worked here, the man who was clueless about birthday gifts.

Liam and I turned left as we left Ryan Westerly's office, and he ushered me into an empty office a few doors down.

"This will be your office."

I hadn't contemplated an office all to myself; most people here were in cubicles.

"Really?"

The office wasn't large, with two lateral files taking a bit of space, but I was still wowed.

"The papers you'll be working with will need to be locked up at night. I'll introduce you to Gwen. She'll get you whatever you need."

He led me to the front and introduced me to a middle-aged, short-haired redhead. He instructed her to give me keys to the entire facility.

"Natalie," she said after Liam left us. "I had a cousin named Natalie——ran off with a musician, and we never saw her again."

"I'll be careful to steer clear of musicians," I said.

"Do that. Musicians are the worst. I ought to know; I married one." She laughed.

She was going to be fun to be around.

"Let's get you outfitted," she said.

Two hours later, I'd been to security and gotten a cardkey and a badge with *Natalie* on it, in big letters, and Spencer as my last name. With a computer on my desk and enough pens, pencils, paper, and file folders to outfit a platoon, I was ready.

"Liam didn't mention what you would be doing for us," Gwen said as she helped me connect the computer monitor. "It must be important. Nobody else gets a keycard to everything."

"I'm going to be helping Dr. Westerly with patents."

Her face fell. "Oh. Good luck."

There was a story there. What the hell did that mean?

"Is there something I should know?" I asked.

She looked behind her. "Maybe over lunch."

Gwen seemed like a nice person, and somebody who could give me the lay of the land. "Okay, that sounds good."

Brosnahand's money was helpful, but I needed this job, and the patent bonuses seemed like the only way I would be able to escape Boston. I wasn't going to do it working at Subway.

"Hey, I'll treat," Gwen said. "Do you like Thai?"

"Thai sounds great."

We agreed on a late lunch.

Shortly after that, Rick from the IT department showed up outside my door. Skinny, in a T-shirt and sandals, and with a scraggly, only partially filled-in beard and hair that could use washing, he earned a wide berth from Gwen as she left. He fit the stereotype of computer geek, except he didn't wear glasses.

"I'll need a laptop for home too," I told him.

"No problem. Got ya covered." He pulled a folded piece of

paper out of his satchel. "You'll need this too, the instructions on logging into the VPN——that's virtual private network," he explained while leering a little too obviously at my chest. "I'll bring a laptop by before the end of the day."

I nodded with a semi-smile, not wanting to encourage him.

Rick sat at the keyboard, loading my computer with various software, eying me every few minutes.

I didn't have to wait long for the come-on.

"Want to have lunch tomorrow?" he asked.

I was the fresh meat around here, it seemed. "Sorry, I have to meet my sister," I lied.

After a half hour of explanations about the network and email systems, he gave me a security fob that I added to my keyring. It had an eight-digit number that changed every minute. The computer wouldn't let me in without the number to prove it was me. He watched as I tried logging in.

I got it right on the second try. This company took security to a new level.

I spent the rest of the morning getting access to the patent office and search websites I'd need, and setting up my tracking spreadsheets the way Dad had taught me. I was amazed at how much of his teachings I remembered from all those years ago.

When our lunchtime arrived, I chanced a peek in the direction of Ryan Westerly's office as Gwen and I left for the restaurant. The door was closed, as it had been each time I'd looked.

Spice Castle Thai, the restaurant Gwen had picked, was a small hole-in-the-wall just off the main drag, but the aromas as we entered were heavenly.

Due to my sister's barren fridge, I'd had to settle for Raisin Bran with water instead of milk for breakfast, and I was starved. I checked my phone again——still no call back from Jasmin. This wasn't like her, and she couldn't be in the air much over twelve hours, even if she'd been on a long haul. I sent her another text asking her to call as we sat down. If only she'd told me her new boyfriend's number or even his last name.

"Boyfriend?" Gwen asked.

"No. Just trying to get in touch with my sister. I'm worried that I haven't heard from her."

She picked up her menu. "Sisters can be like that." She laughed. "If mine found a hot new guy, she wouldn't return my call for a week. Tells you where I fit on her priority list."

"I don't think that's it."

Jasmin could be like that, but we'd talked last week, and she had gone to LA to be with her boyfriend. She hadn't been having any problems, at least not any worth mentioning to me.

I studied my menu; the list was endless.

When the waitress came by to take our orders, Gwen chose the beef pad thai, and I settled on Panang curry with chicken.

"How long have you been with Chameleon?" I asked after our waitress had retreated.

"A year and a half now. The place has grown a lot in that time. Most of the back was empty when we first moved into the building, and now it's almost all built out."

"You like the industry?" I asked.

"The costs of new medicines are obscenely high, but hell, they save lives. And the people are dedicated, and nice to boot."

I wondered how the *nice* characterization squared with her opinion of Ryan.

"It seems a pretty security-conscious place," I added. "I mean, with the security fobs to use the computers and everything. Is that normal for the industry? They even took my phone when I came in to interview."

"No, I wouldn't say it's normal, but it's understandable given what happened."

Our waitress interrupted us with our hot and sour soup.

"What happened?" I asked after she left.

"A theft of some of our experimental data and a drug design. Very valuable stuff."

"How?"

"Nobody knows for sure, or if they do it's above my pay grade. There's even a court case going on about it."

"Wow, serious, huh?"

"A hundred-million-plus worth of serious is what I hear. That's why all the new safeguards. Same old, same old——closing the barn door after the horse is out, if you ask me." Gwen shrugged. "But then that's sort of why you're here."

"How's that?" I asked.

"The patents. If we had filed a patent application on the drug before the data theft, it wouldn't have really mattered, because we'd have the patent and that Valestum company would be up a creek."

"What does Valestum have to do with it?"

"They're the company that ended up with the data, and they filed the patent on our discovery, if you can believe that."

"That's not right."

It wasn't right, but I knew the America Invents Act of 2011 had changed the patent owner from first to invent, to first to file, and if Valestum got to the patent office first, they would get the patent even if it wasn't fair.

"That's what the court case is about."

"You hadn't filed a preliminary?"

I knew a lot of companies didn't file preliminaries to avoid tipping off the competition.

"Not my field." Gwen shook her head. "I don't even know what a preliminary is, but I'm guessing we didn't, based on all the concern."

The waitress arrived with our plates.

My first taste of the curry confirmed that this place was as good as the aromas had promised.

"This is really good." I'd found a wide range of quality at the Thai restaurants I'd tried, and this one was near the top.

"The best food is in these little hole-in-the-wall places. If you want, I can show you an Indian joint not far away that's just as good."

I agreed, and we attacked our plates. This was the first substantial food I'd had in more than a day.

"You seem to be on good terms with the big boss. I take it you knew him before?" Gwen asked between forkfuls.

"I did some part-time paralegal work for him."

"That's a good introduction."

"That and he married my college roommate." I smiled.

"I've heard his penthouse has a view to kill for," she said, awaiting confirmation.

"I wouldn't know." Being Amy's old roommate had gotten me invited to the wedding, but never over to their home.

"Oh," she said sheepishly, going for another bite of her lunch.

"So what's the deal with Ryan?" I asked. "Is there some secret to working with him?"

Gwen put a finger up while she swallowed hard. "Good luck with that. First rule, if you want to last till the end of the day, he's Dr. Westerly, not Ryan. And the last three people assigned to work with him——none of them lasted longer than two weeks."

"He can't be that bad," I countered.

"Better grow a thick skin before you go anywhere near him is my best advice. I got my ass in a sling the one and only time I ventured into his office. That's like radioactive ground zero. You don't go in uninvited." She scowled. "The man may be uber-rich and a genius, but he sure got sent to the back of the line when they were handing out manners."

I didn't dare tell her I hadn't found him that bad yesterday morning. Buying me a cup of coffee had been a genuinely warm-hearted gesture. "So how am I supposed to get my work done?"

"I don't know. Maybe get the bossman to escort you in? Dr.

Westerly was always talking back to the last CEO, but he doesn't try it with the big boss."

"It said on the website that Dr. Westerly founded the company?"

"Yeah, serial startup guy, I guess. He sold his last company for, like, a billion dollars. If I had his money, I'd be shopping for tropical islands instead of working 24/7 starting another company."

I ate in silence, digesting the advice. Don't talk to him, don't go into his office——those ground rules weren't going to work. It wasn't in my DNA to do a half-baked job of this.

"The website also said Chameleon is working on orphan drugs?" I asked.

"That's why I joined. Orphan drugs are drugs for rare diseases. For the longest time, nobody could develop drugs for them, because there weren't enough patients to run the normal-size FDA trials. Now we get exemptions to work with smaller numbers of patients, and it's a large part of what we do."

We finished lunch with a casual discussion of our backgrounds ——carefully constructed, in my case——without returning to the topic of the enigmatic Ryan Westerly. Thankfully Gwen was either unaware that my last name had been Winterbourne, or she was in the minority who didn't care.

Back in the office after lunch, Gwen introduced me to more people on the science staff——enough that I was going to have trouble remembering all the names. The looks I got when Gwen announced that I was here to help with patent applications seemed enthusiastic enough, until she added that I'd be working on Dr. Westerly's as well. Only one of them spit out his coffee, but the reactions mostly mirrored Gwen's. *Good luck with that* seemed to be the sentiment.

Returning to my office, I opened the first of the three folders of unfinished patent applications left by the last resident of this office, a Brian Smithersnott. He must have gotten a fair amount of hassle about his name when he was younger.

The first application was on a chemical process for synthe-sizing one of the precursor compounds for Chameleon's work. It had been submitted by Dr. Sydney Roundhouse. The prior-art section looked pretty thin to me, so I logged on to the computer and started searching. My father's lessons came back to me quickly. It only took a few hours to find the problem; this applica-tion wasn't going anywhere if I could find prior art invalidating it this quickly. The rules were simple: if the technique or discovery had been published before, no patent could be issued, period, full stop, end of sentence.

I moved on to the second, also by Roundhouse.

A couple hours later, I hadn't finished the search, but it was after six. The office was slowly emptying, though I could still see light under Ryan's door.

He was in his office, doing God knows what——obviously a hard worker.

Before closing down my computer, I sent myself an email with the relevant search terms to check tonight from home. With Ralph needing food, and *me* needing food, I gathered up my purse and the laptop Rick had brought by and set out for the grocery store. With Brosnahand's money in my purse, I could now afford to feed us.

Once outside it occurred to me again that I should have heard from Jasmin by now. I punched up her contact and dialed.

It went instantly to voicemail.

~

WITH THE LAPTOP IN ONE HAND AND A HEAVY GROCERY BAG IN THE other, I trudged back to the apartment, my feet hurting. I paused and switched arms. A bag of cat food and another of litter made the grocery bag weigh a ton, even with just a few breakfast things for me. More people food could wait until tomorrow. I was limited to what I could carry.

I stopped at the ATM on my way, a chance to put the bag down without looking like an idiot. Anyway, it was worth a try. The machine ate my card and refused to cough it back up, or even let me see the balance.

Fucking FBI.

Without a working bank account, how was I going to cash my paycheck? Another problem caused by that asshole Willey because he thought I knew where Damien would hide money.

Opening the door, I couldn't wait to put down the bag and shuck off my heels. At least Ralph was happy to see me. He rubbed up against me and tried to lead me to his empty food bowl.

As I put away my meager haul, Ralph turned up his nose at the dry food I'd poured him and walked away, giving me the dirty you-must-not-love-me look.

"Hey, suck it up, Ralph," I told him. "We're both on limited rations here. This is all I can afford right now, so get used to it."

He ignored me and curled up on the couch.

Ungrateful.

He stared at me while my dinner cooked in the microwave. This was my second, and hopefully last, frozen dinner.

I parked myself at the table and forked the first bite of my turkey and vegetables from Jasmin's freezer.

Ralph jumped into the seat next to me and meowed.

I cut a small piece of turkey, scraped off the sauce, and put it on a napkin for him. "Okay, but just this one time. If I can eat frozen, you can learn to like dry food."

He scarfed down the meat and meowed again.

By the time I had finished, Ralph had gotten three chunks of my meat, and he was less than happy when I got up to throw the plastic tray away without giving him more.

After three hours of computer work on the patent search terms I'd emailed myself, I was convinced that this second patent was a waste of time as well. Roundhouse was an idiot if he thought it was going to fly. If the third was as bad as the first two, I was not going to find any easy money in the patent bonuses Liam had promised me.

My phone rang from its perch on the counter.

I promptly tripped over the heels I'd kicked off as I moved to answer it.

It was Brosnahand. After his kindness in lending me money, I was happy to take his call, even if he was still trying to get me to visit Damien.

"Natalie, I've looked over the forfeiture paperwork, and I found a significant error——or more properly, a loophole in it."

My heart sped up and I suppressed a smile. "Does this mean I can get my house back?"

"I'm afraid not."

I slumped against the counter, the air let out of my sudden balloon of hope. "What then?"

"It names your husband, of course, and you by your married name, but omits you or any of your assets under your maiden name, and the divorce decree has a name change in it for you back to Natalie Spencer."

"And?" I asked.

"Did you get the name changed on your bank account or credit cards yet? Those would be safe."

A day late again. "No, I'm still waiting for my new social security card in the mail." I'd checked, and the banks needed a new driver's license, and the state wouldn't give me one without a new social security card.

"It was a thought."

"Thank you for trying. I really appreciate the help."

He sighed. "Have you perhaps given any more thought to meeting with Damien?"

"It doesn't take thought, Mr. Brosnahand. No way am I spending any time or effort on him."

"Just consider it again, please. And it's Mason."

"Okay, Mason. I'll think about it."

With the help Mason Brosnahand had given me, I owed him at least that.

We hung up, and I logged in to the Social Security Administration website.

The news was good and bad. The card had been mailed; that was the good news. It was too late to give them Jasmin's address instead; that was the bad news. I was going to have to get back to my house to check the mailbox. That would be my before-work task tomorrow.

I checked my call history one more time. Still no return call from Jasmin, so I tried her again——straight to voicemail. A little needle of fear poked at my heart.

Where are you, Jasmin?

CHAPTER 6

Natalie

I WOKE EARLY THE NEXT MORNING. CLOTHES SHOPPING WOULD HAVE to be added to my list. Jasmin and I were the same size, so a few of the things in her closet would do for work, but most of them were too casual. I'd laid out a nice skirt and blouse combination for work today.

Jasmin had an armband holder for my phone that would come in handy. It reminded me how many simple things I didn't have, and Brosnahand's five hundred dollars wouldn't go very far in replacing them. I rechecked my phone——it wasn't on silent, and I hadn't missed a call back from my sister. The voicemail log was empty as well.

I tightened the laces on my running shoes. Exercise had always helped to calm me, and I needed to get home to check the mail for that social security card. Hopefully the FBI wasn't confiscating my mail.

Downstairs I turned toward Brookline, started the timer on my phone, and slipped it into the holder. I didn't have a good gauge of how long the run would take me, and I might need to repeat this for a few days to catch the particular letter I wanted.

Even with Jasmin's Lululemon leggings, it took several blocks for me to warm up with the early morning spring chill. My path back over the BU Bridge and on to my neighborhood was a familiar one, but running on the sidewalk instead of driving, I noticed all the little changes from block to block that were just a blur in the car.

Reaching my street, I found Mrs. Garnsey out collecting her paper. The sneer on her face grew fierce as I approached. Her husband's company had lost pension money with Damien.

I mentally crossed my fingers and closed my eyes before opening the mailbox.

Bingo.

Under the junk mail I found an official white envelope from the Social Security Administration with my maiden name in the clear address window. I left the junk mail. Clutching the envelope containing my escape from the Winterbourne name, I sprinted past Mrs. Garnsey with a wave.

A middle-finger salute was her response.

I just swallowed my pride and smiled; they didn't deserve what Damien had done to them any more than I did. My day was brighter now that I could see an end to having anything in my wallet with Winterbourne written on it. Reaching the end of the street, I turned left toward the bridge over the Charles River and slowed to my long-distance jogging pace.

Stopping two intersections down, I pulled my phone from the armband holder. After a quick search, I located an RMV office downtown a few blocks from the Park Street MBTA station. A visit there became my lunchtime priority.

The run was invigorating, a link back to a better time——before Damien when a morning run had been a part of my routine. Now that I could see a path to a semblance of normalcy, I decided today was the day to get back to the real me, starting with a longer run.

Clutching the envelope containing my future, I picked up the pace and reached the bridge quickly. There were more pedestrians now, and I had to weave around them. Instead of crossing the bridge, I veered down the steps onto the path by the river.

There a stiff breeze cooled me. The grass would have been softer footing, but Canadian geese were foraging nearby. That meant staying on the pavement and avoiding the goose-shit land mines amid the greenery.

A couple walking their toy poodle took up almost the entire width of the path.

I dodged right around them.

The dog barked and lunged at the man running toward me.

He and I collided with a thud, and I went sprawling.

I rolled onto the grass, shielding my face with my hands.

My precious envelope had blown over the fence and landed in the traffic lanes of Storrow Drive. It got run over by one car and then another.

"Jesus H. Christ, you fucking idiot," I yelled at my attacker as my future fluttered farther away down the road.

~

R YAN

THE COUPLE WALKING THE TOY POODLE HAD ONE OF THOSE fucking retractable dog leashes that could let out ten yards of line for Fido to run away with.

I shifted left to avoid the little fur monster.

Without warning, the brainless dog darted toward the railing, and its leash tripped me.

I braced for the fall and rolled toward the grass to my left.

Like an idiot, the girl jogging the other way zigged around the dog when she should have zagged and wasn't looking up either. She ran straight into me as I tumbled to the grass.

We ended in a tangle of legs and arms on the ground. Since I was so much bigger, she took the worst of it.

"Jesus H. Christ, you fucking idiot," she yelled at me, turning and springing to her feet.

I tried to untangle my foot from Cujo's leash. "Me? You should look where you're going," I yelled back.

I had my eyes on the wicked fur ball with teeth, ready to give it a kick it wouldn't forget if it got close enough. I got my leg free, and the owner reeled the little fiend in and picked him up.

A car honked. I turned to see.

Idiot Girl had jumped the low fence and gotten into the roadway, trying to retrieve a piece of paper. Storrow Drive was no place to mess around.

I did the stupid thing and jumped the fence myself, out into the traffic lane, and put one hand up high and the other pointing at the car barreling toward us. I could see an older driver behind the wheel, and I hoped to hell Grandpa was awake.

Tires screeched, and I backed away from the skidding car, ready to jump, if needed.

He stopped ten feet from me and started yelling obscenities through the windshield, laying on his horn the whole time.

When I turned, Idiot Girl had caught her paper and was picking it up.

"Get out of the fucking road," I yelled at her as Grandpa honked again.

She didn't move or look. I grabbed her and pulled her to the narrow curb, shielding her from Evil Grandpa as he sped by, his side mirror missing us by inches.

Evil Grandpa flipped me the finger out his open window. An audible crunch sounded as he ran over the phone Idiot Girl had evidently dropped in her paper quest to get run over.

Boston drivers.

The guy with the poodle let the little yap monster down, this time on a shorter leash. The woman with him just shook her head.

Idiot Girl turned my direction.

"Natalie?"

"Ryan?"

Natalie fucking Spencer, the hot-as-hell new patent lawyer or assistant or whatever she was at work. The girl I had spent all day yesterday avoiding. The girl whose face and body kept interrupting my concentration.

I hopped back to the safe side of the low fence.

She did the same.

"You all right?" I asked.

"Yeah, no thanks to you."

The girl had a serious attitude problem.

"Me? You're the one that ran into the damned street."

"I wouldn't have had to if you hadn't knocked me down," she spat back. She patted her armband phone holder. Finding it empty, she surveyed the ground around her.

"Don't bother, it's road kill," I shouted over the traffic noise. I pointed to the crunched electronic carcass on the roadway. I couldn't take my eyes off the heaving of her full tits under the tight Nike tank top.

She stomped her foot. "You…"

She looked even hotter when she was mad, I decided.

I was unsuccessful at stifling a laugh.

"You think that's funny?" she fumed, pointing at the mangled remains of her smartphone.

"No, not that." I pointed to the side of my head. "You might want to get cleaned up before work."

She put her hand to her head and came away with fingers full of goose crap. She flung the shit to the ground and screamed. She definitely had a temper.

My cock was taking too much notice of her shape in that tank top, and those tight yoga pants. The fact that I'd jerked off last night thinking about her wasn't helping.

"See ya." I turned and continued my run.

Any more time with the distracting Natalie and the condition in my running shorts was going to become a serious embarrassment.

∽

NATALIE

THE CRUNCHING SOUNDS WERE SICKENING AS ANOTHER CAR AND then a truck ran over what was left of my phone——my lifeline, the only thing of value I still owned. A tear escaped down my cheek. Mason's money wasn't enough to replace it. I was going to be the only girl in Boston without a phone.

Ryan turned and ran off.

How could he?

The audacity of the man. My phone ends up in a million bits on Storrow Drive because he bowls me over, and not even an apology? Yesterday, I'd thought Gwen had him wrong. Today was another matter. She had understated his rudeness.

"Asshole," I called after him.

"How could you?" It was the lady with Poodle Man.

"Pardon?"

"He risked his life to keep you from getting run over a minute ago, and now you're calling him names. Shame on you."

A car honked.

I jumped to the side, remembering the honking as the car had barreled toward *us* moments ago. Looking toward the noise, I realized it was one impatient driver honking at another.

Us?

Maybe I'd been too hasty judging Ryan. He had hopped the fence to stop traffic for me.

"Sorry," I said. "You're right."

I turned the direction he'd gone and started after him——not just to follow him, but to get back home so I could clean the crap out of my hair. If I got myself financially secure by Thanksgiving, I was going to cook goose instead of turkey to get even.

Now Jasmin had no way to reach me. I could try to email her, but she was almost allergic to that form of communication.

Holding my mangled envelope tightly, I sped up my pace.

Ryan was ahead on the path, still in sight. It was a pity he was so rude; he did have a nice ass.

Such a pity.

But he had been gallant, jumping onto the road like that.

Running faster to catch up, I decided his shoulders were even better than his ass, if that was possible. And no need for me to feel self-conscious, I decided. I'd been whistled at a fair number of times. If men could objectify women and judge us on looks, it was fair turnaround for me to do the same.

Here I was running after a man who was as rude as they came, and fantasizing about him, just because I liked how his ass looked, and of course his shoulders, and those arms. How I needed to be held in arms like that.

Down, girl.

He ran at a brisk clip, his fanny pack bouncing above that gorgeous ass. I still hadn't caught up as we crossed the bridge into Cambridge.

Ryan turned down the path on the north side of the Charles River, making a loop.

I was getting too winded to catch him, and the goose crap in my hair was bugging me. Instead of turning to follow him, I slowed and went straight toward the apartment.

Does he run here every morning?

He slowed and looked back in my direction. He waved.

I waved back.

I might have to go on more morning runs, preferably with cleaner hair, and without making such an ass of myself.

Ass, *there was that word again.*

～

R YAN

NATALIE FOLLOWED ME FOR A BIT. I KEPT A FAST ENOUGH PACE TO stay ahead of her. The last thing I needed was for her to see the reaction she'd caused in me. Taking the turn off the bridge down the north side trail, I looked back. She didn't follow me, and I slowed my pace.

A young coed running the other direction shot me a disgusted look and gave me a wide berth. She'd no doubt noticed the bulge in my shorts.

I might as well have *pervert* printed on my shirt. Massachusetts, being the home of the Puritans, probably had a law against going out in public in my condition.

I looked back again.

The coed had pulled out her phone——no doubt reporting the pervert on the trail.

A few minutes of contemplating my experiments while running, and my cock deflated.

Why did Liam have to hire *her*? My experiments were coming to a head, and I needed to concentrate more than ever. What I didn't need was Natalie distracting me the way she had yesterday. If this morning's encounter was any indication, it was likely to be a losing battle.

I'd resorted to jerking off last night because I'd been unable to get her out of my head. It hadn't helped. It had given me temporary release, but her visage kept appearing everywhere I looked. And after this morning, with the way her tits strained against that tank top with her every breath, calling me to hold them, feel them, taste them, my obsession was only getting worse.

"Hey," the old man on the bike yelled.

I jumped out of the way. Good thing there weren't cars nearby, or I'd be road kill.

"This is a bike path, ya know," he yelled as he pedaled away. *Duh.*

The official name of this trail was the Dr. Paul Dudley White Bike Path, but there were way more runners than bicyclists this time of day.

I turned off the riverside path as soon as I could. Concentrating, I made it back home without any more incidents.

It was obvious I couldn't continue like this. My work had to come first. If I couldn't concentrate, I wouldn't make the progress I needed to.

I had to talk to Liam. The work was just too important.

I couldn't let David down.

CHAPTER 7

NATALIE

I MADE THE MISTAKE OF BRUSHING MY HAIR BEHIND MY EAR AS I closed the apartment door behind me. My fingers came back coated with disgusting crap——literal crap.

Yuck.

Ralph sidled up to me. That lasted about five seconds, which was all the time it took for him to get a whiff of my goose-poop hairdo. He quickly scooted off and hid under the couch.

"Fair weather friend," I said. "This wasn't my fault, you know."

I set the mangled envelope on the table and started stripping off my clothes as I made my way to the shower.

I made the mistake of looking down at the drain to see the black and white goo rinsing off my head. I closed my eyes. If I'd had anything to eat this morning, it would've been coming up right now.

The hot water continued running over me, rinsing away this morning's debacle. Typical of Jasmin, she had five different choices of shampoo in the shower, including my favorite, the orange blossom I'd given her to try. After two long applications of the heavily scented shampoo, I felt human again.

I hoped I wouldn't get fired after this morning's altercation with the founder. I could end up on the street if Ryan——er, Dr. Westerly——was as bad as Gwen had made him out to be.

A smoothie would have to wait until tomorrow. I fried my eggs and sausage from yesterday's grocery run and sat down to breakfast with the social security envelope in front of me. With the tire tread marks and rips, I was afraid to open it and find my new social security card unusable.

Ralph emerged from under the couch and meandered over to rub up against my leg. "Meow."

"It wasn't my idea to roll in goose shit."

He walked over to his food bowl and looked back at me, his unspoken request for fresher food.

"Toughen up, Ralph. I can't afford to throw away half your food anymore. You get fresh food when you finish that."

His expression didn't change.

I took a sip of juice. The time of reckoning was at hand. If this was bad enough, I would be making an emergency visit to the social security office instead of the RMV.

I carefully opened the carcass of the envelope and closed my eyes, saying a silent prayer that the news would be good.

Inside I found the top half of the letter torn in several places. But I sighed in relief. My new card on the bottom half was intact. I'd never read more welcome words than my maiden name on my new social security card. After smoothing it out, the new card went in my wallet.

Hello, Natalie Spencer, and goodbye, Natalie Winterbourne. For good.

~

MY KEYCARD CLICKED OPEN THE LOCK, AND I PASSED FROM THE lobby into the interior of Chameleon. The room was already bustling with activity. No slackers here; a surprising number of people had beaten me into work.

I was going to need to reassess my schedule. I couldn't afford to be seen as lazy. I hadn't had a real job since college, as Damien had been adamantly against it. But I knew I could excel at this, given half a chance.

My office door was oddly unlocked. I could have sworn I locked it when I'd left last night. Carelessness was not usually one of my traits. I tried the key again, locking and unlocking it.

Gwen came around the corner.

"Am I doing this right?"

"Oh, don't worry, you got it right. I just unlocked it for IT this morning. They do virus sweeps early to stay out of everybody's way."

I let out a breath. "Cool." I wasn't losing my mind after all.

"The big boss wants to see you later," she told me.

I almost shit my panties. I grabbed the doorframe to hold myself up.

"Have you seen Dr. Westerly this morning?" I asked, hoping for a negative response.

"Yeah, but he was in one foul mood when he left the big boss's office. Like I said, you don't want to poke that tiger. I'd stay clear of him today. I sure plan to."

Her words disheartened me. I rounded my desk and fell into my chair.

"Lunch today?" she asked.

"Sorry, I can't. I've got an errand to run downtown." I didn't add the caveat that it was dependent on me still having a job come lunchtime.

Gwen excused herself and continued down the hallway, humming.

If Ryan had been to see Liam, and Liam wanted to see me, that was as bad as it got. I should have been able to control my temper, but at the time, he'd just bowled me over, and then the goose poop?

I closed my eyes and took a deep breath. I needed to settle myself. Nothing good could come of me hyperventilating. I still had a lot of Mason's cash left, and if high school kids could handle jobs at Starbucks, so could I. I just had to make sure it was somewhere the customers wouldn't recognize me——if there was such a place around here.

I logged onto my computer and sent an email to Jasmin, explaining that I'd broken my phone and to please email me back that she was okay, as I was worried about her.

I took another three deep breaths. With my analysis of the two Roundhouse patents I'd finished in hand, I held my head high and walked toward my doom in the corner office. At least I wouldn't go down without a fight. I could show how much I'd gotten done in just my first day here. That ought to earn me a second chance, at least in my book.

I knocked on the door.

"Come in," came from the other side.

Even with a door between us, Liam's voice carried the weight of a man not to be trifled with. My friendship with his wife had gotten me the chance here, but the way Liam Quigley operated, that was likely as far as it got me. He hadn't gotten where he was by being a softie.

I lifted my shoulders and opened the door.

He was head down in paperwork. He glanced up as I closed the door.

If I was going to get yelled at and fired, at least it would be in private, not with the door open for my shame to be broadcast to the whole company.

He smiled. "Hi, Natalie, come sit. I have something I want to talk with you about."

He motioned to the chair in front of his desk, the execution chair. At least he didn't have plastic on the floor, like in one of those movies where they walk the person into a room and there's plastic over the floor to make cleaning up the mess easier.

I sat. "Before you say anything. I want to say how much I appreciate the chance you've given me here, and I want to show you what I've accomplished so far." I needed to get my side of the story out as quickly as I could to stand a chance.

He cleared his throat. "Okay, but——"

"Please," I interrupted him, opening the folder I'd brought.

He smiled and nodded.

"There were three applications in process when I came in yesterday, all by Dr. Roundhouse. Yesterday and last night I went through two of them. This one…" I laid the first partial application on his desk.

He picked it up. "Yes?"

"And this second." I handed it over as well.

He appraised me warily.

"I did thorough prior-art checks on them, and in my opinion, they're both a waste of time. Neither is going to pass muster at the patent office. It's our duty to disclose this prior art, and frankly, if I can find disqualifying papers so easily, they won't stand a chance."

Liam smiled at me again, for some reason I couldn't fathom.

"Natalie, that's very good," he said. "Very impressive, as a matter of fact."

The praise washed over me like a warm wave. I so needed something to go right in my life.

His smile vanished. "I'm not so concerned about these." He put the applications down and steepled his hands. "I wanted to talk about Dr. Westerly. He came in for a chat this morning."

Here it was. The hammer was about to drop. I tried to swallow but couldn't. My mouth was drier than the Sahara.

❦

R*YAN*

I CHECKED THAT THE LAB DOOR HAD LOCKED BEHIND ME, A HABIT of mine after the theft.

Paul, my lab tech, was busy at the centrifuge. He nodded in my direction and waved a finger. Paul didn't engage in idle chit chat, one of the reasons I'd chosen to bring him over with me from Luxxamin. He kept his head down and never made mistakes. Carpenters had a saying: *measure twice, cut once.* With Paul it was more like a constant triple-check that he had everything set up properly.

He pointed to the microscope at the rear. "Batch seventy-four is ready for you to check. I think you'll like what you see." Paul had a good eye. If he thought it looked promising, it almost always was.

"Thanks." I double-checked the preparation worksheets before I sat down to use the microscope. I'd made the mistake once of assuming I remembered which protocol I was looking at and had mistaken it for another. By the time I realized my mistake, the samples had been discarded and three weeks' work lost.

As I moved between samples, the stage on the scope seemed a little too stiff. I pulled out my lucky Swiss Army knife and adjusted the tension down just a bit.

Paul had been right. This batch looked encouraging. I logged onto the computer next to the scope and started typing my notes. I found it easier to type them on the keyboard than to write them longhand in a notebook the way many people still did. My handwriting was so bad even I sometimes had trouble deciphering it if I was writing fast.

Paul waited silently nearby.

"You're right. These look promising. Let's start up two more batches. Up the incubation temperature two degrees on one and three degrees on the second."

Paul wrote down my instructions on his tablet and read them back to me. He gave me his signature two fingers to the eyebrow salute

I continued my examinations and expanded my notes.

With any luck, by now Liam was handling Natalie for me.

~

NATALIE

"I HAVE A PROBLEM," LIAM BEGAN.

I couldn't take another blow. I really needed this job.

"I'm so sorry," I blurted. Tears clouded my eyes.

Liam put up his hand to stop me. "Natalie, let me finish, please."

I nodded.

"We're involved in a patent trial," he continued. "It's in recess for a few days, but our lawyer tells me it's not looking good."

This took me by surprise. I'd never been involved in litigation; I hadn't even graduated yet.

I blinked back my tears and waited on his words. If he was going to fire me, this had to be the oddest firing speech ever.

"It's about the theft of some of our work."

"Valestum?" I asked, hoping I'd remembered the name right from my lunch with Gwen.

"Yes, so you know about that?"

"Just that there's a case. That's all."

He leaned forward. "Let me get to the point. We're doing a lot of really good work here that will be quite important, but we can't bring any of it to market if we can't protect it with patents. The problem with Valestum is half that they stole from us, but also half that we weren't proactive in filing paperwork last year. If we had, this wouldn't be a problem."

He had a bigger problem than he thought, from what little I'd seen. "Pardon me, but I just told you the two of the three applications I looked at are frankly not going anywhere."

He laughed. "Yeah, because those were Sydney Roundhouse's. He's a fine follow-up guy, but he's not the brains of the operation here. Dr. Westerly is, and that's where you come in."

"Me?"

"Yup, you. I'm going to force Dr. Westerly to give you what you need to write up his applications. He's got two dozen, maybe more, locked up in his head. The problem is, to him, freeing up the time to write applications takes second place to moving his work forward. We're going to solve that problem by having you do all the paperwork."

I'm sure that sounded simple to Liam, but he didn't understand.

"I can't write up applications without him spending time explaining things to me," I said. "It's still going to take time out of his day."

"Details. You two can figure it out, I'm sure."

"And he's on board with this?"

Liam laughed again. "Absolutely not. I think he saw this coming and came in this morning to tell me to keep you away from him——a preemptive strike on his part."

Exactly as I'd expected, our morning run-in had caused Ryan to want to get rid of me.

"I'm not sure you understand what he meant." Having the founder intent on firing me was more than a minor problem.

Liam waved me off. "I don't care. You two are working together on his patents until they're done. I understand that he can be intimidating, but you have to be tough. Don't let him push you around too much. He and I share a vision for this company, and it's one that will be dependent on our patent position later. He'll see the light. Trust me."

I doubted that, but arguing the case now was useless. I had one last question to clear up.

"What if he——"

"No more questions, Natalie. No more self-doubt. You have my full support. This project is critical, and we need to get moving *now*, not next month. I need somebody I can trust on this. I'll talk to him again and make it clear."

His full support. That certainly sounded good.

"I'll talk to him later this morning," Liam continued. "I'll have him come see you this afternoon to get started."

"That sounds great," I replied, not certain I believed my own words.

I wasn't looking forward to facing Ryan Westerly after this morning, but that's what work was all about: doing what you had to, not just what you wanted to.

～

R YAN

"BUT CAN'T IT BE SOMEONE ELSE?" I ASKED LIAM.

He was a formidable presence, even though I was the one behind the desk. I wouldn't admit to him how distracting I found Natalie. It seemed unprofessional.

"No, it can't," he said. "She's the one we have, and I think you'll find she's a lot better at it than Smithersnott."

I snorted. "That's a pretty low bar. But that's not the point. I can't spare the time to babysit her through everything."

Liam leaned forward, the way he did when he had something profound to say. "Ryan, we can't afford to wait on this. Losing CTX-13 to Valestum was bad enough——"

"We haven't lost it yet," I argued.

"I've talked to Dillard, and reading between the lines, he's not optimistic. And what happened with CTX-13 could happen again. We have no idea how they got the data. The only protection is prioritizing the patent work. It's the only way for us to succeed at our mission."

I rolled my eyes. "Okay. I'll give her an easy one, but if she can't handle it without taking up all my time, you agree to get someone else."

"What is your problem with her?"

That was a question I wasn't about to answer.

"I just doubt she's up to the task," I lied.

Liam got up to leave. "Try her out. I think you'll be surprised."

He had no idea how badly I wanted to try her out——over the desk or against the wall, or on her knees under my desk. I blinked hard and tried to rid myself of the image of her lips on my cock. That wasn't how he'd meant the phrase.

"I've got too much to do to get to it today."

"It's not a request," Liam added as he reached the door.

I needed time in the lab to concentrate on work and get my mind straight before my hospital visit, not time with that woman.

After he left, I pulled the photo out of my wallet for a second to remind myself of the importance of the mission. When I'd tucked it safely away again, I put my earbuds in to listen to the message.

CHAPTER 8

NATALIE

EXITING THE STUFFY RMV OFFICE, I INSTINCTIVELY REACHED IN
my purse for my phone before realizing the futility of it. Who the
hell didn't have even a phone to their name these days? Or credit
cards, for that matter?

I stepped around a homeless person sitting on the concrete,
looking off into space. No phone, no credit cards, no home to call
my own——I seemed to have quite a bit in common with him.

But I was making progress, though it had taken forever——
first one line then the next——until I was finally handed my slip of
paper.

I had it tucked safely in my purse as I boarded the Red Line
train back from Boston to Cambridge: a temporary driver's license
for the Commonwealth of Massachusetts with my new legal name
of Natalie Spencer. I'd given them Jasmin's address, as I no longer
had a home of my own. The official plastic card with my picture
would arrive in due time, they'd told me. They kept the old one.

I smiled as I took a seat. Natalie Winterbourne was now officially in my past. I'd cut up the useless credit cards with her name on them last night. I was determined to rid myself of any vestige of those years.

The man in the sportcoat who'd gotten on the train through the other door glanced in my direction. He looked oddly familiar.

Avoiding eye contact, I studied the floor. The last thing I needed was to be accosted by one of my ex-husband's victims while stuck here, unable to flee.

The wheels of the train screeched as we rounded a corner. I continued ignoring the man and wondered how Liam's conversation with Ryan had gone. I had to decide how to handle my meeting this afternoon with the man who wanted me gone from the company.

How my world had changed. Six months ago my biggest decision after lunch would have been yoga or Pilates.

By the time I stepped off the train, I'd decided on firm. I had the training to back up my presence at Chameleon, after all. I could do this job well if he'd give me a chance. And, I might be a pawn in the chess match between Liam and Ryan, but I had the backing of the stronger chess piece in this fight.

"*You have my full support*" had been Liam's exact words. Amy had told me Liam never said anything he didn't mean, not ever. I was counting on her being right.

Looking back over my shoulder after I reached street level, I saw the man in the sportcoat behind me taking a selfie, another reminder of the gulf between me and everyone else in this town ———no phone.

I sped up my walk. The relative safety of the Chameleon building lay ahead.

Another look behind and he was still moving my direction. He seemed a little old to be taking selfies; this time he was talking on his phone.

Pulling open the lobby door, I found Selfie Man had changed to the other side of the street, still walking this direction.

After the lobby door closed behind me, I let out a breath. Some of Damien's victims were real nut cases. Having your life savings go up in smoke could make somebody more than a little upset, and early on some of his victims had made pretty vile threats.

I plopped my ass down behind my desk. My legs were shaking. Winterbourne-haters were bound to be around every corner in this town. It just emphasized the importance of moving away. But that was out of the question until I had some money. My job now was to confront Westerly and force myself to work with him——and more importantly, him with me.

With the protection of the king, even the pawn could be a strong chess piece.

∾

*R*YAN

"ENTER."

I'd ignored the first knock, but the second was firm, and the third insistent.

Natalie strode in and closed the door after her. "Dr. Westerly, do you have a minute to discuss patent applications?" Her chest heaved slightly under a dark blue blouse.

I tried to guess her bra color today. Red, I decided. Red to match her lips——the lips I imagined wrapped around my cock almost every time I closed my eyes.

"Dr. Westerly?" she asked again.

This was intolerable. She needed to leave. "No," I answered. "Later."

She didn't move to leave. Instead she lifted the folders I kept in my visitor's chair specifically to prevent anybody from taking a seat, and sat herself down. She placed the folders on the floor.

Nobody but Liam had ever dared to do that.

She crossed her legs, and I blinked. I imagined her recrossing them *Basic Instinct*-style, giving me a glance up her skirt, but it was all in my head. Like every guy alive, I could still remember the first time I'd run that scene in slow motion. I'd moved closer to the television and re-run it more than once.

I clenched my eyes shut for a moment and took a deep breath. *Concentrate.*

"I'll wait," she said, meeting my stare. She remained planted in the chair, right where I couldn't possibly ignore her.

I scanned her for a sign of weakness and came up empty. "I said later."

Her posture was almost military, her chin up high——not snooty, but unintimidated.

"And I said I'd wait."

If she had this attitude in bed, I'd break her of it. "You can wait in your office," I said firmly, without raising my voice. My eyes returned to my desk. I'd seen this maneuver work for Liam a hundred times. It didn't work for me today.

"Liam told me to get started on your patent applications today." She'd played her card, and it trumped mine.

This might be my office, but it was Liam's building. There was no disputing that.

I let a slow grin grow on my face. She'd asked for it, and Liam had insisted she was good, so I'd give her a small test. At least it would get her out of sight and let me get back to work.

"Every one of these piles is a new experimental path." I pointed to the towers of papers I had placed in order around the room.

Her pale blue eyes widened as she looked around.

The scent of oranges wafted my way, momentarily distracting me. "In each stack are printouts of all my experimental notes for that series, including the objectives, along with the relevant papers I've found in my morning searches of the literature."

"Very impressive," she said, nodding. "There must be over two dozen here."

When she turned her head to survey the room, I took the opportunity to stare at the hint of cleavage that showed above her top button. A button that needed to be undone. Cleavage that needed to be nuzzled. Tits that needed to be squeezed. She needed a hand-bra ——my hands squeezing her tits, holding them up.

She looked back in my direction.

I shifted in my seat to accommodate my growing cock. "Thirty-eight," I told her.

"Which should we start with?"

She didn't get it.

"No." I shook my head. "Not *we*. You. You can start with the short one closest to the door." I pointed. "Number twenty-six."

I knew where every experiment pile was and what it included. My filing system might be unorthodox, but it helped me keep track of things, and I didn't give a shit what anyone else thought of it.

"And if I have a question?"

"Look," I said, leaning forward to emphasize the point. "I can't lead you through everything. I can't spare the time. If you're not up to the task, recommend someone who is."

Her eyes narrowed.

"My deal with Liam is you help with this without taking me away from my work," I lied. It was worth the bluff. "If you have a question, ask Paul."

"Paul?"

"My lab assistant, Paul Mayer."

She wrote the name down. "Where can I find him, if I need him?"

"He's around. He spends most of his time in the lab. Lab One, the smaller one on the right along the back wall. He usually comes out at the end of the day."

"I've got a key, thanks. I'll find him." She didn't realize that

Liam, Paul, and I had the only keycards other than security that opened the door to Lab One.

Stack twenty-six was a short one, less than three feet tall. She hefted the top half of the pile. "I'll be back for the rest."

I waived her off without looking up. The last thing I needed was to see her leaning over, the skirt tightening around her hips, and that ass…my God, that ass. My cock was already about to bust my zipper.

"And don't screw up the order," I told her when she returned.

"There's an order?" That attitude was back.

I didn't rise to the bait.

She closed the door on the way out, and I was alone again. The stack would probably exasperate her, and I could get back to normal when she left. I needed normal. I needed to concentrate.

Liam was constantly overstating the importance of patent filings. We'd upped the security, and if no more data escaped, the filings could wait while I finished the current series of experiments. They were too important to delay.

It wasn't patents that cured patients, it was the compounds we discovered by doing the hard lab work. The quicker that got done, the sooner treatments would be available to the children who needed them. The truth couldn't be simpler.

Until then, there was something I needed to get. I googled the store number and dialed. They picked up on the first ring.

CHAPTER 9

NATALIE

MY GOD, THE MAN NEEDED A PERSONALITY TRANSPLANT. RUDE was an understatement when applied to Westerly. No wonder Gwen disliked him.

The pile I'd retrieved was smaller than most in his office, but still massive. The man had evidently never heard of filing cabinets, or electronic filing and retrieval. It took two trips to get it all to my desk, ready to sift through.

I sat at my computer and checked my email yet again.

It was overflowing with hate messages from Damien's victims ——par for the course. My email had been leaked to the media and published in the name of "public service." Those reporter trolls had no concept of the hell they'd unleashed on me in the name of ratings and circulation. Fuck the First Amendment; what about my rights?

I'd tried replying to the first few dozen I received, expressing my sympathy and explaining how I was a victim as well. That had been a waste of time and mentally draining when the return messages were even more vitriolic than the first had been. Their senders wanted to vent, not discuss or understand. They were volcanoes of anger, hurricanes of hatred.

I'd given up changing my email address, too. It hadn't helped. The new one always showed up on the internet within days of the change. All I could do now was delete the messages without reading them. Initially, their volume had grown every week, but it seemed to be ebbing recently.

There was even a support group on the internet for Winterbourne victims. I'd visited the page once. They recounted to each other what they planned to do to me if they met me, or even worse, what they planned to do to Damien if he ever got out. It was frightening to see what severe financial loss did to the human psyche. *Hate* was much too mild a word.

After clearing the daily hate mail, I found I still had no word from Jasmin. Her radio silence was not good. I couldn't imagine what had happened, but it had to be bad.

A week, hell, a few days ago, I would have booked a plane to LA to look for my sister. But without cash, I was stranded, helpless. Though my heart squeezed again, I pushed my concern for my sister to the side for the moment.

After setting up my spreadsheets, I pulled the first paper from the top of the pile. I gave it a quick review, logged it on my sheet, and laid it upside down, starting a new pile. I would maintain Ryan's sequence. Per his rule.

He would be itching for a reason to complain about my work, and I wouldn't give him such an easy one.

Two hours later, I had logged all the research papers he'd printed out——by title, journal, and authors——in the order he had stacked them, and I started through his notes.

The man was thorough, and his notes were unusually clear for a scientist. Doctors may have had the worst handwriting, but scientists were often the most haphazard note takers. Ryan seemed the exception that proved the rule.

Reviewing the prior-art papers had given me an understanding of the importance of the drug he was working on. He was trying to cure an intractable disease.

Rule number two: talk to the assistant, Paul, and don't bother Ryan. By five o'clock, I had a series of questions prepared for Paul Mayer.

I went to the source of all knowledge, Gwen.

She was at her desk.

"What can I do you for?" she asked.

"I need to find Ryan's——sorry Dr. Westerly's——lab assistant, Paul, but I don't know what he looks like."

She rose and led me toward the break room. "I'm guessing Dr. Mayer is getting a caffeine fix. The man drinks Diet Cokes like nobody's business."

One of us was confused. "Dr. Mayer? No, I'm looking for Dr. Westerly's lab assistant."

Gwen stopped and turned to me. "Paul Mayer is his assistant, and also a PhD. in biochemistry."

"And he works as a lab tech?"

"Don't call him that. He's a lab assistant, and good enough to have his own lab at any other company, if you ask me. He's not much of a talker, but he's as sharp as they come. Dr. Westerly only hires the best. They make an odd pair, but there's no arguing with the results."

We reached the break room, and Gwen pointed out a lanky, balding man, probably twenty years older than Ryan——certainly not who I would have picked out of a crowd as his assistant. He had a Diet Coke in front of him and was eating a package of Fig Newtons.

I thanked Gwen after she introduced me.

"I'm writing up patent applications for Dr. Westerly, and he suggested I ask you if I had any questions about the work."

He looked at me intently and waited for me to continue.

"Dr. Mayer, would you have time now to go over a few things, or should we schedule this for later?"

He motioned to the chair across from him and nodded. "Paul" was all he said.

"Yes, Paul, thank you." I took the seat.

I had arranged my questions in the order they'd occurred in the processing. I slid across the printout of Ryan's notes for the first question.

"It's on CTX-26. It says here that the sample was subjected to successive centrifuge cycles."

He nodded.

Gwen's description of not talkative fit.

"And how fast would that be?"

He stroked his chin. "Nine-hundred thousand."

I waited for a more complete explanation. None was forthcoming. "RPM?"

Paul snorted. "Gs."

Apparently nine-hundred thousand RPM was absurd, but nine-hundred-thousand times the force of gravity was not. He bit off another sliver of his Fig Newton and looked at me expectantly.

I asked several more questions from my notes. For each, I had to be very specific to elicit a useful answer from Paul.

In the end, I thanked him for his time. He returned a smile and a nod.

I stood.

"Natalie. Your questions were quite insightful."

The six-word reply surprised me. Until now, he hadn't strung more than four words together. There was definitely more to Paul Mayer than I'd originally thought.

"Why, thank you, Paul. I'm sure I'll be back with more later."

He reverted to silent mode and merely raised his Diet Coke in salute. Paul Mayer was definitely an odd bird, but quite a nice man.

Shuffling back toward my desk, I saw Wanda, the ever-present security guard, emerging from my office.

"Just dropped off a delivery that arrived up front for you," she said. "You got some awfully nice friends." She walked away.

I didn't understand the comment, nor did I know who would be sending me anything. I hoped one of Damien's fans hadn't tracked me down again. They'd sent numerous packages of foul things to the house. The worst had been the dead chicken——even worse than the box of dog shit. I didn't need that kind of aggravation at work.

I crossed my fingers and opened the door.

A small white box was dead center on my desk.

Walking closer, the unmistakable picture of an iPhone on the top of the box made clear what it was. Still wrapped in cellophane, the box was a brand new phone. I set my papers down and turned it over. The label said it was a 256-gig version of the latest model, top-of-the-line iPhone——in rose gold no less, the same color as the one that had lost its life on the roadway this morning.

I hadn't told Gwen; I hadn't told anybody here. I racked my brain. Nobody knew I'd lost my phone.

I gasped.

Nobody but Ryan.

I couldn't suppress my smile, or the warmth that overtook me. This morning I'd resigned myself to at least a few weeks without a phone.

He had a soft side after all. He didn't need to do this, and yet he had. Just as he'd bought me a coffee when my credit cards wouldn't work. Ryan Westerly was certainly an enigma. He'd said his mother made him do it, but I wasn't buying that.

Maybe he was like an M&M, a hard shell and sweet on the inside? I settled on a prickly pear, with spines on the outside. Thorns fit him better than just a hard shell.

How to handle this?

I slid the white box into a drawer and put my computer to sleep. I stood from my desk and headed back to the break room.

The biotech industry knew how to take care of their employees. Chameleon hadn't skimped when it came to providing a high-tech coffee machine for the break room. I made two mochas for my encounter with Mr. Prickly Pear. It wasn't going to be as good as Peet's, but at least I knew his preferred brew.

My luck had changed today, and I needed to thank the responsible party.

Reaching his closed office door, I put one mocha down and knocked.

No answer. Naturally.

I knocked again, and then again.

"Enter!" The barked order came from within. Who the hell said *enter* these days?

I opened the door, picked up the coffee, and approached the desk.

He didn't look up for the longest time. "What do you want, Miss Spencer?"

"Natalie, and I brought you something." I offered him the coffee concoction.

He scowled and didn't move to accept it.

I set it on the edge of his desk. "For later, then."

A shiver went through me as he appraised me from head to toe, stopping perceptibly at my chest. It wasn't a co-worker's scan, but a man's, a look I hadn't gotten in a long time, a look that set my hairs on end.

"And?" he asked.

I tucked a stray hair behind my ear. "I came to say thank you for the phone."

"No need. It seemed the right thing to do." The man's face was impassive as his eyes held my gaze like a tractor beam.

Fumbling to get my mouth to operate, I finally found my voice. "Aren't you exceeding your quota for the week?"

A hint of a smile tugged at his mouth, just a momentary glimpse behind the prickly thorns on the exterior. "It's a minimum, not a maximum."

"Still, it was nice of you. But your secret is safe with me. I won't tell."

His eyes narrowed, and the hint of a smile disappeared. "You can close the door on your way out." He looked back toward his computer screen.

He thought our meeting had run its course, it seemed. But I wasn't done with him yet. I still had a job to do.

"I have some questions on your experiment, if you have a moment." It was the truth, but I had left off the part about wanting more time to peek past the prickly exterior.

"I don't have the time," he growled without looking up.

"It's mocha, by the way," I said as I turned to leave. I reached the door in several quick steps.

God, the man could be rude.

"Thank you," he said as I opened the door.

I turned to see that faint hint of a smile poking out through the thorny facade once more. It lasted only an instant, but I'd caught him. He couldn't hide it from me forever.

"Natalie," he added before returning to his computer.

"You're welcome, Ryan."

I closed the door and left with a spring in my step. I'd gotten my peek. A different Ryan Westerly hid beneath the gruff exterior.

I grabbed my purse on the way out. I still had to stop by the phone store to get my shiny new present activated. How quickly things could change. A week ago I wouldn't have given a second thought to a phone. Today, it was my most prized possession—— and my most prized gift.

Mr. Prickly Pear, I know your secret.

CHAPTER 10

R YAN

THE NEXT MORNING, I WOKE UP WITH A RAGING HARD-ON.

On my normal schedule, I would've gone hunting at one of the Harvard-area bars last night for an appropriate coed, but it hadn't appealed to me. Instead I'd gone back to the lab. A pile of samples awaited my analysis. I'd fallen behind my usual pace yesterday.

Natalie-on-the-brain had been the cause, and it was a condition I needed to cure myself of. A longer morning run had always helped in the past.

I laced up my running shoes and set out.

Turning left on the sidewalk, the chilly early morning air raised goosebumps all over me for the first few blocks. If somebody invented a blood pre-heater for runners in cold climates, I'd be front of the line to buy one.

The riverbank path I always took was thankfully devoid of arrogant bicyclists at this time of morning. I passed a few other runners going the opposite direction. Their breath left trails of fog in the cold air. We exchanged good-natured nods and hand raises, the camaraderie of early-morning exercise nuts.

As I crossed the river, I could see cars full of commuters sucking down coffee from their travel mugs on the BU Bridge. I went down the stairs from the bridge to the southside path and turned back toward the east to complete my loop.

She came from behind a tree. "Good morning, Ryan."

I almost tripped, turning to take in the sight. Natalie wore tight yoga pants like yesterday, but blue this morning instead of gray.

Her tits bounced enticingly in her tight top.

I went eyes-forward to avoid the sight, lest I embarrass myself again. "Aren't you going the wrong way?"

Why did she have to be so damned attractive?

"No, this is the right way," she said between breaths. "At least if I run the same direction you won't knock me over again."

I lengthened my strides.

She kept pace. "You said you didn't have any time for me yesterday."

I avoided looking over. "Sorry, today's even busier." I picked up the pace just a little more.

She laughed. "It won't work, Ryan. I ran cross-country in college."

I didn't acknowledge my attempt to leave her behind.

She had her phone in one hand, the phone I'd bought for her yesterday.

"I thought I could ask you about your experiments during your morning run," she said. "That way it won't cost you any extra time."

Her logic was frustratingly irrefutable. Damn her.

I slowed to my normal pace. There seemed to be no way to avoid her on this.

She glanced at her phone and drifted toward me.

We brushed against each other for just a stride.

The electric jolt of her brief touch shot up my arm. This girl would be the death of me.

"Sorry," she said, moving away.

I didn't answer, because I wasn't sorry in the least. I ran because I should, because it was good for me, because it cleared my mind, not because I enjoyed it. Until today.

"My first question is…" She read from her phone. "What do you see as the significant difference between your approach and that in the Jefferson paper?"

Her question surprised me. Jefferson was the most important prior-art paper to deal with, and she'd figured it out in less than a day. She was much sharper than I'd given her credit for.

Unless?

"Did Paul mention that paper?" I asked.

"No. We discussed the gaps in your experimental notes."

We dodged to the right, off the path, to avoid two cyclists riding abreast, taking up the entire trail.

"What gaps? There are no…" I made the mistake of looking over and catching a glimpse of her bouncing tits again. "No gaps."

Focus, Ryan, focus.

"Maybe you'd be happier…" We angled back onto the pavement. "…if I called them something else."

I was careful to keep my eyes on the path. "It doesn't matter what you call them. There aren't any discrepancies in my notes."

"Have it your way. Help me understand them," she said as we jogged along, passing a slower runner.

We continued pounding the pavement eastward toward the Longfellow Bridge, my normal turning point.

"About the Jefferson paper," she started.

Her breathing had become more labored. She may have run cross country in college, but that was clearly a few years ago.

I slowed my pace a tad.

"I noticed that they didn't do the first centrifuge step; is that the only distinction between your experiments?" she asked.

This girl was good. She had caught on right away. A lot of professionals would have missed that.

I slowed further as we approached the bridge. "Why do you need me, if you already know the answer?"

"I didn't want to go off in the wrong direction," she said between breaths.

"The earlier centrifuge step increases the purity prior to the first incubation." We dodged a teenager on a bicycle. "That and the pH adjustment later are the most important distinguishing characteristics."

Another cyclist came at us, and I let Natalie go ahead. I followed.

Big mistake.

I couldn't take my eyes off her ass and those legs. I sped up to get alongside her where I could look straight ahead and not be distracted.

We crossed the bridge and turned back westward on the MIT side of the river. She asked a series of questions, and I answered as we ran, no different than if we'd been across a table, but all without looking at her. That was the one thing I couldn't do.

When we reached the BU Bridge again, she begged off.

"I need to make Ralph's breakfast," she said as she turned off toward central Cambridge. "Thanks for the time, Ryan."

Ralph?

He had to be a loser with a name like that. She deserved better.

I crossed the river for my second lap. I was going to need it, and possibly a third to get my head straight after this time with her. It wasn't going to be easy to unsee her in those tight pants, or her bouncing chest——especially her bouncing chest.

∽

Natalie

. . .

OPENING THE APARTMENT DOOR, I ALMOST TRIPPED ON RALPH AS he ran up to me, chastising me with loud meows. I'd been so concerned about being late and missing Ryan that I'd broken Ralph's rule number one: I'd left without feeding him.

I took down my notes from the run as quickly as I could.

Ralph visited his empty food bowl and gave me a disgusted look. He wasn't happy about being in second place for my attention and wanted me to know it.

I finished my notes, realizing I'd forgotten one of Ryan's answers. Maybe it would come to me later.

This early-morning run wasn't the best way to ask questions, but seemed like the only way right now with his constant refusal to grant me time during the day. It had been a mistake, though, not to record his answers as we ran on the trail.

I knew the reason I'd missed that one answer. I'd been distracted by him. He wasn't merely a one-hundred-octane man who dripped sex appeal, but he was brilliant to boot——and kind, although he tried to hide it behind his quota explanation.

I'd gotten a peek behind the curtain of rudeness he put up to hide from everyone else, and I was certain more surprises lay there to be discovered.

It had been a mistake to suggest his notes had lacked clarity. I should have found a better way to phrase it——an item to remember for our next encounter. Gracious acceptance of criticisms was not one of his attributes.

Keeping up with him during the run hadn't been easy, and I would have died if he hadn't slowed a little on the return leg. Yoga and Pilates had filled my schedule more often than cardio, but that was going to change. Daily runs with Ryan had just moved to the top of my priority list, and not just for the workout value.

I fixed Ralph's food and set the bowl down for him. "Breakfast, Ralph."

He ignored everything, remaining curled in a ball on the couch, intent on punishing me.

Jasmin still hadn't been in touch. My stomach knotted at the thought. What could have happened to her? I had no way to reach her, and no way to get to LA if she needed me.

∾

WHEN I REACHED THE OFFICE, RYAN'S DOOR WAS CLOSED, AND NO light showed under it. I'd beaten him back. He obviously did more than one loop of the river trail each morning.

Ryan's stack of papers greeted me when I opened my office door. It was unlocked again, but Gwen had told me she let the janitor in to empty the trash before most of us arrived. I would have to ask her to lock it again after he finished. Liam had been insistent that I keep my work behind lock and key.

My computer started up quickly, and a check of my email yielded a surprise.

I let out a relieved breath. Jasmin had finally responded last night. Her message said she'd dropped her phone in the toilet just before a long string of overseas flights. She'd returned yesterday and hadn't gotten a chance to replace it yet. I giggled, imagining Jasmin debating whether to put her hand in the toilet to retrieve her precious phone. No doubt she'd made Corbin do it for her.

Knowing she was safe put my mind at ease.

I typed a quick response saying how good it was to hear from her, and asking if she could please give me the full name and contact number of her boyfriend in case I needed to contact her. I signed it Natalie SPENCER and hit send; my electronic missive was on its way.

My shitty circumstances with the asset seizure and this harassment by AUSA Kirk fucking Willey could wait for another day, as could news of my new job, and most of all, any mention of the hot prickly-pear billionaire Ryan Westerly.

I loved her dearly, but playing fast and loose with ways to

reach her was something I would have to break her of. She'd caused me more than a few sleepless nights.

CHAPTER 11

*R*YAN

I LEFT THE LAB AFTER FINISHING THE LATEST AFTERNOON SAMPLE summary. Paul had been right; it was turning out interesting.

I turned the key in my office door, but it was already unlocked. It had been locked when I left after lunch——I was nothing if not conscientious about locking up.

The faint scent of orange gave her away as soon as I opened the door. Natalie was on her knees, picking up papers from a stack by my desk she must have knocked over.

"How did you get in?" I asked.

"I have a key."

A key?

"Liam gave it to me," she said, a reminder that she was Liam's special hire, and there was nothing I could do about it.

"This is why I don't allow visitors," I barked. "You've ruined the organization."

"I can fix it," she answered, still on her knees by my desk.

Her red lips trembled as I approached, the very same lips I'd imagined clamped around my cock a dozen times since this morning. She'd better get out, unless she was assuming the position to suck me off right here.

She looked up at me, lips parted. "I know your system; I can put them back."

"You are supposed to be helping with patents, not distracting me." I instantly regretted uttering the words.

"I was picking up another experiment to start on. I'll be out of your way in a second." She shuffled forward a few inches to reach the papers at my feet and looked up at me from the perfect angle, perfect to look down her blouse.

The canyon of her cleavage drew my eyes. I could imagine getting lost there.

She had chosen a pale pink bra today, a color that likely matched her nipples. Nipples she would beg me to suck, to lick, to nip.

"What am I doing to distract you?" she asked innocently, breaking my stare.

As if she didn't know.

I shouldn't have said a word. I'd said what I meant, but it wasn't something I should have admitted. Anyway *distracting* was much too meek a word for what she did to me.

Did she have no idea how tempting she was? How utterly sexy? Her tight skirt over those hips that were just meant to be grabbed, the way she filled out her blouse with tits that begged to be sucked, begged to be handled?

The pink lace of her bra down the opening of her top from this angle was enough to make me lose it. I stepped back. I'd stared too long——much too long.

She likely realized I'd been taking in every aspect of her body, committing it all to memory to jerk off to later. Instead of objecting to my stare, or getting up to leave, she gathered up the last of the fallen stack.

"Take a minute to pull the stick out of your ass and be little nicer," she said. "I'm just doing my job."

"Nicer?" The gall of this girl. Nobody talked to me like that.

"Yes, nicer. You can cut the rude-asshole routine with me. I'm just trying to help." She held the papers up to her chest, shielding herself.

"Me be nicer? You're the one who just called me an asshole." That ought to be good enough to get her fired.

"So you know the word?"

She stared up at me, still on her knees, her face just a foot from my straining dick. Her tongue darted out and wet her lips. She got to her feet and smoothed her skirt with one hand, still clutching the papers to her chest with the other.

"Natalie," I said.

I couldn't come up with any other words. I didn't trust myself to not grab her, lock my mouth over hers, and tell her how beautiful she was just before I took her on my desk, fucking the attitude right out of her.

The sexual electricity between us was hot enough to set off the fire sprinklers.

My heart hammered, and my cock strained against my zipper as she looked me up and down, pausing noticeably at my crotch, giving me the same treatment I'd given her moments ago.

She cocked her head back and parted her lips. "Ryan, you can be a little distracting too." She licked her lips again.

I didn't look away, and neither did she. Her next move, or mine, could start fireworks that wouldn't be quenched without ripping clothes and grasping flesh.

"Natalie," I said again, slowly.

She bit her bottom lip, considering her next move——a move that would determine how this would play out between us. There was no doubt she felt the static in the air. No doubt at all.

I reached out and smoothed my thumb over the lip she bit, perhaps crossing a line that couldn't be uncrossed.

"I think you should let me get some work done." I pulled my hand back.

She didn't move.

I wished silently that she would refuse and tell me she wanted to stay. I'd wanted to fuck plenty of girls, but none as badly as I wanted to fuck Natalie Spencer at this moment.

If we'd been in a more casual setting, away from work, I wouldn't have held back. But here in my office, mere feet from the rest of the company, I had to control myself. The walls weren't thick enough to contain the screams of ecstasy I intended to force out of her.

She nodded and stepped back and then around me. Her faint orange scent followed her.

I wouldn't have been able to control myself more than a few seconds longer. I faced the desk, away from the door, afraid I'd change my mind and yank her back to me if I watched her go.

I heard her open the door.

"The application for CTX-26 is on your desk for your approval. I have just one question remaining to be cleared up."

I turned.

She stood in the doorway. "What does CTX stand for, by the way?"

"Chameleon Therapeutics Experimental," I answered.

"Tomorrow." She winked and shut the door.

Fuck me.

I took a deep breath. I'd almost lost my load when she winked at me from the door. Or, did I just want it so badly I'd imagined it?

I took another deep, calming breath, adjusted my dick in my pants so I could sit down, and opened the folder she'd left for me.

A half hour later, I'd gone over the application and couldn't fault a single thing in it.

She'd done a masterful job understanding the experimental sequence, as well as the distinctions from the prior art of other scientists. Liam had been right; she was good at this. And she'd accomplished this application in a day, without taking hours of my time the way the previous occupants of her office had attempted to do.

She was more than a beautiful distraction. This morning's questions and this afternoon's application proved she was sharp as a tack and talented. She was the complete package——beauty and brains.

With the coeds I normally pursued, brains had never been much of a criteria. Sure, they were all smart enough to get into Harvard or MIT or one of the other several dozen colleges nearby, but I doubted any of them could hold a candle to Natalie.

This morning, I'd done my best to keep my eyes off her for fear of getting distracted. That ship had sailed, and I would have to learn to deal with it. Imagining how her tits were going to feel in my hands when I got her into bed made my cock strain against my pants again.

And I *was* going to get her in bed. There was no doubt about that anymore. She knew it too. Now it was only a matter of timing.

~

NATALIE

"THAT TOTALLY SUCKS," JASMIN SAID. "I'LL TRANSFER YOU SOME money."

We were on the phone——after dinner my time and late afternoon in LA. I'd finished explaining the horrible day I'd had when the FBI had taken everything.

"Jaz, that'll have to wait until I can get a bank account set up. They froze everything I had under Winterbourne, and until I can get one set up under Spencer, I'm a cash-and-carry girl."

"I never did think you should have taken his name. I mean, Winterbourne? It just sounds evil."

I couldn't have agreed more right now. "Water under the bridge. I got my Spencer driver's license today——sort of the beginning of the rest of my life."

"Nat, you know you can stay at the apartment as long as you need to."

"Thanks, Jaz. I'll take care of everything here."

"Just don't let that demonic cat of yours climb my curtains again."

I flinched, remembering how Ralph had been a less-than-stellar house guest last time.

"I'll see to it." I would need to get some of those glue-on claw protectors tomorrow before Ralph made a liar of me.

As if on cue, Ralph rubbed up against my leg and meowed.

"Hey, where's Corbin? And when do I get to meet the mystery man?"

"He's at work, and I don't know when we can get out there really. I'm signed up for all far-east flights for the rest of the month, nothing going your way for a while."

"Can't a cop take some time off to meet his girlfriend's sister?"

"He's tied up on some secret task force. He's not allowed to talk about it. You know how it is. Maybe later."

"Sure."

I had no idea how it was with cops, but after Damien, I understood completely about being left in the dark by the man in your life. If only mine had been a cop instead of a crook.

"Is there anything that lawyer can do for you?" she asked. "It sounds so illegal what they did."

"He said it would take a while."

My phone dinged with an incoming text. I held it back to read.

LIAM: Good work

"I heard that," Jasmin said.

"It was just work."

"Right," she said in disbelief.

"It was," I protested.

I would rather it had been Ryan, but I didn't have his number, and he didn't have mine. Then I got an idea.

"Gotta go," I told Jasmin. "Work calls, and I need this job."

"Talk again soon, Nat. I'm off to Tokyo tomorrow, but I'll have a break in the schedule in a few weeks. Let's say we do another spa weekend, out on the cape this time?"

I smiled, remembering the time we'd had together last year, just the two of us. "I wish I could afford it, but——"

She stopped me mid-sentence. "My treat, Nat. I can't wait to see you again."

"You're the best, Jaz."

She had always been there when I needed her. And a weekend away with her sounded heavenly. I really needed a break like that.

"I'll set it up. I found a place in Provincetown. Be good and don't do anything I wouldn't do."

Her last statement didn't limit me much; Jasmin had always been the wild one.

"Sure, and you keep your phone away from the toilets."

She laughed, and we hung up.

Liam's text could only be referring to the patent application. I composed my message, checked it, then erased *Ryan* and replaced it with *Dr. Westerly*.

ME: Thank you. Could you please send me contact info for Dr. Westerly?

A moment later, Liam's return text arrived with Ryan Westerly's cell number.

I didn't hesitate. I wasn't into half measures today. This was my new life as Natalie Spencer. I composed a message to Ryan.

ME: BU bridge at 7?

I didn't get anything back right away. Maybe I should have signed the text.

Just as I put the phone down, it dinged.

RYAN: 6:30

Why change the time? It didn't matter really.

ME: Ok

I sat back, and warmth swept over me. I'd just asked Mr. Prickly Pear on a date of sorts, and it felt good. I had no idea why he wanted to start earlier, but I didn't care. I wasn't sure what had happened in his office today, but the way he'd looked me over, the hungry glint in his blue eyes, had me hoping I'd read the signals right. Tomorrow was just the two of us running together, but it was a start.

I powered up my laptop. I still needed a cogent set of questions.

~

*R*YAN

THE MESSAGE HAD ARRIVED JUST AFTER MY REGULAR EVENING visit at the hospital.

The text from Natalie had been a surprise. I hadn't given her my cell number.

She was obviously resourceful because almost nobody had it.

As I lay in bed, sleep didn't come easily. I'd played out the scenarios in my head a million times. I closed my eyes, and the million and first started.

Instead of leaving my office, she undid the first button of her top and reached for my belt. That had been all it took. I lifted her skirt, ripped off her panties and bent her over the desk. She came like a banshee, yelling so loud the whole building had heard, but I didn't care. She wanted me, and I wanted her even more. And now they would all know she was off limits——she was mine.

My eyes jerked open as I realized how absurd that scene was. Loud and quick in the office was all wrong. It might be right for some girls, but not her.

It needed to be here in my bed, long and slow. That's what she deserved, and that's what she would get.

Or maybe she liked it up against the wall. Or in the kitchen, or...

I went back and forth many more times before sleep finally overtook me.

CHAPTER 12

R YAN

I REACHED THE BRIDGE EARLY, NOT WANTING TO MISS HER. I waited to see the voluptuous Natalie running toward me. I'd imagined it a hundred times on the run over, like a slow-motion running scene in a movie——her tits bouncing with each step, straining against the fabric.

Right on time, she jogged toward me in the early morning light. She was a sight to behold, and she bounced even better than I'd imagined.

"Morning. Are you ready for two loops today?" I asked as she reached me.

"If you think you can tolerate me that long."

I laughed, and we started out. This was going to be a good run.

All business, she began by repeating a question from yesterday. She was carrying her phone to record my answers today——very efficient.

By the time we started the second loop, she had exhausted her work questions.

"That's all?" I asked as we traversed the steps down to the southside path.

"Wasn't that enough?"

"Quite," I responded. "You can stop the recorder now."

She shot me a quizzical glance before she closed the phone app. "Why? You want to go off the record?"

"You're very thorough," I told her, slowing to let her go ahead as we passed a gaggle of runners going west. "And I was hoping you could remember a compliment without the recorder."

When we had to go single file, I let her go first. The view was magnificent from back here, simply magnificent. But then I hadn't found any bad angles to view her from.

"Thanks."

"How did you end up working for us? You seem like you could have a job at any of the local law firms."

We passed a slower jogger.

"They only hire lawyers, and I'm not a lawyer," she said after a few strides.

That threw me. With her obvious knowledge of patent law, I'd just assumed she was a lawyer, same as Smithersnott had been.

"I did two years of law at Columbia, but my marriage interrupted that."

That answer pointed out how little I knew about Natalie Spencer.

"You're married?"

"Not anymore."

That was a relief.

We trotted off the path for a few strides to avoid cyclists coming the other way and continued on in silence.

I'd obviously introduced a painful subject. "You don't need to——"

"My married name was Winterbourne," she said, breaking the awkwardness between us.

"I like Spencer better," I told her between breaths.

"I was Damien Winterbourne's wife."

"His loss, I'm sure."

"You're okay with that?" she asked as I let her go ahead again.

"Why wouldn't I be?"

I'd never considered divorced women one way or the other. Everybody was entitled to make mistakes in their lives.

She stopped by the side of the trail. "I said *Damien Winterbourne*."

I was missing something here. "The name doesn't mean a thing to me. Should it?"

She started jogging again, and I followed to catch up.

"What am I not understanding?" I asked when I got alongside her.

"Don't you watch the news?"

"Never. It's a waste of time." The only news that interested me I found in the journals I perused every morning.

"Read a newspaper?"

"Why bother?"

We reached the Longfellow Bridge and started across to the Cambridge side. She sped up, and I followed. She wasn't going to outrun me, of that I was certain.

"You should do your research," she said before we reached the other side.

There was some history she felt I needed to know, but I didn't care. Right now, I knew everything I needed to about Natalie Spencer. She was quite a package: brilliant, hard working, and beautiful; and she made my cock ache. The electricity I'd felt between us yesterday was real. She was just denying it.

At the turn onto the northside path, she continued straight into Cambridge. I turned on my normal loop; I had another lap to go.

"See you at work, Dr. Westerly."

I didn't run with my phone, so research would have to wait till I got home.

Fuck research.

I reversed course, sprinted back to Main Street, and turned left, the way she had gone.

After a few blocks, I still couldn't see her ahead. She was faster than I'd given her credit for, or she'd turned off on a side street. I sprinted to the Chameleon building, which wasn't far away.

Reaching the lobby, I yanked open the glass door. My lungs ached.

It was early, and the receptionist wasn't in yet.

I pressed the after-hours buzzer, and the ever-present Wanda appeared from inside.

"I need Natalie Spencer's home address," I panted.

"Dr. Westerly, the manual says——"

"Screw the manual, Wanda. I need it now," I said, definitely louder than I should have.

"Okay already, but don't tell Gwen." She logged onto the receptionist's computer and gave me the address.

I knew the street, so I just had to remember the house and apartment number. "Thanks, Wanda. Sorry. I shouldn't have yelled."

"It's okay, because it's you," she said as I left.

That was an odd statement I didn't know how to take.

I left for Natalie's street at a slower pace. I knew where she'd be, and I wouldn't be able to speak intelligently if I was too out of breath.

Her building number turned out to be on the right side of the street.

I crossed between cars and checked the mailboxes. Number six had J. Spencer listed. *It had better not be her father*, I thought as I ascended the stairs to the second floor. That would be more than a bit awkward. *"Hello, Mr. Spencer, is Natalie home? I just want to tell her how much I want to fuck her."*

There was no way in hell that conversation went well.

Number six was on the left, and I knocked.

No response.

I knocked again.

A careful listen close to the door yielded no discernible sound from within. I often stopped for coffee on the way home. If she did the same, I might have beaten her here.

I knocked again, harder this time.

A faint "Just a minute" came from inside.

Moments later, the door opened the width of the security chain.

Her hair was wet, and she had a towel wrapped around her. She'd come from the shower.

Her eyes popped wide. "Ryan?"

"Natalie," I said, at a loss for anything else. My usual lines for girls about *coming over to my place* didn't fit.

She unchained the door. "Come in."

"It said J. Spencer downstairs. Your brother?"

"No, sister," she replied, closing and chaining the door behind me.

"Oh."

"She's in LA. I'm staying here because…" She looked away. "Well, just because."

"And Ralph?" I asked. I'd almost forgotten the guy she'd mentioned.

"Ralph is my cat."

I let out a relieved breath. We were alone.

"I wanted to say…I don't care to do any research." I stepped closer. Her faint scent of orange wafted my way.

I didn't know how to say the only research I wanted to do was between her legs.

She bit her bottom lip in that seductive way again. "I'm not sure."

I was. I closed the distance and pulled her to me. Her breasts pressed against me with only the damp towel between us, our lips inches apart.

She lifted up on her toes and snaked a hand behind my neck, pulling herself up to meet my lips. She wanted this too.

I squeezed her closer, my firming erection pressing against her. Her mouth opened to me, and we began the exotic dance of lust. We exchanged breath and our tongues sparred as we caressed each other. I longed to explore her body.

I pulled at the towel, and it came loose. I flung it to the side. One hand found the softness of her breast as the other grasped her ass and pulled her tightly to me.

She tasted of grape juice and desire. Her hair carried the familiar orange scent I'd come to associate with her.

None of my imagined scenarios were playing out, but this was better. She felt warm and soft against my hardness, and she pulled herself to me with the intensity of pent-up desire.

"Ryan," she said, pulling away for a moment. "You need to know."

I shushed her with a finger to her lips. "No words. Close your eyes and just feel."

"But——"

"Ssshhhh. Close your eyes and stop arguing, girl." I should have said woman. There was nothing girlish about her; she was all woman.

She hesitated before giving in and closing her eyes.

She squealed as I picked her up and deposited her on the edge of the couch.

Her eyes opened again, wide with concern, almost alarm. My finger went to her lips and she calmed down, closing her eyes again, giving in to my request.

I spread her legs and knelt between them. I kissed my way slowly down from her neck to between her breasts. After a quick visit to each hardened nipple, my mouth continued the journey south, stopping briefly at her belly button and then on to the final destination.

She leaned back, and her legs quivered as my tongue made the first swipe up the length of her folds. Her breath hitched when I began to circle and suck at her clit. Then I darted to one side and the other, watching her shiver with delight as I did.

She was responsive to the lightest lick, the softest suck, the gentlest flick of my tongue. A gasp escaped her as I inserted a finger. She was soaking wet and slippery——and tight, oh so tight around my finger.

My cock ached, anticipating her tightness surrounding me.

She threaded her fingers into my hair and pulled me snugly to her pussy, craving more.

I gave her more. More finger action, more tongue action, more sucking on her little bundle of nerves.

She arched her hips into me and pulled at my hair.

I raised up to look into her lust-filled eyes. "I'm going to fuck you straight into next week," I told her, my chin rubbing against her clit.

"Then fuck me already," she panted. She tried to pull me up to her.

"Not 'till you come for me."

She gave in and arched her mound into my mouth as I tongued her rapidly.

Before long she shuddered and gasped as her climax overtook her. Staccato gasps were her only sounds. Her legs shook as her fingers clawed at me.

I lapped up her juices as she rode the wave down from her high, slowly regaining her breath.

Her eyes opened to look into mine. "That was——"

A loud knock sounded at her door.

"Natalie Winterbourne? FBI," came from the hallway.

I jerked up, not sure I'd heard it right. I struggled to reposition my cock to make my erection less noticeable in my shorts. I shifted the fanny pack to the front and wiped my mouth with my sleeve.

Natalie ran to the bedroom.

"What do you want?" I asked through the door.

"Open the door, sir."

I could see Natalie climbing into some clothes through the open door to her bedroom.

"Just a minute," I said.

"Now, sir." They were insistent, and they carried guns——not people to have pissed off at you.

I left the security chain in place and cracked the door. "Can I see some ID?" I expected that would slow them down.

Two men in suits stood in the hallway. The first took his ID from his coat and flipped it open.

"Special Agent White, FBI," he said.

I'd never seen real FBI credentials, but this set looked official enough to me.

I looked toward Natalie's room. She wasn't quite dressed yet.

"And you?" I said to suit number two.

He presented his ID as well. "Special Agent McNally," he said in a tone that indicated his displeasure.

Natalie came up behind me. "It's okay. I'm used to this."

"You don't have to," I told her. And who the hell is used to the FBI knocking on their door?

"It's okay."

I closed the door, undid the chain, and opened it again. I stood in the doorway, blocking their entrance.

"May we come in?" White asked.

"No," I said before Natalie had a chance to object. "State your business."

I knew my rights. We didn't have to let them in.

Natalie didn't overrule me.

"Mrs. Winterbourne, you need to come with us," White said.

"It's no longer Winterbourne. The name is Spencer," Natalie said from behind me.

That didn't slow him down one bit. "No matter. You need to come downtown to the US Attorney's office to talk with AUSA Willey about a few things."

With an arm, I urged her to stay behind me. "Are you arresting her?"

She tugged me back by the shoulder. "It's all right, Ryan. You go into work, and I'll be along when I can." She walked past me into the hallway with her purse.

I had nowhere to go but out with her.

She locked the door after us. "I'm used to this."

Neither agent said another word. Downstairs, they loaded her into the back of a black SUV and drove off.

She waved to me as they pulled away from the curb.

Taken by the fucking FBI?

She was right; I did need to know more. I started the jog back to my place.

CHAPTER 13

NATALIE

THIS WASN'T THE FIRST TIME I'D BEEN *INVITED* DOWN TO THE federal courthouse to talk about Damien's misdeeds, but this was the first time they'd shown up at my door first thing in the morning, insisting on driving me there.

Thankfully neither of them spoke for the entire trip. I recognized White as the one who'd kicked me out of my house, and the other had probably been there as well, but I hadn't paid that much attention at the time.

On the way, I dialed Mason Brosnahand's number and left a message telling him where they were taking me.

Once through the metal detectors, they escorted me into a small conference room upstairs, for what I expected to be the same set of questions as always. The one thing I'd been told was never to deviate from my story.

The papers had said Martha Stewart was arrested on insider trading charges. But the only charge brought against her was the one she went to jail for: lying to the FBI. First you tell them you walked down the left side of the street, then you tell them it was the right, and just like that you're a criminal. Martha learned the hard way.

I wasn't going down that road. She'd probably gotten off easy because of her celebrity status, but I didn't have that advantage. I had just the opposite reputation. They'd be happy to lock me up and lose the key for a decade or two.

I waited alone in the cold conference room, staring at the tiles in the ceiling. Today had started so well, and now I was going to waste another morning reviewing things I didn't know about what Damien had done while we were married, before this whole nightmare began. I reviled the man for what he'd done to me. But they couldn't understand that, or didn't want to.

I squeezed my legs together, remembering this morning with Ryan. My one bright spot: Ryan. This morning the sun had finally shone on my future. Then this.

Without a knock, the door opened and the two agents entered, followed by another man, whose nametag around his neck said Willey, the asshole AUSA who had threatened me a few days ago, the asshole behind the seizure of my house, my car, my future, my everything.

Fuck you, Kirk Willey.

~

R YAN

I POWERED UP THE COMPUTER AS SOON AS I GOT HOME. I GRABBED a water while it booted.

A quick search for *Winterbourne* yielded pages of results as soon as I figured out how to spell it correctly.

Damien Winterbourne, the mini-Madoff of Boston, had been arrested and now sat in prison awaiting trial on dozens of federal counts of financial fraud. His schemes had wrecked thousands of lives in the New England area and had dominated the news for months, based on all the articles on the web.

It came back to me in a flash. Damien Winterbourne's company had been in talks to invest in Chameleon before Liam bought us, and I had completely forgotten the name.

The pages contained a few stories of Natalie divorcing Damien, all with the slant that as his wife, she must have been involved somehow. But she had not been charged. The implications were clear: she'd had a hand in it and gotten away with crimes against the good people of Boston. There were even pictures of crowds gathered outside the house chanting ugly slogans.

A few articles voiced the opinion that she had brought him down, but that seemed to be the minority perspective.

Natalie must have gone through a terrible ordeal. No wonder she'd divorced the dickhead and renounced his name.

Walking around this town with her married name had to be akin to visiting New York with a nametag that read Osama bin Laden.

The most recent story, from a few days ago, showed federal agents at a suburban house. The subtitle indicated her property had been seized. The sources quoted in the story made it clear they thought it was overdue.

I shut down the computer. A shower was next on my agenda.

The poor girl had been through hell, and based on the tactics of the FBI this morning, it wasn't over yet.

The other thing I could be fairly certain about? She didn't deserve it.

Liam Quigley was nothing if not thorough. He wouldn't in a million years have hired her without being certain of her innocence. Liam didn't take risks like that.

The ex-Mrs. Winterbourne had been through the wringer, and it wasn't over yet.

∾

NATALIE

KIRK WILLEY INTRODUCED HIMSELF; HE EVEN SPELLED HIS NAME.

I didn't take his extended hand. The last thing I intended to do was shake with one of these lowlifes.

Willey placed a digital recorder in the center of the table and started it. He stated the date, time, and who they had on their side of the table. "Continued interrogation of Mrs. Natalie Winterbourne."

I surprised him by opening my purse. "Can't you guys get a single thing straight?" I slid over my precious temporary driver's license. "It's Natalie *Spencer*," I told him loudly.

He read the paper with a smirk. "The continued interrogation of Natalie Spencer, previously Natalie Winterbourne, wife of Damien Winterbourne."

The reminder of my bad judgment for having married Damien stung.

"Natalie——" he started.

"Ms. Spencer," I corrected him.

I had no intention of being on a first-name basis with this asshole who had taken everything from me.

"Very well, Ms. Spencer. It has come to our attention that your husband kept a ledger of certain off-the-books financial trans-actions."

"You'd have to ask him about that."

"We have, and he hasn't denied it," Willey said.

The two FBI goons stayed silent.

I knew this trick. "Did he say he had, or did he just decline to answer?"

I couldn't lie to the FBI, but they could lie to me trying to elicit a confession of some kind, to trick me.

Willey smiled, not answering. His silence provided the response. They had asked Damien, and he hadn't said anything.

This was our first meeting. Willey had been handed Damien's case when the previous attorney was found to be biased because his wife's IRA account had been managed by one of Damien's victims. That mistake had delayed the trial.

"We need to find that ledger to prove your innocence."

What a crock. They cared about convicting Damien of as many counts as they could. It already added up to a hundred and eighty-seven years in jail, but that wasn't enough for them. Charging me with something would appease the pitchfork crowd in this town and earn these jerks kudos from on high.

"When did you first start working for Liam Quigley?" Willey asked.

This was the first time my work for Quigley-Fulton had come up.

"Last year."

Willey's eyes narrowed. "Getting back to the ledger, did you pass it to Mr. Quigley?"

"I told you, I don't know anything about a ledger. I've never heard of one before today."

"You need to think back carefully about this, Ms. Spencer. We are attempting to recoup as much as we can for the victims of your fraud as possible."

"Not my fraud. Damien's. I told you I don't know anything about a ledger. If he kept one, he didn't tell me."

"Yes, your husband's fraud. I'm sure you want to do what you can to help the victims."

The questioning went on like this for over an hour.

I repeated the same answers. I'd never been told about a ledger, I'd never seen one, and I didn't know anything that could help them.

Then the door from the hallway opened.

A big man filled the doorway. Mason Brosnahand entered, wearing one of his signature brown suits.

"Natalie, don't say another word." He rounded the table to my side.

I sat back in my chair. Finally this would be over, at least for today. On TV, when the lawyer arrived, the questioning ended.

Willey leaned forward to turn off the recorder. Today was apparently no different.

"Willey, I told you not to question her out of my presence," Mason bellowed.

The two agents squirmed, but Willey sat expressionless. "She came willingly."

"The next time you would like to question Ms. Spencer, you request it through me."

Willey didn't respond. "We'll talk again," he said to me, more threat than suggestion.

Mason urged me to stand, which I did, and he escorted me out of the building and led me to his car.

He offered me a ride back home.

"To work would be better," I answered.

"Work? I didn't know you had started a job."

"Just did. Chameleon Therapeutics." I gave him the address.

"No problem," he replied.

On the drive, he asked what they'd wanted to know, and I told him about the million questions on the supposed ledger.

"What about the money?" he asked.

"This time money didn't come up. It was all about a ledger." Before they had always focused on what I knew about Damien's business dealings, and about money they thought he'd stashed.

He turned right toward the bridge. "They probably think the two are hidden in the same place."

"Today they only asked about a ledger," I repeated. "They took my house. If they think there's a secret hiding place, they can tear it down looking. I don't know where it is."

"They'll probably do that next."

I felt nauseated at the thought of them tearing my house apart. Until now, I'd held out hope of getting it back with Mason's help.

We halted at a stoplight, and he turned to me. "What did they say about the ledger?"

"Nothing much. Just that they think it has records of some sort."

"Nothing about money laundering?"

We crossed the bridge.

"No, those words didn't come up."

"Good, then they're probably not trying to broaden the case to include you."

We were getting close to Chameleon.

"Why would they think I have anything to do with money laundering?"

"It's just a way to pressure you to tell them where he hid the money."

We stopped in front of the Chameleon building.

Mason turned to me. "Natalie, think hard. There must be a hiding place you can remember?"

I had no idea. I'd told everybody the truth a million times. "If Damien had a hiding place, he didn't tell me." I undid my seatbelt. "Thank you for the ride."

"If you come up with an idea of where the ledger might be, call me first. I can make sure you get credit with them for cooperating. It's the best and fastest way to get your house back."

I opened the door. "I will."

The part about getting my house back sounded good. Too bad I had no information to trade. Though I did have one avenue to get information for them…maybe. Damien had been the one to suggest a meeting. I discarded the thought. He was the reason I was in this mess in the first place.

"And don't agree to go with them again without calling me."

"I won't." I closed the car door.

Volunteering for another meeting with fucking Kirk Willey was already on my never-again list. The guy gave me the creeps.

Tear down my house?

I might have to rethink a Damien meeting if it could save my house.

CHAPTER 14

R YAN

I KNOCKED ON THE DOOR.

"Come in."

I let myself into Liam's office.

"Ryan, have a seat," he said as he got up from his desk. "I'm glad you approve of the work Natalie did on that first patent application. She really knows her stuff, doesn't she?"

I shut the door behind me. "Can we talk about her?"

"Sure, but don't tell me you don't care to work with her, because that's not changing. We need her, and she's here to stay."

I sat down.

Liam retook his seat, his face changing to one of concern. "What is it?"

Unsure how to start, I hesitated.

"Ryan, just take your time."

Liam had this uncanny ability to read me that I hadn't run in to with previous managers.

"It's about Natalie. What can you tell me about her ex-husband?"

A darkness descended on his demeanor. "That skunk deserves whatever he gets." He took in a deep breath. "Let me start at the beginning. Damien Winterbourne and I were in competition when I was at Quigley-Fulton, before coming over here. He was outbidding us at every turn, intent on taking us down, trying to ruin us. It turns out, he had the help of a spy in my organization."

I waited for more.

"But that's the minor story," he continued. "In the bigger picture, he had been fleecing people in this town for years, and nobody realized it until my sister and her husband got onto his trail and turned him in to the FBI. It was big in the news a few months back. Mini-Madoff they called him."

"And Natalie?" I asked.

"In college, Natalie was my wife's roommate, and a dear friend. I've learned Natalie is as good as they come. I hired her for some part-time work at Quigley-Fulton before all the crap hit the fan.

"After his arrest, though, it got tough for her——the innuendos and all——so she stopped working for us. She divorced him, and she was getting her life back together until the feds swooped in a few days ago and took everything, and I mean everything."

I shifted in my chair. "You knew about that?"

"Sure. I learned about it the day it happened. Amy and I knew she was too proud to ask for help, so I offered her a job here. But don't get me wrong, her dad was a top-notch patent lawyer in his day, the best of the best, and she has two years at Columbia Law under her belt. I knew she could handle this work. She's one bright lady."

"She is good. The work she showed me yesterday was excellent," I told him.

He nodded. "So now you know the story. Don't hold her past against her. She's had a hard time of it."

"I'm not," I assured him. "But I have some bad news."

Liam leaned forward.

"The FBI took her in for questioning at seven-thirty this morning."

His fist came down on the desk with a bang. "Assholes."

"Is she in trouble?" I asked.

"They put a new guy on Damien's case recently; that's all I know, but I'll see what my uncle can find out. We'll support her any way we can."

Having Liam and his influence behind her could help a lot.

"So you're not in a hurry to get rid of her anymore?" he asked.

I shook my head. "Nope." I tried unsuccessfully to keep my face blank.

Liam smiled. "Good."

I let myself out.

Married to a crook, that's some baggage.

~

NATALIE

AFTER MASON DROPPED ME OFF, THE DOOR FROM THE LOBBY closed behind me and locked with a reassuring click. I was safe inside Chameleon, insulated from the cruelty outside for the time being. My first priority was the break room. A microwaved breakfast burrito and a hot cup of mocha were at the top of my list. I abhorred microwaved food, but that fucking Agent White had whisked me away before breakfast, and I didn't have a choice.

A quiver went through me as I remembered what else the FBI had interrupted. If we'd ignored them, they probably would have broken down the door, the fuckers. FBI agents must take a class in how to annoy the citizens that paid their salary, because White had been short on words and even shorter on tact.

It had been a long time since...well, since anything. Things had been rocky with Damien even before his arrest. And the short time with Ryan this morning had reminded me what I'd been missing. For just a second I considered barging into his office, locking the door, and picking up where we'd left off. I looked around at the others in the break room and realized how inappropriate that would be. This wasn't the place.

Self-restraint needed to be my watchword, for today at least.

The microwave finished, and I carried the burrito and my coffee to the office. Ryan's door was closed, sparing me the temptation to go in and talk to him, at least for now.

The burrito didn't last long, and I started work on the next pile of Westerly documents.

Every little while I took a break, walking through the rows of cubicles to the break room. Ostensibly I was freshening up my coffee, but in reality, I hoped to run into Ryan. Knocking on his door was tempting, but seemed too forward.

Rick from IT approached me, and I begged off on lunch with him again. A cardboard imitation of a cheeseburger from the vending machine became my lunch companion instead. The afternoon developed into a repeat of the morning, as I finished up the patent application as quickly as I could, taking frequent breaks and hoping to catch sight of Ryan.

As the end of the day neared, I had three questions for Paul, and they would give me a pretext to go into the lab and maybe find Ryan there, since I hadn't had any luck in the rest of the building.

My cardkey unlocked the door labeled Lab One and let me into a small room with a restricted access sign. I passed through and entered the next little chamber, which immediately started blowing a hurricane-force wind down from the ceiling.

I moved quickly out of the windy closet into the lab beyond, and the giant fans stopped. The lab proper was nearly all white, with stainless steel tables and wire rack shelves. This was completely unlike high school chemistry, which was the only lab I'd ever been around.

I didn't see Paul down the first aisle and poked my head around the corner to the second.

Ryan was seated at a microscope halfway down the corridor. For some reason, he was wearing a white hazmat-style suit. He looked up as I approached.

"What are you doing here?" he yelled. "Get the hell out." His arm stretched out, pointing back the way I'd come. "Now, goddammit," he yelled even louder as he stomped toward me.

I scurried back through the hurricane room and out to the cubicle area. I made it back to my office and closed the door before the tears started.

So much for a warm welcome, or concerned questions about how my FBI interview had gone.

Ryan hadn't called, he hadn't texted. He hadn't stopped by my office.

I gathered my things and locked my office door behind me.

Before she had become a flight attendant, Jasmin had endured an office affair gone sour. She'd quit her job to get away from it.

I should have learned from her example. Getting interested in Ryan fucking Westerly had been a terrible idea.

I escaped the building and turned on the sidewalk toward home. The sun was out, but it didn't cure my mood.

Mr. Prickly Pear was a lot more thorns and a lot less sweet inside than I'd thought. That was clear now. He could have at least asked nicely. Why did I deserve to be yelled at? Even the turd Willey hadn't yelled this morning, nor had jerkus maximus Agent White.

Ryan was rude with a capital R. Actually, *insulting* and *abusive* were better words. *Obloquious* or *vituperative* were descriptions my father would have used.

The walk didn't take long, and I soon turned onto my street. Odd how I now considered this my street, and Jasmin's small apartment my home. Almost nothing in it was mine——except Ralph, of course. It would be staying that way until I got paid. After that, we'd have to see.

It seemed I would soon find out how far Liam's support of me went. I couldn't possibly do a good job on any more patent applications without *some* cooperation from Ryan, and the rage on his face when he'd yelled at me to leave the lab made cooperation unlikely now. My inability to secure that would end my usefulness.

I unlocked the door and was greeted by Ralph instantly rubbing up against me. At least I had one friend, so long as I fed him.

After putting things down, I dished out Ralph's early dinner. I'd soon need another trip to the market to restock his food.

The ding of an incoming text announced itself within my purse. I pulled the phone out.

RYAN: Where are you

Not an apology, just a demand. Add *insensitive* to *rude* and *cold-hearted*.

I poured a glass of wine from the fridge and lay down on the couch without responding to the text.

Someone knocked on the door.

I ignored it.

They knocked again.

"Natalie Spencer, FBI."

Those assholes again?

At least this time they got the name right.

I opened the door for the duo of White and McNally for the second time today.

Why did they always appear in pairs?

~

*R*YAN

120

. . .

As I walked toward Natalie's apartment, the black SUV turned the corner from her street two blocks away and drove past me.

I couldn't see inside the back, but the pair in front looked like the agents who had taken Natalie away this morning.

Once I reached her building, I climbed the stairs and knocked on the door of number six. It was the second time I'd come knocking on her door today.

Nothing but quiet from inside the unit.

I knocked loudly several more times.

No response.

The door to number five opened across the hall. "Get a clue. If she don't answer, either she ain't there or she don't want you here."

"I'm worried about her," I told the old lady who peered out from behind her door.

"Let an old lady get some sleep. Get yur ass outta here before I call the cops," she snarled.

I lifted the bag and turned for the street. Doing battle with Natalie's neighbor wasn't going to get me anywhere.

This could take a while, so I texted Briana at the hospital.

ME: Can't stop in this evening - sorry

Her response was quick.

BRIANA: Not a problem

I took up residence outside Natalie's building. After a bit I started walking up and down the street, keeping her doorway in sight. Not knowing if she was inside and just ignoring me, or had been taken by the FBI, I decided to text her instead of calling.

ME: Waiting for you outside

Stalking wasn't my MO, but I needed to talk to her. Checking the phone again and again didn't do anything to speed up a response. Instead it just made me more upset that none came. I put the phone away.

I turned back toward the apartment building for the millionth time.

Why would the FBI have come for her a second time?

CHAPTER 15

NATALIE

"RYAN?"

He was standing, or rather pacing, outside my building when I got back.

"Natalie, where were you?" he demanded.

I pushed past him. He didn't have the right to harass me and demand explanations.

He followed me up the steps. "I was worried."

I stopped and turned. "I don't deserve to be treated like this."

"Like what?" Mr. Clueless asked.

"Like what? I get carted off by the goon squad, you ignore me all day, and then when I come looking for you, you yell at me and order me away." I could barely control the tears that threatened, so I started up the stairs with my treasures: my new checkbook, and a carton of Ben & Jerry's.

He followed me. "I'm sorry. I can be a little brusque. But I'd be happy to explain——"

"A little?" I slid the key into the door.

"I'm sorry. Can we start over? Maybe you can help me with my manners."

Helping this man with his sensitivity deficit would be like trying to load a dump truck with a teaspoon.

"You really should see someone, a professional, about your issues, before you open your mouth again." I turned to see puppy-dog eyes.

He lifted the bag he was carrying. "Dinner? I brought Chinese."

How could he know Chinese was my weakness? I was dying for some good Chinese. My fear of being harassed had kept me away from any of the restaurants near my old home for the longest time.

"Please," he added. "I'm really sorry, and I promise to grovel."

I turned the key, mentally debating.

"And this morning, I thought you liked my mouth open."

I couldn't contain my chuckle. He had that part right.

"Dinner," I said. "Groveling, and no yelling."

"Got it; no yelling."

I opened the door and let us in.

My wine glass was still on the coffee table from when the FBI dudes had arrived. They'd come to return the driver's license I'd left downtown when Mason had whisked me out of their interrogation room. It had been their first sign of humanity.

I'd taken the temporary license instantly to the bank and opened a checking account with one of Mason's bills.

I picked up the dirty glass and lowered it into the sink. The Chunky Monkey went in the freezer, and I brought over two clean wine glasses and the remainder of the chardonnay.

Ryan was laying out his loot from Chef Chu's Palace. I'd heard they had great food.

I returned for plates and silverware.

He wagged his finger. "No, no. Chinese can only be properly enjoyed with chopsticks."

I put the forks away and brought over serving spoons.

I'd never mastered the slippery little sticks. "I'll need some help."

"Got you covered, Nat." It sounded good to hear him using the shortened version of my name like Jasmin always had.

He served up portions of cashew chicken, sweet and sour pork, and a beef dish I didn't recognize.

"Tangerine beef," he said, noticing my look. "I think you'll like it."

"I'm sure I will."

"Do you like your rice steamed or fried? I didn't know, so I got both."

"Fried," I told him.

"I want to hear how your day with the feds went, but let me start by explaining why I yelled at you in the lab." He spooned rice onto the plates.

"You could start by apologizing," I suggested.

"Maybe I shouldn't have yelled——"

"Stop right there," I said. "Maybe? You promised to grovel."

"If you'll let me finish," he said firmly.

I shut up and waited. So far this was not my definition of an apology.

"I apologize for yelling. You jeopardized lives today with that stunt."

"Me? It wasn't like I spilled some deadly chemical on the floor. I didn't even touch anything."

"Yes, you. The lab is a clean room with thousands of patient samples. You can't go in wearing street clothes without risking contaminating them."

Now I felt dumb. I'd seen a clean room in the movies, but I hadn't put it together this afternoon.

"If a patient's sample gets contaminated, we may not be able to identify a treatment for that person, and that could be catastrophic."

I shrunk in my seat. "I'm sorry. I didn't realize."

"Thousands of lives hang on the research we're doing. Contaminating the samples could set us back and cost lives. It's terribly important. That's why I was upset." He reached out to hold my hand. "But I am sorry I yelled, very sorry."

"I'm the one who should be sorry. I didn't mean to screw anything up." I felt like a total schmuck. I'd spent too much time on the defensive these last few months. This time I had actually been in the wrong.

He squeezed my hand. "I know. No harm done. The samples were all closed up. Let's eat."

The warmth of his touch and his rich voice calmed me.

He broke apart the wooden chopsticks and handed me a pair. "Let me also explain why I avoided you all day."

"Is this the groveling part?" The piece of chicken I tried picking up slipped out of my chopsticks.

"Let me help you." He picked up the food and lifted it to my lips.

I sucked it from his grasp. It tasted every bit as good as I'd expected.

"I was afraid," he said before filling his mouth with some of the beef. He chewed. "This is really good."

I was hanging on his explanation, waiting for the words.

"I was afraid that if I saw you in the hallway, I wouldn't be able to control myself. I'd drag you to the nearest closet to ravage you."

The words instantly raised my temperature. No guy had ever said anything remotely as hot to me.

I couldn't control my grin. "In my version, it was your office," I said, watching for his reaction.

I'd also never dared to say anything so racy to a man. He was a bad influence tonight, the right kind of bad.

His hand stopped partway to his mouth, and instead he offered me the piece of pork.

I took it and licked my lips.

"I like your version better," he said with a widening smile.

I shifted in my seat. This was getting almost too risqué. "And what happened in the closet in your version?" I couldn't resist trying to embarrass him.

"You were scared," he said.

He fed me another morsel.

I could get used to having him feed me like this. It was decadent.

"What scared me, the dark?" I took a sip of my wine.

"No," he said chewing another bite. "The size."

I coughed on my wine as I laughed.

"But in the end," he continued. "You screamed your head off, it was so good."

We both smiled.

An hour ago I'd thought him rude, when he was actually trying to preserve the integrity of the patient samples, and cold-hearted because he hadn't cared how my visit downtown had gone. Wrong on both counts.

Most guys exaggerated when it came to size, but I couldn't wait to see what Ryan was packing. He didn't seem like the exaggerating type.

He fed me another bite of beef. "What happened in your version?"

I chewed for a moment. Every guy I'd ever known would want to hear that I started by sucking him off, but after this morning, I had a different idea.

"First, you went down on me."

"We already covered that ground."

"A second time," I said before a sip of wine. "Then you fucked me straight into next week. And you screamed *your* head off, it was so good."

He chuckled.

"With that big tool of yours," I added.

He eyed me ravenously. "You take me for a screamer, do you?"

I nodded, and he offered me another piece of pork.

"Now, tell me about your meeting with Tweedle-dee and Tweedle-dum this morning," he said. "I was worried."

He kept feeding us, alternating the dishes as I slowly filled up on Chinese. Between bites, I explained the repetitive questioning I'd endured about this stupid ledger I'd never heard of, and how Mason had rescued me.

I split the remainder of the wine bottle between us.

"So the ledger issue is a new one?" he asked.

"Completely."

He finished chewing. "It's odd that it just came up. What did they say?"

I fished in my memory for the exact wording. "It *recently came to their attention* is what he said."

"That sounds like they got a tip from somebody. Why else would they be at your apartment at the crack of dawn?"

I took another sip of wine. "I guess so, or maybe they found something in the house."

"Yeah, that could be it too. Regardless, I'm with the lawyer. What's his name?"

"Mason Brosnahand," I told him.

"Stop accepting their invitations to talk."

I got up. "That's the plan." I walked over to the fridge and found another bottle of Jasmin's wine. "Should we open it?"

"No way," he responded, approaching me with a wicked grin.

I put the bottle back in the fridge.

He wrapped his arms around me from behind. "I want you sober when you answer me," he said into my ear.

"And what's the question?"

"Are you ready to continue where we left off?"

"Depends." I giggled.

He tightened his embrace and whispered again. "On what?"

I wiggled my ass against him and moved my hand behind me to stroke his bulging crotch. "If you're packing the right tool."

He spun me around and lifted me up.

I went up on my tiptoes.

He pulled me in tight, my breasts pillowed against his chest. "You can give me your verdict in the morning." He squeezed my ass as he pulled me into the hardness of his erection.

"Deal," I said, just before I pulled myself up to meet his lips.

The kiss began slowly as he swiped his lips over mine. I opened, and his tongue caressed mine. Everything with him was slow and tantalizing. I pulled harder on the nape of his neck and strained on my toes to meet him. Without heels, he was so much taller than me.

His grip on my ass lifted me higher, and I deepened the kiss, getting lost in the sensations as time slowed and the room melted away. My heart accelerated as the heat within me built.

I closed my eyes, and the woodsy pine scent of his hair transported us deep into the forest. Just the two of us. Alone. No work, no city, no worries, just a man and a woman.

We explored each other's mouths, our chests pressed together with mere layers of cloth separating us. My nipples ached to pierce the fabric that would soon be gone as skin met skin and we mingled sweat.

I stroked his wide, muscular back, and he pulled me more firmly against him. I ground into the monster in his pants, certain he'd brought the right tool to the party.

We traded breath, and he tasted like a man on fire, desire with a side of passion. I reveled in being the object of his desire, while burning with the same passion.

His hand found my breast as he came up for air. "Does your sister have anything harder than wine?"

I had trouble concentrating on the question with his hands so active on my body. "She might."

He released me to go look.

I checked her liquor shelf. There wasn't much. "Fireball," I told him.

"No way. Anything better?"

"Smirnoff, and..." I moved those two aside to find the shorter bottle behind them. "And, cognac, Grand Marnier." Jasmin had hidden the good stuff at the back.

"The cognac is perfect."

I pulled the bottle down and located two glasses.

I poured the first one.

He put his hand over the other to stop me. "One glass. All in the one glass."

I did as he asked. We were sharing, I guessed.

He lifted the full glass to my lips. "Take a sip."

I did, and he took the glass in one hand and led me to the bedroom with the other.

~

R YAN

THE THOUGHT OF HER HAD TEASED ME ALL DAY, AND THE REALITY of her with me here had tormented me all evening.

"I want you so fucking badly," I growled as I led her to the bed. I put the glass down and snaked my arms around her. She felt so good there, so warm, so soft, so inviting.

She clung to me, pulling herself close. The taste of the orange cognac on her tongue as we kissed was a stronger version of the scent in her hair. My hands explored her body.

She rubbed herself against my aching cock. I slid a hand down the front of her jeans, through her curls, and moved a finger the length of her slippery, soaked slit up to her clit.

She moaned into my mouth as I teased her little button. She

broke the kiss. "Oh my God, keep that up." Her hand found the outline of my cock and rubbed me through my pants.

I'd been waiting all day to feel her. I pulled my hand from her pants and almost lost it when I brought my finger up to taste her.

I pushed her back against the bed, yanked off her shoes, and pulled her jeans down and off.

She struggled to get out of her blouse while I pulled the condom from my wallet and tossed it on the bedside table.

Her pink panties were next to go, leaving me with the sight of her glistening pussy. In my mind I'd already plunged deep inside her a dozen times today, but the sight of the real thing upped my hardness from steel to diamond.

She sat up at the edge of the bed after shedding the last of her clothes. Her black lace bra came off, and the tits she'd freed from their confinement were world class. Creamy white mounds of delectable flesh topped by pink nipples, which stood at attention, saluting me.

I moved to hold and caress them as she struggled with my belt. They were soft, warm in my hands.

She was trying to undo my belt one-handed, using the other to rub my bulging cock.

I wasn't complaining. Her hand on me was what I'd been waiting for. "Tell me your fantasy."

She decided to devote both hands to the belt. "I want you inside me."

"That's not a fantasy; that's a future event. Tell me a fantasy you've wanted to try," I said as she got my belt free.

She pulled at my pants, along with my boxer briefs. "I want you inside me," she repeated.

"I won't be able to grant your wish if you don't tell me."

My cock sprang free and her eyes went wide.

"Mega-cock," she laughed.

Mega-cock? I liked it. Make way for Mega-cock.

She pulled me toward her, and I gave up asking questions. She was about to be mine. She was obviously too shy to say. In time she would loosen up for me, but time was not something we had in abundance tonight.

I urged her legs apart and knelt between them. She was a visual feast spread out before me, and I was going to have a hard time holding off.

She squeaked as I dove in to taste her again, and again. Her breath caught as my tongue traced her folds and found her clit.

I looked up to see her eyes wild with desire. I inserted a finger into her tight, slippery, wet heat, eliciting another gasp. As I worked my tongue over and around her little nub, she clawed at my hair, urging me on, pulling me into her for more, more pressure, more tongue, more finger.

I reached up to caress a breast with my free hand. Her hitched breaths, her soft moans and shivers guided me as I brought her closer to her undoing.

"Come for me, baby," I urged.

Her eyes slammed shut. She arched her hips into me, tugged at my hair, and her words came in quick bursts as I tongued her more rapidly and added a second finger to the mix.

"Fuck…fucking hell…God, Ryan… Oh, God." She shuddered her way through her climax, her pussy clamping down rhythmically on my fingers.

I watched the pleasure wash over her, mesmerized by the bliss written across her face. I moved up to kiss her nipples and ran my length over her clit.

She clamped her legs around me and ground against me as I moved forward and back.

I pushed up and reached over for the packet of protection on the nightstand.

She took it from me and tore it open with her teeth.

I rolled over on my side, giving her enough room to work. The feel of her hands on me as she slowly rolled down the latex was almost too much to bear.

She pushed against my shoulder, guiding me to lay down.

So she was a rider.

I lay on my back, and she straddled me with lust in her eyes.

She teased me, gliding her slick folds the length of my cock, back and forth, before grabbing hold of me and settling down, guiding the tip into her slippery entrance.

I let her take me at her own pace, while I fondled her marvelously soft tits. She was so tight, so amazingly tight.

She moved up and then slid down a little more, the slightest grimace on her face. She wasn't used to my size. A few more strokes, and she took all of me with the broadest smile.

She leaned forward to rub her chest against mine. "You promised me something this morning."

I couldn't remember. "I did?" In my current state, I was applying all my mental power to holding off my orgasm. I had to last more than a few embarrassing seconds, but she felt so unbelievably good.

She started to ride me, up and down more rapidly now. "You promised to fuck me——"

"Straight into next week," I said, finishing the sentence.

The light in her eyes told the story.

"Not till you come for me again," I told her as I reached between us to thumb her clit.

She ground down on me and purred. Her breathing became shallow and rapid as she rose up and slammed down, again and again while I worked her little bud. Just in time, her contractions began, and the words spilled out of her.

"Oh yes...fucking yes...my God yes." With several panting breaths, she shattered and fell forward against my chest.

I grabbed her and rolled us over, me on top of her now. I braced myself with my arms on either side of her and started to pound into her, the tension building to an intolerable level as she urged me on with her ankles wrapped behind me, pulling me in.

With each thrust, she rocked into me, and I came closer to my end. She pinched my nipples, and I slammed deep into her. The tension broke, and I shuddered as I came unglued with a final, deep push.

I rolled us to the side and settled into the bed, exhausted, but satisfied. My cock continued to throb inside her.

Her eyes looked into mine. "That was——"

"Fucking incredible," I said. I tucked her hair behind her ear.

She smiled, kissed me, and got up to use the bathroom.

I followed when she was finished and disposed of the condom. I picked up my pants and went searching for my underwear.

"You don't have to go," she said, patting the mattress beside her.

I was tempted. "I can't stay, Cupcake. I won't be able to resist you, and I only brought the one condom."

Her smile converted to a frown. She got up while I continued the underwear hunt.

She returned with a sneaky grin. "You don't have to leave."

Unprotected sex was not on the menu. "Yes, I do."

With a flourish, she produced a box of condoms from behind her back. "I found my sister's stash."

I laughed and dropped the pants I was holding. "Ultra ribbed ——your sister is kinky." I started to get hard again.

She squealed when I picked her up, plopped her on the bed, and pinned her down, straddling her thighs.

I reached over to get the glass of Grand Marnier I'd forgotten about. I dipped two fingers in and painted her nipples with the sweet orange liqueur. I leaned over to lick them off.

She retaliated by dipping her fingers in the glass and coating the tip of Mega-cock.

This was going to be a long evening.

CHAPTER 16

RYAN

THE MORNING SUN SNEAKED AROUND THE EDGES OF THE BLINDS, and I rolled over and kissed Natalie on the forehead.

Her eyes opened slowly. "What time is it?"

"Time for me to go. It's after seven, and I have to stop by home and get changed."

She closed her eyes. "Be careful of Ralph. He likes to hide by the door, hoping to get out." She put the pillow over her head.

I climbed out of bed and searched unsuccessfully for my underwear in the dim light. "Any idea where my underwear went?"

"Check under the couch," she mumbled. "Ralph likes to hide things."

I pulled on my pants. I'd go commando before I'd fight her damned cat for my underwear. "See you at work."

"Don't know if I'll make it in today," she said sleepily.

I pulled on my shirt and sat on the side of the bed. I stroked her exposed arm. "You have to. If Liam finds out I caused you to miss work, he'll kill me."

She lifted the pillow off her face and squinted at me. "That wouldn't be good." She reached for me.

I leaned over and kissed her. A long kiss that brought back memories of last night, good memories.

She let me go. "See ya."

"You have no idea what you do to me, do you?" I asked.

"Who, me?" she asked with a wicked smile.

She knew exactly what she did to me.

I got up. If I didn't leave now, we'd both be an hour or two late to work, and our secret wouldn't last long.

As expected, I spied the cat lurking under the table by the door, ready to make a dash for it. I stared Ralph down as I opened the door and shut it behind me. He got the message and didn't challenge me.

The air outside was brisk. I took up a jog to warm up.

~

NATALIE

"He sounds dreamy," Jasmin said over the phone a few hours later.

I had closed my office door so I could fill her in on yesterday, including my night with Ryan.

Recounting the dinner and after-dinner wrestling got me tingly in my lady bits. I omitted everything after midnight. She didn't need to know that much.

"Wait, is he the first since Damien?" she asked.

I told her everything——well, almost everything——so she already knew the answer.

"Yes."

"Shit," she hissed.

"What?"

"That makes him little r instead of a big R."

I was lost. "Come again?"

"If he's the first, he's little r for rebound. Good for sex, but not big R, the real deal. He comes next."

"Get outta here."

"Look, a little r just wants to take you to bed, and you want the same thing, so you hook up. A big R wants to take you to dinner. He's the one you want to find. Problem is, the first one you find is always a little r. It's pheromones and shit."

"Where did you read that horseshit?"

"No," she insisted. "It's science——like, a hardwired hormone thing, propagation of the species and all that. You have to get in the sack with someone before you can move on to the next big R. But just once, or maybe a few times. They can be tempting, even addicting, but don't get tangled up with a little r. That never works."

"You're being ridiculous."

She huffed. "Listen, I've been through enough of these to know."

She had that partly right. Jasmin had gone through more men than I had shoes.

"You're certainly no relationship expert," I countered.

"I'm not the one who married a criminal mastermind," she shot back.

I had nothing to say to that. The truth stung.

"Thanks for the advice, Jaz. I have to get back to work."

"I'm sorry. Love you, Nat. I just don't want you falling for a little r."

After we hung up, I tried to settle down. Looking around my office, I decided it wasn't bad. I did have a small window in one corner. I could look outside and see the parking lot, with people coming and going, and I could tell the weather without having to consult my phone. But there was none of *me* in here. There was none of the previous occupant either. It was just bland, beige walls in every direction. That would have to change.

I opened my door and headed to the break room. The coffee machine and I had a date. A nice hot mocha or two would get me started.

Gwen came into the break room just as I did. "Hi, you look happy today. Things going well?"

I waited in line while someone else finished with the coffee machine. "Pretty good. No, make that great. I got one application for Dr. Westerly pretty much done, and the next few should be even easier." I didn't mention that they would be *much* easier with Ryan agreeing to help as he had.

"So, yesterday was good?" she asked.

I also wasn't going to let on how good I felt after last night ——tired, but good. Actually, better than good, great. Ryan had certainly been the prescription for what ailed me.

"Yes," I told her. "I heard from my sister."

"She okay?"

"Yeah, she dropped her phone in the toilet before a set of flights overseas and wasn't able to replace it until she got back."

That wasn't the real reason I had a happy face today, but the bit about Jasmin was the truth.

"You wouldn't catch me going after that phone."

"Me either," I said, punching the buttons on the machine to get my extra-large mocha. "She made her boyfriend get it out."

"I guess that's one reason to have a man around the house," Gwen said.

I pulled my finished cup out of the machine, and Gwen placed hers under the spout.

"You have a man in your life?" I asked.

Her expression made me regret having asked. "Not any more. My husband passed a while back."

"I'm sorry to hear that."

"What about you?" she asked, changing the subject.

Unsure what to say, I settled for a partial truth. "Divorce just became final."

"Oh. I'm sorry."

"Don't be." I didn't feel like letting everyone in the building in on my married name. Someone here could be a certified member of the Damien-haters group. "Let's just say I'm glad it's over."

She pulled her finished cup out, and we made room for the next person in line. "A pretty girl like you will be reeling in another one in no time."

"We'll see," I said with a smile.

Back in my office, I wondered what Ryan was doing, and how long it would be before I could see him without arousing suspicion. I decided it wouldn't be right to approach Mr. Prickly Pear much before the end of the day.

I powered up my computer to start on the next patent stack. While the machine booted up, a smile crept onto my face as last night's memories replayed in my head. I'd sampled a one-hundred-octane man, and all I wanted was more Mega-cock, lots more.

I logged in, started up my spreadsheets and word processor, and pulled the first paper from the stack. The sooner I got this done, the sooner I would have a legitimate reason to knock on Ryan's door.

A reminder popped up on my phone. Today was my day to pay the utility bill at my ex-house. Great, bills on a house I didn't own anymore.

I googled the phone numbers for all the services I needed to terminate at the house. I started with the internet and finished with the gas company. Like parrots, they all wanted a forwarding address. I gave them all Jasmin's address for the final bill, and declined the offers to put it on a credit card.

I sat back in my chair and closed my eyes to think. My first paycheck couldn't come soon enough.

Finally I dialed the number I had been avoiding. It seemed like my only avenue to getting my house back.

"Yes, set up the meeting with Damien," I told Mason.

CHAPTER 17

*R*YAN

I GOT INTO THE OFFICE LATER THAN USUAL AFTER MY NIGHT WITH Natalie and decided to skip checking with Paul until later. As I walked up to my door, I noticed her office was open. She'd made it in to work. Good girl.

I closed my door after me and started on my morning journal research. It went surprisingly well. I was able to concentrate for the first time since I'd met Natalie.

Maybe I'd gotten my fill of her and things could get back to normal. *I* could get back to normal. Normal was good.

I moved to the next paper, read it, and decided it didn't apply to anything we were doing or wanted to do. I moved it to the ignore folder.

After an hour of reading scientific papers, I'd had enough normal.

Putting this morning's printouts in their respective piles, I noticed one pile askew. It hadn't been that way yesterday. I would have to remind Natalie to be more careful if she came in here while I was out.

I took a quick trip to the coffee machine for a refill, and my office didn't seem right on my return.

I could still feel the tingling. I repositioned my dick in my pants. It didn't change; the aftershocks of my night with Natalie were something I wasn't used to. I realized then that we weren't done; we had just started. I wasn't even close to finished with her.

Beyond the sex, I couldn't put my finger on it, but I needed more of her. She irritated me and put me at ease at the same time.

I sat down behind my desk. The chair across from me seemed wrong. It *was* wrong. The files I always kept there to deter visitors were on the floor where Natalie had moved them, and I hadn't put them back.

Now the chair looked odd because she wasn't sitting there giving me lip.

Perhaps I hadn't put the files back because I wanted her to come in and sit there again. More importantly, I wanted her to *want* to be here.

There was so much I wanted to know about her. How had she survived the ordeal she'd been through? From the outside, the news stories were clinical about it, but on a personal level, it had to have been ten times worse than any of us could know.

I closed my eyes and leaned back in my chair. Her face came into view, with those light blue eyes, and that infectious smile. She couldn't handle chopsticks for shit, but last night's dinner had been a breath of fresh air. I hadn't had fun like that since…well, since I lost my brother.

Bob had known how to get me out of my shell.

I remembered the last time we'd gone bowling. Bob had suggested I not try the sixteen-pound ball. He'd been right, of course. My thumb didn't fit in the hole, but I wouldn't admit it had been a mistake. The longer the game went on, the more swollen it got, until in the end I fell down because I couldn't release the ball.

It took loads of olive oil from the kitchen to get me loose. We'd kept drinking beer, and our aim got worse and worse. I'd almost lost my right thumb that night, but it had been fun.

A week later he was gone. He and my parents.

Bob had been my rock, the one person who could call me on my crap when I needed it. The one to get me to move past serious.

Somehow dinner with Natalie had been another one of those fun times where I could let myself go. I could tell she'd had a good time too. Even when I'd dropped a piece of sweet and sour pork down her shirt...kind of on purpose, and offered to fish it out, she'd been the right mixture of funny and sassy.

Natalie was special, very special. Just thinking about her made my heart speed up.

Someone knocked on the door.

The door opened, and Liam entered. Anyone else would have waited for me to respond.

When he closed the door behind him, I realized I'd hoped for an instant the knock had been Natalie.

"I just got a call from Dillard," he said as he sat down. He cocked his brow at the files already moved from the chair to the floor. He'd noticed the difference.

"Yes?"

"The news is not good," he started. He shifted in his chair. "The judge has denied our motion, and it looks like the case will go to the jury on Monday. Dillard thinks we have zero chance. With the jury instructions as they stand, we can't possibly win. I'm sorry, but CTX-13 is a lost cause."

I let out a long breath. I'd tried to prepare myself for this, but still the news hit me hard. "It's just not fair. They stole it, and we all know that." They should be going to jail for what they did, not be rewarded with a patent for something they didn't create.

"I know it's not fair, but the justice system in this case is long on system and short on justice. They have the rules on their side, and you can't fight the rules."

"The rules suck," I lamented.

"We can agree on that, but we have to let it go and focus on the things we can impact."

"Let it go? What about all the patients they'll screw over? You know their reputation. They'll jack up the price, and half the patients won't be able to afford it, even with insurance. And what are they supposed to do? Die quietly because the rules are the rules?"

"Ryan, I get it. I'm on your side, you know that. But there's nothing we can do."

I huffed. "So we just sit back and watch people die?"

"You know better than that. What we do is develop more and better treatments. We come up with a better treatment than CTX-13."

"But there isn't a better one."

"Yet," he said emphatically. "Aren't you the one that told me there are always alternatives?"

I hated when he used my words against me. I nodded silently. There was nothing else to say.

"That brings me to my other topic. I was watching, and you haven't spent a single hour with Natalie on patents since she started."

"That's not true," I objected. "I answered questions for her on my run yesterday."

Predictably, that didn't satisfy him. "Your run? Great. That's not good enough. You know the only way to keep from having a repeat of CTX-13 is to get these whipped into real patent applications." He motioned to the piles around the office.

"But——"

"Hold on, I'm not done. How many do you have here?" he asked.

"Thirty-six beyond the one she has now."

"Starting today, I expect you to devote two hours a day minimum to working with Natalie to get these filed."

"One hour," I countered.

"Hour and a half, minimum. Remember, in the end, it's for the patients."

I didn't respond. I knew he was making the right call, and unlike two days ago, I was now aware there wasn't an alternative.

"We're agreed, then," he said rising from the chair.

"Agreed," I repeated.

He stopped at the door. "You can start by going to see what she needs from you now."

"After I check in on the lab."

"Right after," Liam insisted before we went our separate ways.

Entering the lab, I could tell something was amiss. I checked the first aisle, then the second and the third. Paul wasn't here. He should have been classifying the CTX-29 samples after last night's incubation.

Fuck!

He'd told me would be out this morning at the dentist. Paul wasn't here, so it had fallen to me to take the samples out of the incubator this morning.

I rushed to the chamber. The elapsed time was over the experimental plan by four hours. I pulled the trays out, but it was too late. Three fucking weeks down the drain.

I kicked the table. The tray skidded around but didn't fall. It didn't matter. We would have to start over again, and all because I'd been getting my rocks off with Natalie. She'd caused us to lose the time by distracting me from my mission.

Fucking women.

I clenched and unclenched my fists and tried to slow my breathing. I was wrong; it wasn't her fault, it was mine. I'd gotten so wrapped up in her, *I* was the one who'd forgotten his priorities.

If I kept this up, David might not make it. It had to stop. I had to stop.

NATALIE

I EXPECTED THE KNOCK THAT SOUNDED ON THE DOOR.

I'd shut it after Liam's visit. I couldn't have just anybody walking by and see how happy I was that Ryan was assigned to spend time with me. An hour or two a day with my one-hundred-octane man. What could be better?

Ryan let himself in. "Liam told me to come talk to you."

"Sure, come on in and close the door."

His demeanor was chilly, nothing like when he'd left this morning. "I'm told we need to work on patents together."

I smiled. "I missed you, and yeah, Liam told me the same thing."

"Will four o'clock work for you?" he asked.

I didn't exactly expect him to return the "missed you" comment——some guys were like that——but I could tell there was a sudden frostiness between us.

"Sure," I replied. "Four works."

He rose to leave, without even a smile.

"What's wrong?" I asked before he reached the door.

He grabbed the door handle, stopped for a second, and returned his hands to his pockets. "We can't do this. Us."

My mouth almost hit the desk. I'd not sensed a single issue last night or this morning. He'd been genuinely concerned about the appearance of the FBI goons, and he'd come to see me again, even after knowing my Winterbourne history. It didn't make any sense.

"Just like that?" I asked.

I'd never been dumped so quickly and coldly.

He returned to the chair and sat, eyes downcast. Something was eating him. "It's not you; it's me."

"Ryan, we can go slower, if you want."

"I got too distracted by you."

There was that word of his again. The one he used in a pejorative sense.

"I ended up forgetting something I had to do early this morning, and the experiment is ruined now. It'll take three weeks to get caught back up. I failed the mission, and I can't let that happen again. It's too important."

My feelings were conflicted. I felt good that I'd been so *distracting*, and at the same time, I felt ashamed to have harmed the company's mission. Sex with me had been *too* good? Was that even a thing?

Whatever it meant for my personal life, I couldn't lose this job. It was my lifeline. "I can stick to business if you can."

He got up again to leave. "Me too." He opened the door and paused, as if wanting to say something.

"Maybe we could do dinner sometime," I offered.

"Maybe," he said before he shut my door.

I could hope, but that was as close to *no* as it got.

Why did Jasmin have to always be right?

Little r.

CHAPTER 18

Natalie

I SHOULD HAVE KNOWN BETTER THAN TO PLAN AN ERRAND BEFORE my visit to Damien. But I'd wanted to be efficient. I'd finally gone back to Cartier to collect my earrings this morning, only to discover the FBI had been there to pick them up on my behalf.

Which meant I could kiss them goodbye.

I sighed. That damned Willey was determined to make my life hell. And now I had to be at the Suffolk County Jail in an hour. Only Brosnahand's suggestion that this might help me get my house back kept me moving forward.

When I arrived, Mason was waiting just inside the door. "I'm glad you decided to meet with him, Natalie. As you can imagine, it's hard being locked away from your loved ones."

The man had no clue. Damien loved me less than his socks.

I wasn't a loved one; I was an ornament and always had been. Damien had needed a wife to host dinner parties, and I'd enjoyed that, not understanding my role in his deception. He'd needed me to complete his persona of a respectable member of the Boston business establishment, all while he was being the complete opposite.

"It will do him good to see you," Mason said as we got in line for the metal detectors and X-ray machines.

I nodded, but I couldn't care less if this helped Damien feel better; I was way past worrying about his feelings. That part of me had been lied to and betrayed, and had died on the funeral pyre of public humiliation long ago.

By staying silent after his arrest, Damien had condemned me as his accomplice in the eyes of the community.

Past the metal detectors, I was asked my purpose here. "Visiting a prisoner" earned me a more-than-thorough pat-down from a female deputy who enjoyed her job just a little too much——as if my underwire might be a saw blade or something.

The sign-in process was marred by the fact that my name didn't match the "guest list" for Damien, because they had Natalie Winterbourne down. It got worse when I showed them my paper temporary driver's license with "not valid for ID" printed on it. They wanted a valid photo ID, which I didn't have.

Mason intervened and got me approved after showing them a copy of the divorce decree he had on his phone, which showed my name change.

If there had been one more bump in this particular road, I would have gladly bailed, but eventually we transited the bureaucratic maze.

"I'll stay out here," Mason said.

I entered the visiting room alone and sat across a table from Damien.

His face was sallow and gaunt. He had always been thin and trim, but he now bordered on emaciated.

"Hi, Natalie. I'm glad you agreed to come." The tone of his voice was as it always had been: indecipherable.

"Hi," I replied.

I didn't bother to ask how he was. It seemed like a silly question to put to someone in prison.

"I've wanted to see you for the longest time," he continued. "How are you?"

"The feeling's not mutual." My brain-mouth filter had failed me, and I didn't care. It was the truth.

He ignored the statement. "Everything I did, I did for you...for us."

"Why?" It was the question I'd never been able to get an answer to.

"I told you, for us, for you."

That crap answer didn't mean anything to me. He'd never thought of anybody but himself. His motivations were clear to me now.

"That's bull." I didn't have the patience for nice talk today.

"In the end, you'll understand it was all for you."

The man was delusional if he thought time would soften the blow and make me appreciate him more.

I decided on the direct approach. Damien had always appreciated directness.

"What did you do with all the money?" I asked.

He grinned. "I spent it." He looked happy with the statement, as if it was an accomplishment.

"Was it gambling?" I asked.

It was incomprehensible that he'd wasted all that money so quickly. To my knowledge we hadn't bought an island or a small country or anything.

"I told you, I spent it on things for us."

His answer was nonsensical, delusional. We'd lived well, lavishly actually, but that didn't account for the millions he'd stolen. A nice house, nice furnishings, nice clothes, nice cars, nice vacations——it just didn't add up.

"Was there another woman?"

I'd considered call girls, but that didn't make sense either. Even a mistress I didn't know about couldn't account for all the money, but I had to know.

His eyes were solemn. "There was never anyone but you, and there never will be."

"If you want to help me, tell me there's some left?"

"No, no money," he said.

His eyes were even darker than I remembered. Impenetrable. I couldn't get a reading out of him.

But that had been my problem all along. That's why I was the witch of Brookline in everybody's eyes. They couldn't believe I'd lived with the man and not known what was going on. No one would believe that he'd lied to me, his wife, just as convincingly as he had to everyone else.

I hadn't been able to see through his deception, and that had been the hardest part to accept.

He coughed. The hack had an unhealthy rattle to it.

"Why did you call me down here, then? The only help I really need is some money to escape this town."

"I wanted to see how you're doing," he said.

I'd lost count of the lies he'd told me, but the number clicked up one higher.

"I'm doing just peachy. I went a whole day without anybody spitting on me or delivering a dead chicken to my door."

"I hear you're staying with your sister?"

"How did you hear that?"

"I have sources. Always have, you know that."

It was one of the things that had first attracted me to him, and now it seemed repulsive. He was plugged in to so many sources that when we met, he had seemed like a powerful and influential man. He knew so many secrets.

"So, you heard they took my house?"

"Yes, I'm sorry that happened. It was inevitable."

"It was not," I protested, raising my voice more than I should have. "You could have told them I wasn't involved," I spat.

"I was advised to not say anything." He smirked. He thought his answer was amusing.

"You think it's funny? Everyone thinks I was in on it. Not a single person in this town will talk to me. Everywhere I go, they think I should be in here with you."

"I'm sorry. I didn't mean for that to happen," he said.

I didn't believe him. Was I finally getting better at deciphering his lies?

"Why did you really want to see me, Damien?"

"You're my wife; why wouldn't I?"

"Not anymore I'm not. You didn't just ruin your life; you ruined mine too."

"I know you met with the prosecutor, Willey."

The sudden switch in topics meant we'd gotten to the meat of the meeting.

"So?" I asked.

He shifted in his seat. "I could make it worth your while not to cooperate with them," he said in a hushed tone.

"I don't know anything."

I didn't have anything to tell them. But Damien's implication that I could be bought was insulting.

"You know they're just going to up the pressure," he warned me.

I shook my head. "There's nothing else they can do to me. They took everything——the house, the car, all the accounts. They didn't even leave me bus fare."

"So how are you getting by?" he asked. He wanted me to think he cared, which I knew he didn't.

"Mason lent me money to tide me over."

His eyebrows shot up. That had surprised him. "Mason, is it now?" he asked slowly.

The dirty implication of his question hung in the air.

"Are you fucking him? Is that how you earned the money?"

I got up. "You're disgusting," I spat.

I turned and left. Coming here had been a mistake. I wasn't spending any more time with this devil, ever.

"I could make it worth your while," he repeated as I walked away.

I didn't dignify that with a response. I'd made an error in judgment when I agreed to marry the man. But that man in the prison garb wasn't the same one I'd married.

"How did it go?" Mason asked when I emerged from the visiting area.

I shrugged. "About what I expected."

"Did you get any clues about where he might have hidden the ledger and the money? Anything we can use?"

Even Mason thought Damien had hidden money somewhere.

I collected my purse and phone from the deputy. "We didn't get that far. He says he spent all the money. There isn't any left."

Mason shrugged and ushered me toward the exit. "Sometimes these things take time. Maybe next visit."

I stopped in my tracks. "I'm not interested in a next visit."

"It's the best way to get your house back."

He had a point; sometimes you had to hold your nose and do something distasteful to make progress. I just wasn't sure there was any progress with Damien to be made. I followed Mason out of the building and accepted his offer of a ride back to work——back to someplace that didn't remind me of *Silence of the Lambs*. Damien might not be a serial killer, but today he'd been just as creepy as Hannibal Lecter.

I closed the door and buckled myself in. "You're his lawyer. Isn't it some sort of conflict if I get information out of him?"

He turned to me and started the engine. "Not at all. He's entitled to the best defense I can provide, and I'm duty-bound to provide that. His best interests would be served by providing the prosecutors some helpful information, showing the court some contrition. In the end, the question is how to minimize the sentence he gets."

I considered his explanation. It made sense.

He pulled out of the parking space. "I'll do the best I can, but expecting he'll get off scot-free is wishful thinking. The US attorney they assigned to the case is a shark, and this is high profile. They'll be throwing everything they have into it. I might be able to get us a hung jury, but there's no doubt the government will retry the case. It's just a matter of time, and if you convince Damien to give us something I can work with, it will help me argue for a lighter sentence. That's my job. The upside is that I get to help you too."

My anger hadn't let me worry about the length of Damien's sentence. The way he'd treated me, I'd only focused on the last part——helping me get my house back was the only aspect of this I cared about.

I hated the idea——right now I felt like I needed a shower—— but I might have to consider seeing Damien again.

How had he become so twisted?

CHAPTER 19

(TWO WEEKS LATER)

NATALIE

TOO BAD RYAN HAD TURNED OUT TO BE A LITTLE R. IT HAD BEEN two weeks, and he hadn't mentioned having dinner once. It sucked that Jasmin had been right. *Science,* she'd said. But if that was it, shouldn't the attraction have worn off by now?

Apart from my unresolved feelings, things had been going well on the work front, and my spa weekend with Jasmin was coming up.

I'd gotten my first paycheck, paid Mason back, and even had vegetables in the fridge. It would be a while before I could afford to leave town, but I felt like my future was finally getting on track.

Ryan and I *had* been meeting each morning for two laps of his circuit up and down the Charles River. Keeping up with him had been easier this last week, even though he'd increased the tempo. I realized he'd been taking it easy on me the first several days we ran, adjusting his pace to what I could handle while claiming it was his usual speed.

I used the running time to get clarification on an item or two, and when I didn't have a question, I made some up. Running with him had become a joy, and I asked questions I already knew the answers to just to have pretext to join him in the morning.

I didn't know if Gwen or anybody else had noticed the extra spring in my step in the morning, but starting my day that way left me feeling energized for hours after.

I had skipped lunch today, trying to polish the latest application for our meeting, and I finally finished with a little time to spare. Rick wandered down the hall just before I went to freshen up my coffee cup.

I returned to my desk shortly before Ryan arrived for our afternoon discussion time, as mandated by Liam.

"Your place or mine?" he asked with a wicked grin.

We had been using my office because it had more space. His was so cluttered with his piles, I was always afraid of tripping and knocking them over.

It still made me wet just hearing him say that. But I kept things professional. It seemed clear that's what he wanted.

We had only been working an hour when he stood. "We have to stop a little sooner this afternoon. I have to go by the hospital early tonight."

"Whatever."

I didn't mean to be mean, but my voice synthesizer hadn't gotten the message. I flinched at how bitchy I sounded.

I stood and rounded the desk, preparing an apology. "I shouldn't have said that." I ventured farther into his personal space than I should have. I bit my lip waiting for a reply.

He smiled and smoothed my lip with his thumb. "I'll see you in the morning." He turned and opened the office door to leave.

I melted a little at the kindness of his gesture. The man had my number.

As much as I shouldn't, I treasured our assigned time together, but sharing him with the hospital couldn't be avoided. At first I hadn't understood the necessity, but having trials underway meant monitoring the patients' reactions to the treatments and making adjustments along the way.

Healing was our business, and visiting patients was part of that. Especially in the orphan drug effort, patients were both our customers and a valuable resource for learning about a drug's efficacy and effects.

Ryan fished earbuds out of a pocket and put them in.

I watched his cute ass recede down the hallway.

Why had I let my bitchiness rise to the surface? I didn't have any claim on his time. We'd had some fun together. I still tingled thinking about him——it had been more than just fun. But for the sake of the mission we couldn't fall back into that.

"The mission is too important," he'd said, and he was right.

Was this how most people felt about their work? I hadn't had a proper job before, but now I was a part of a mission, a mission to alleviate suffering, even death. We had a purpose here.

I straightened my posture. The mission was a noble one ——"*one worth sacrifice,*" he'd said. I only regretted that I had to be part of the sacrifice. But that was a decision he alone could make.

Rick passed Ryan in the hall, continuing in my direction.

"Natalie, glad I caught you," Rick said before I could escape back into my office.

I pasted on a smile.

"Wanna catch some pizza tonight? I've got a coupon for Round Table," he said.

Going out for pizza with Rick wasn't at the top of my list, but I hadn't had a good pizza in forever.

I'd already turned Rick down three times, but he hadn't gotten the message.

"Sure, that sounds fun," I lied.

I caught sight of Ryan turning back to look.

"Six?" Rick asked.

"Okay, six."

Ryan scowled.

Tough. A free dinner is a free dinner, and I crave pizza.

~

*R*YAN

SOUNDS FUN?

Natalie's words to that little snot Rick grated on me the rest of the afternoon.

Things had changed significantly since she had arrived at the company. I looked forward to our morning runs, and our afternoon patent sessions had been productive, which was in the company's best interest. Knowing I had another meeting with Natalie around the corner fueled me each day.

A month ago, I would have considered it impossible to look forward to seeing the same woman day after day, but each day with Natalie was better than the last. She continually surprised me with her knowledge, her drive, and the quickness with which she grasped the intricacies of what we did.

I pulled the photo from my wallet, and after a glance, I left for the hospital earlier than usual, listening to my brother's old message again on my earbuds. My visits didn't need to be scheduled, and David's charts had been worrying me.

The locker room was busier than normal, but that was probably because I was here earlier than usual. I changed into scrubs and gathered my clipboard from the locker. I donned the white coat signifying my faux-doctor status and slung a stethoscope around my neck.

I wasn't a medical doctor, and I didn't use the stethoscope, but it made the patients more comfortable. To the people here, I was Dr. Westerly, and it didn't matter that I wasn't an MD. I acted like one, and that made it so.

To the doctors and nurses, I was a source of lifesaving medicines for several of their patients, and a fount of knowledge regarding several of the rare diseases they faced. That had made this hospital the regional center of excellence for nine of these diseases and the national center of excellence for three more.

When we had first started here, the chief clinical officer had been skeptical, but my breadth of knowledge had won his support. I read all the journals and consumed much more data than he or any of his doctors had time to. I had become his personal walking encyclopedia. I got at least a phone call a week from him on one subject or another, and I always quoted him studies and statistics if any were available on the topic.

Making him look smart had worked. I got all the access I requested, and his support meant none of the other doctors questioned me. I had become a part of their team.

When I reached my first patient, a little boy named Tommy, he was receiving a nebulizer treatment from the respiratory therapist.

He waved and smiled as much as the mouthpiece would allow. Tommy's chart indicated his progress was slow, but his lung function was improving steadily.

I asked him a few questions, and he mostly nodded his answers. Our treatment seemed to be having the desired effects and without any serious side issues. He only complained of cold feet today. I added a request for daily ankle/brachial blood pressure tests to the bottom of his chart. I hoped the ABI testing would prove just a precaution.

I got a thumbs-up response from Tommy when I told him I'd see him again in a few days.

The second patient was out of bed and off with the physical therapy team. Renee's progress also looked good, as far as the numbers went, but it was always better to get a reaction from the patient herself. Not everything could be condensed to a chart. This was the downside of varying my routine and coming earlier than usual. I didn't have time to wait, so I wouldn't catch up with her until next time.

I moved on to the third and most perilous patient. His eyes were closed when I entered the room. A check of his chart showed no change, which was disappointing. I'd hoped for improvement. But no matter how much I squinted at the chart, the numbers didn't improve. Each recent visit had been the same. I left David's room wondering what to do next.

I took the long route back to the MBTA station. A month ago on a Thursday night, I would have planned to hit one of the college bars to find a suitable exercise partner, but since my night with Natalie two weeks ago, that had been off the menu.

I had dragged myself to a bar near Harvard on one occasion since our encounter in an effort to get back to normal. But the girls had all seemed so different, younger than I remembered——lithe bodies, but somehow less-complete persons. I'd made the mistake of asking one a question beyond the normal bar banter, and her blank stare told me more than her words.

Before, these girls had seemed a perfect fit. They didn't want or expect anything more than I was willing to offer. Now something was wrong. Natalie had somehow changed the yardstick by which I measured the college girls. She had warped my perception, and I needed to figure out how to get back to normal.

CHAPTER 20

NATALIE

AFTER OUR PIZZA DINNER, RICK WALKED ME BACK TO MY apartment building——not that I needed it, but it was a sweet gesture.

My sister's text surprised me.

JASMIN: Call me

"Everything okay?" Rick asked.

I'd stopped walking.

I hesitated. "I don't know. It's my sister. I need to call her. I composed a reply message.

ME: Almost home - call in a min - everything ok?

When I didn't get a reply, or bouncing dots, I lengthened my stride.

Jasmin was the queen of instant text replies.

I crossed my fingers that she wasn't in trouble.

When we reached my building, Rick stayed on the sidewalk.

"See ya tomorrow," he called.

"Yeah, tomorrow." I waved and took the steps quickly.

I pulled out my phone and dialed Jasmin's number as I unlocked the apartment door.

"I can't make it this weekend," she said when she answered.

My heart fell with her words. "Why not?"

I'd so looked forward to our spa weekend at the cape.

"Nat, I'm sorry. Kelly was going to fill in for me on tonight's Sao Paulo trip, but she caught the flu in Shanghai this week, and I'm the only other bilingually qualified attendant available today. I won't be able to get back in time. We'll reschedule later. I promise. I was looking forward to this."

"Me too."

I had been counting the days until I saw Jasmin again. Provincetown, on the tip of the cape, was going to be a rare treat. We had planned to hang out at the spa and enjoy a decadent weekend of pampering.

"I wanted to see my favorite sister," she said.

She was always calling me her favorite sister, as if she had more than one.

I plopped down on the couch. "I miss you too."

"Maybe you can take somebody from work."

"I don't know anybody well enough," I mumbled.

"What about that guy you told me about?"

I laughed. "He's not the mud-bath-and-pedicure type."

"I hope not. I like macho better than metro any day. But he still might be fun to have along."

Jasmin's idea of fun always meant between the sheets.

"Like I told you, it was just the one time." It had been twice if you counted the session the FBI had interrupted.

"I'll bet you could change that if you put your mind to it, or rather your mouth. Just kneel in front of him and beg for it. That works for me."

And based on her stories, it had *always* worked for her. Offering a blowjob seemed to be her go-to approach for dealing with a guy.

"Not happening. He was pretty firm about it."

She laughed. "Firm is good in a man."

I had to giggle. "You know what I mean. We work together, and I can't mess this up."

"Then forget him and go yourself. It would do you good to get away," she said.

That had been the idea——getting away, just the two of us, like old times.

I didn't want to do it alone. But by the time I hung up with Jasmin, I'd agreed not to waste our pre-paid reservations.

I decided who I wanted to ask.

I composed a text and sent it.

~

*R*YAN

NATALIE'S TEXT LAST NIGHT HAD CALLED OFF OUR MORNING RUN for the second time in two days, and I'd done an extra lap wondering if it meant anything.

After checking in with Paul in the lab, my morning paper review at my desk was going slowly. Every time I blinked, I saw her eating pizza.

Across the table from Rick, of all people.

Natalie's confident double-knock sounded on my office door before I started the next paper.

My watch said eight-thirty. I didn't bother to tell her to enter.

She opened the door, as she always did whether I invited her in or not. She had adopted Liam's approach.

"Can we move our meeting up to one o'clock?" she asked.

"No," I answered without looking up.

Looking into her eyes would only make my problem worse. She sounded happy, carefree, while I was dying to tell her what I couldn't.

She didn't say anything, and the door didn't close.

I looked up to see her staring at me.

She put her hands on her hips. "What's your problem?"

"I've got work to do, same as always."

She huffed and turned. "I'll be back at one." The girl had backbone. She closed the door behind her.

I smiled.

Real backbone.

My paper review took almost an hour longer than it should have. After discarding the last one as unimportant, I got up to stretch. Another cup of coffee beckoned, and I headed for the break room.

Beside the coffee machine, Natalie was talking with Gwen.

"My sister can't make it, so I'm looking for someone to go with me," Natalie told her.

I'd lost track of time. This was the weekend Natalie's sister was coming out to see her, and they'd booked a resort for themselves for the weekend.

Gwen grabbed her cup from the machine. "I hear the Land's End Spa is positively decadent. Let me check and get back to you. I might have to babysit, though."

"Let me know. It'll be fun." Natalie sipped her coffee, then noticed me. She raised her cup. "One o'clock?"

I didn't answer.

"Please?" she asked again. "I have to catch a bus at three."

"Sure. One o'clock," I answered. I'd been enough of a jerk this morning——actually too much. "I can make it any time you want," I added.

She smiled back. "One is fine," she said before leaving.

I put my cup under the machine's spout and pushed the button to get it started.

~

NATALIE

WHEN I HAD TO LEAVE, GWEN WAS STILL CHECKING ON HER babysitting obligations for the weekend. Without a car, I would be taking the bus to Provincetown. Lack of credit cards ruled out Uber or a rental car, and a taxi would be more than I wanted to shell out. But the bus meant I had to leave early.

I gave Gwen the information on my way out, and she promised to call as soon as she knew.

Ryan had been frosty during our early-afternoon session to go over the latest patent application. It had been a short meeting because I'd already asked Paul about several of the items, not wanting to bother Ryan with what I thought were simple questions. He could get testy if he thought I was wasting his time.

Just before I turned the corner down my street, I looked back the way I had come.

He was still walking my direction on the other side of the street ——a man I'd noticed before. It was Selfie Man again.

It couldn't be a coincidence.

I was being followed.

A chill ran through me.

I turned the corner, and just out of sight, I started to run. My building was ahead. I sprinted. If I got to the door before he made the corner, I'd be able to get inside before he saw which building was mine.

Taking the steps quickly, I grabbed for the door and looked back toward the corner.

I had made it. Selfie Man was not visible yet.

I'd called the spa, and no thank you they did not welcome pets, so this would be a solo trip. Ralph was set for the weekend with a second food bowl, extra water, and an extra litter box. He wouldn't be happy about it, but he'd survive until I got back.

After getting my things together, I called the taxi company for the ride to the bus depot. Downstairs, I scanned the street in both directions through the tiny window. No sign of Selfie Man.

When the cab pulled up, I left the safety of my building and looked both directions again. No sign of Selfie Man.

Perhaps I was getting too paranoid about the Damien-haters.

~

RYAN

MY QUICK AFTER-LUNCH SESSION WITH NATALIE HAD BEEN EVEN more formal, more business-like than usual.

She hadn't smiled between subjects. Actually, I hadn't noticed any of the normal Natalie happiness peeking through. She'd scurried out of my office without any reference to when we might get together again.

I hadn't questioned her decision to not join me for my morning runs. It hadn't felt appropriate.

Since when do I care about being appropriate?

The woman had upended my world. Things were no longer as black and white as they had been. She had me questioning what normal was, and that screwed everything up. I was a scientist; normal was the natural order of things, but it wasn't clear what that meant anymore in my world.

I pushed back from my desk. Another coffee, that's what I

needed. Sitting behind the desk, looking at the computer monitor was like staring at a screen with her face as the wallpaper. I held my hand outstretched and watched for tremors or shaking.

None. I was good to go. I could have another coffee.

I opened the door and passed by Natalie's closed office. She was obviously already on her way to the weekend retreat with Gwen. I would spend the weekend here, in the lab, or in my office ——comfortable places, places where my work normally flowed easily.

There was that word again. Work wasn't easy or smoothly flowing anymore. Not since Hurricane Natalie had blown in.

I stopped at Liam's door and considered going in to give him an ultimatum: either she went or I did.

That little snot Rick and another IT rat in a dingy Rolling Stones T-shirt passed me in the hall as I stepped aside.

I considered how to word my ultimatum for maximum effect.

The stale odor of BO followed them.

At least I showered after running.

I knocked once on Liam's door.

"She's hot," I heard Stones Fanboy say. "How far did you get?"

"Come in," Liam called from beyond the door.

I stood frozen outside his door and strained to hear the retreating IT guys' conversation.

"Pizza was a hit. She told me she'd been wanting it..." Rick said. The rest of the sentence faded out.

I left Liam's door and followed the IT pair.

"So when you guys gonna go out again?" Stones Fanboy asked.

"I figure next week. I got her number, but I won't call. Kinda get her wanting it," Rick said as they reached the break room.

She gave him her number?

"Yeah, I could tell she was into me," he continued. "I gave her the look, and she licked her lips like..."

I missed the next few words as the sounds of the vending machine dispensing a sandwich drowned them out.

"She'll be puttin' out by next weekend," snotty little Rick said.

I turned and retreated toward the safety of my office. Coffee would wait; my stomach couldn't handle it at the moment.

My computer wouldn't cooperate. Every screen I pulled up had a shadow of her smiling face in the background, taunting me. After half an hour, I'd made zero progress. This was intolerable. I couldn't work like this.

I marched to Liam's office door for the second time this afternoon. We needed to settle this, and now. I knocked on the door.

"Come in."

I shut the door behind me. "We need to have a talk about Natalie."

CHAPTER 21

NATALIE

M Y CHOICE WAS EASY AS I BOARDED THE BUS. I SKIPPED THE SEAT next to the man with the scraggly beard and the stain on his shirt in favor of the seat next to the older lady. I wrestled my small bag into the overhead rack.

"Hi. I'm Agnes," she offered as I took the aisle seat.

"Natalie."

She looked out the window as the bus lurched into motion and then back to me. "A lovely name. I have a niece named Natalie." She removed her glasses.

I nodded. "I was named after my grandmother."

She cleaned her glasses with a cloth from her purse and replaced them. "You look familiar. Have we met?" she asked, studying my features.

If she knew me from the news, this was going to be a very long ride to Provincetown.

"I don't think so; I'm sort of new around here."

True enough if you stretched the meaning of the word *new* beyond the breaking point.

She looked out the window again, seeming satisfied with my answer. "Go to P-Town often?"

"My first time."

Ever since the arrest, I'd avoided public transit. I'd even taken my car and braved the parking nightmare when I had to go downtown. Finding myself trapped with a Damien-hater on a bus or a train with nowhere to run was a recurring nightmare. This time I hadn't had a choice. The call of the spa was too much to resist.

"I go this time every year. My Archie, God rest his soul," she said, crossing herself, "he took me to the Land's End Spa every year for our anniversary. I still go every year."

"That's where I'm headed too."

"I throw a rose off the pier every year. It's what Archie and I used to do to celebrate our anniversary."

"That's very romantic."

"Archie started it. He'd throw one for every year we'd been married…until one year he got a ticket for littering. Can you believe that?"

"No?"

"Yes. I think the damned cop was a communist. He was going to let us off with a warning until he saw Archie's VFW ballcap."

"That's terrible."

"That's what I say."

She then gave me a nonstop recitation of everything she and her late husband had done in P-Town, along with a grading of the restaurants——from *great* for a seafood place that sounded too expensive for me this trip to *good* for a hamburger joint that sounded like something I could afford.

"Who are you meeting there? At the spa?" she asked.

"My sister was supposed to come along, but she couldn't make it."

"Poor dear. I hope she's okay."

I was liking Agnes a lot. "Work got in the way is all. She insisted I go."

"Nice sister, if you ask me."

I totally agreed. "She's the best."

"Family's important. Just remember to tell her how you feel."

"I like that idea."

Embarrassed, I knew I didn't tell Jasmin often enough. I pulled out my phone and sent her a text.

ME: Miss you - wish you were here

She was probably seven miles up right now and would get it later.

"What does your sister do that they make her work on the weekend?" Agnes asked.

"Flight attendant."

Agnes perked up. "That sounds fun. I wanted to be a stewardess at one time."

"She likes it, and she's senior enough now that she gets the international routes."

Agnes sighed. "I wish I could have done it, but Archie wouldn't hear of it. He was in the Air Force. Crashed twice. He said it was too dangerous for me."

For a moment, Archie reminded me of Damien, restricting what his wife could do.

She leaned over close. "I'm sure you'll like it at the spa. Just don't drink their green goddess smoothie," she whispered.

I matched her whisper. "Got it. No green goddess." This was a problem because I liked smoothies.

"It smells like crap, and tastes worse."

We both laughed.

The trip continued with Agnes filling me in on more of her favorite things in and around P-Town.

My phone dinged.

RYAN: Hope you and Gwen have a nice time at the spa

I smiled and composed my reply.

ME: She couldn't make it

The dots bounced around, and his response arrived quickly.

RYAN: Have a great time Nat

I closed my eyes and smiled.

He hadn't called me Nat since the time we'd been naked. After pushing me away to *concentrate* on work, he'd reverted to Natalie.

I clamped my thighs together to calm the tingling the memory gave me.

"Who's that?" Agnes asked, pulling me away from my daydream.

"Just a co-worker."

Her eyes narrowed, and she pointed a finger at me. "Now don't try to kid a kidder. I saw that look."

I'd been caught. I did wish Ryan was more than *just* a co-worker.

"He's a guy I work with." Even thinking about him gave me goosebumps.

"If he's special, maybe you should invite him to take your sister's place."

It was a thought, but not a good one. "He's not the type for a spa. Too macho."

Agnes laughed. "You'd be surprised. Archie and I always liked the couples massage. And let me tell you, Archie was no girlie-man."

My blood heated at the thought of Ryan on a table next to me, naked with just a towel over his ass. And a twinkle in his eye.

"And there's still the food. They have great lobster in the restaurant. Every man likes a good meal."

I shook my head.

"What's his name?" she asked.

"Ryan."

"Archie always told me, victory goes to the bold. Ask Ryan to join you."

I lifted my phone and composed a reply message to Ryan. Then I had second thoughts and added the word *try*.

ME: I will try

"Did you invite him?" she asked.

I shook my head. "No."

"Shame." She sighed.

CHAPTER 22

R YAN

I DOWNSHIFTED, AND THE CAR'S ENGINE SCREAMED AS I ROARED past another slow-poke on Route Six. I had to be careful with all the power this car had available under the hood.

"Turn left ahead," Siri announced.

I was almost there. I applied the brakes——hard. The car decelerated swiftly from over a hundred.

I double-checked the phone.

NATALIE: She couldn't make it

Siri guided me through the final turns to the entrance of the Land's End Spa.

I parked at the far end of the lot and locked the car. My watch read six-fifty, ten minutes to spare. I was taking a chance. This was my best idea ever, I thought, or possibly my worst. I was about to find out which. I'd rushed home to change into the suit I'd worn the first time we met. I wasn't comfortable in it, but it was Brioni, and she deserved the best.

Alyssa had been the one to remind me of my own words: *nothing could be known without experimenting.*

Natalie had been cold at our last meeting, but that was probably my fault for being curt with her in the morning.

Why did I find being an ass so easy? That was a question for another day.

I was about to find out how burned the bridge was.

Inside, I took a seat and waited. I had called the restaurant desk and learned that Natalie had a dinner reservation for seven o'clock. My plan was simple, if not stupid: wait here and surprise her.

I heard her before I saw her. Even from around the corner, her laugh was infectious as always.

I stood, buttoned up my jacket, and straightened my tie.

She turned the corner and laughed again.

A man laughed too. "It's right this way."

Fuck me. She was with a man.

My jaw clenched. I moved for the door to escape.

"Ryan?"

Trapped.

I stopped and turned.

Natalie walked toward me, a vision of beauty and elegance in a black dress.

"I'll see you tomorrow then," the nameless man said and turned the other way.

She mesmerized me. A slinky black cocktail dress with a deeply cut neckline floated my direction, shapely long legs carrying her atop sexy red heels.

I took a deep breath, focusing on her eyes in an attempt to avoid staring lower.

Startled, she stopped, just out of reach. "Ryan, what are you doing here?" Her mouth turned up with the hint of a smile.

Speech eluded me. If she'd been one inch closer, I would have grabbed for her and kissed the living daylights out of her. The delicate line of her neck framed by her long blond hair captivated me, and the faint scent of orange wafted my direction.

I swallowed. "I thought tonight would be a good night for our dinner."

I watched for a response. It was the line I had worked on the entire drive here. It was lame, I knew, but it was the best I had. For the first time in my life, I wished I'd been an English Lit major instead of a science geek. Then I could have come up with something sappy——perhaps a Shakespearean quote.

Her smile grew. "You came all the way here to have dinner with me?"

I couldn't help myself. "Only for you."

I regretted the words as soon as they cleared my lips. It sounded sappy. It *was* sappy. It was something an English Lit major would come up with.

"That's so sweet. And you got dressed up for me?"

"Only if I'm not intruding on…" I tilted my head in the direction Mr. Nameless had departed.

"Of course not," she giggled. "He's a meditation instructor here and was helping me find the dining room."

I could breathe again. "Shall we?"

I offered my arm, and she accepted it. We strolled to the hostess desk.

"Seven o'clock reservation for Shakespeare," I told the hostess.

She checked her book and smiled as she picked up two menus. "Right this way, Mr. Shakespeare."

"Shakespeare?" Natalie whispered as we followed the young hostess.

"Later."

We were led to a table by the window, just as I'd requested on the phone while driving.

Natalie took her seat.

I slipped two crisp hundred-dollar bills into the hostess's hand, as I'd promised her on the phone just after she'd told me there was no way she could fit me in at seven o'clock. Money sometimes came in handy.

She smiled, and the bills disappeared in her pocket.

I hated flaunting wealth, but tonight was special. Natalie was special. This was going to be special.

"Shakespeare, really?" Natalie asked again.

I tugged at my collar. "I prefer to remain incognito."

"And you think that blends right in?"

I hadn't thought about it that way. "You have a point there. Maybe I'll change to Hemingway next time."

I had started using Shakespeare at restaurants after having my name called and getting into an argument with a guy who thought they'd called *Brian*. The evening hadn't ended well.

Our waitress arrived with ice water and a bread basket.

I took a sip of water and perused the wine list. I wasn't a wine snob. I normally would have settled for the house red, but for Natalie, I selected the most expensive merlot on the list.

Satisfied, the waitress disappeared.

"Or Patterson——at least that blends in," she offered.

It was hot in here. I loosened my tie.

"Go ahead. Lose it," Natalie told me.

"Lose what?"

"The tie. You've been itching to get out of it. I can tell."

I pulled the tie completely off and undid the top buttons of my shirt. "I have no idea how people wear these things all day long." I folded the tie and stowed it in my jacket pocket.

"Next time, get a shirt with a half-inch more in the neck. That will help."

"Easier to never put on a tie." I'd let the store clerk talk me into a special dress shirt he said would go with the suit. It had been a mistake.

"You're going to have to put one on to accept the Nobel."

I huffed. "That's not happening."

"Whatever you say."

Her comment perplexed me, but I let it slide.

We perused the menus just in time. Our waitress was back with the wine.

She offered to have me taste it, but I deferred to Natalie, who approved of the bottle.

"I think I'll go with the New York strip," I told the waitress, requesting it medium when she asked.

"I hear the lobster is good," Natalie said, looking at me.

"It's your choice, Nat."

The waitress held her pen over her pad, waiting for a definitive answer out of my date, which wasn't forthcoming.

"The lobster," she finally decided. "And a mixed green salad, please."

"Sure thing. Follow me, and you can pick him out."

"What?"

The waitress tapped her pad. "Come with me to the tank and pick the lobster you'd like to have. I think we still have a few big granddaddies."

"Uh…" Natalie murmured. She opened her menu again. "I think I'll go with the cucumber-dill salmon instead."

The waitress nodded and left.

"I thought you wanted the lobster."

She toyed with her fork. "Not if I have to look him in the eye and pick the one that dies."

I lifted my glass. "To saving lobsters one at a time."

She raised hers. "One at a time." She smiled before taking a dainty sip. "Thank you."

The sight of her smile warmed me more than the alcohol. "For what?"

"For this. A dinner away from the office."

"Only for you," I said, repeating my English Lit line.

It worked again. The blush rose quickly in her cheeks. "I thought you had work this weekend."

"Sometimes you have to prioritize."

Her blush deepened. "This is nice, being able to go out to dinner. I haven't been able to since…"

She didn't need to elaborate. The when was obvious. Her ex-husband had ruined her life.

I tore off a piece of bread. "You want to tell me about it?"

She also took a piece of bread, without answering me.

"Only if you want," I added. "I can be a good listener."

She picked up her wine glass, but put it down without drinking. "Sure. I don't have anyone to talk to about it outside of my sister."

I buttered the bread while I waited.

She paused, as if considering how much to reveal. "When I met Damien, it was sort of a whirlwind romance. I don't know if *courted* is the right word to describe it, but it seemed so romantic at the time——the things he did for me and all. Anyway, we married after I finished my second year at Columbia Law."

She took a drink of water.

"Liam mentioned you had done a few years at law school."

"As soon as we were married, Damien insisted I move to Boston with him and postpone finishing my degree. I thought I'd transfer to Harvard or BU or somewhere to finish a year late, so no big deal."

"But that didn't happen?" I asked.

"Things changed. I got involved in all the social things associated with his business, and I didn't have the time anymore."

I was ahead of her on my piece of bread. I slowed down.

"Shit." She grimaced. "That's not it. That's the way he put it, but what really happened was he kept convincing me to put it off. He wanted me full time as his version of a wife, and I was trying hard to please him——too hard."

I reached across to put a comforting hand over hers, and she gave me a heartwarming smile.

"The worst part was he wouldn't let me work."

"How could he stop you?"

She nodded. "I finally realized it was my fault for acquiescing. That's when I met Liam."

I waited, wanting her to tell me more.

"I figured if I got a part-time job I could do from home without Damien knowing, I could show him my working wouldn't affect anything. So I called Amy, and she introduced me to Liam. He gave me part-time paralegal work I could do from home. That was going really well…until the arrest."

She took a bite of bread.

Our salads arrived, halting the conversation for a moment.

I sipped my wine. "I don't know anything about what he's accused of except what I read online."

She fiddled with her salad. "Why don't you tell me a little about the reclusive Ryan Westerly?"

I sighed. "There's not much to tell. I work all day every day, so my life is pretty boring."

"Bull," she mumbled with her mouth full. "Tell me about your family."

"What does your sister do that she's away so much?" I asked.

It took her a second to finish chewing. "Jasmin's a flight attendant, but stop evading."

I stuffed my mouth with salad greens to delay the inevitable.

"She's trying out a new boyfriend in LA, which is why she's not here. Your turn. Tell me about the wonderful Westerlys." She waited for me to swallow.

"I have a sister. Her name is Alyssa."

"The lucky girl that got the ruby necklace for her birthday?"

"Yup." I put the wine glass to my lips and pulled down a big slug.

"You know you overdid it, right?"

I put my fork down. "She bitched for a minute, but it got me out of the doghouse for screwing up last year."

"A pretty expensive way out of the doghouse," she said.

"She deserves it."

She watched me with intense eyes. "And? What about the rest of the wonderful Westerlys?"

The next part was hard for me. "My parents and my brother were killed in a plane crash."

Her face fell. "I'm so sorry, Ryan. I didn't mean to make fun."

"It's something I'm still coming to grips with."

"Is that why you work so hard?"

I nodded. "I guess."

Indirectly that was the reason, but talking through all of this was not my style. I hadn't had a conversation about the crash in over a year. It was safer to avoid the subject altogether. The pain was still too real, too fresh.

We shared this pain, though. Liam had told me she'd recently lost her parents as well.

She twisted her glass. "My dad was a lawyer. That's what got me interested in the law in the first place, sort of carrying on the family tradition."

"Liam told me he was a good one... Actually the word he used was *great*."

She put her glass down after a sip. "That's what they tell me. He taught me a lot about patents. On the weekends, I would sit with him and we'd analyze them together."

"That's what makes you so great at this."

"I'm passable, but I haven't even taken the bar."

"Don't sell yourself short. Remember, I've seen your work."

The beginnings of tears showed in her eyes. "Dad died of a heart attack."

"I'm sorry."

"Mom went six months later. He was her everything. She died of a broken heart." She sniffed. "So, now it's just Jaz and me."

For anyone else, I would have corrected them——medically there wasn't any such thing as a broken heart. But in this case, I kept my mouth shut.

She took another bite. "Liam said you and he share a unique vision for Chameleon, but he didn't elaborate."

"That's because it's not something we talk about publicly."

She ate some more and waited.

It was weird that we had to keep this part of the plan secret. I hoped Natalie was worth the risk.

"The vision we share is that a portion of the projects we work on——right now it's one-third, but hopefully we can get it up to half by next year——will be orphan drugs."

"I'm not sure I follow," she mumbled, making good progress catching up to me in the salad race.

I took a small bite and continued. "Orphan drugs are drugs for rare diseases. Since there are few patients to test the drugs on, the FDA has reduced the threshold for testing them, making approvals easier to get. They make a lot of money for some companies, because the drug maker is granted exclusivity. Exclusivity leads to pricing power. Which leads to exorbitant prices."

"So what's so secret about that plan?" she asked.

We paused the conversation while the salad plates were cleared and the main course arrived.

"The secret part," I continued, "is that we plan to make our orphan drugs affordable. These patients are the most vulnerable. Because they've had the misfortune to get a disease that's rare, they're often misdiagnosed, sometimes for years. There's no focus in the medical community on their diseases, no experts. To compound that by making the drugs they need expensive is cruel. My goal in starting Chameleon was to remedy that where we can."

She rushed to finish her bite of salmon. "That's great. Why keep it secret?"

I cut another piece of my succulent steak. "The financial guys aren't fans of underpricing."

"But maybe there's a way to turn that into a positive for the company."

"We need the support of the venture community right now, and it would make us a pariah."

She cut another piece of fish. "Now I think I understand what you meant when you said it was for the patients."

I put my fork down. "They are our ultimate customers, and a good business has to put its customers first."

She reached across and offered her hand.

I took it, another shock of electricity running up my arm as I did.

"You do the research; I'll help with the patents," she said, squeezing my fingers.

She withdrew her hand and sipped her wine.

I lifted my glass in toast. "To patent success."

She clinked her glass with mine and repeated the toast.

Coming here had been the right choice.

She was the right choice.

CHAPTER 23

NATALIE

RYAN WAS SUPPOSED TO BE A LITTLE R, ACCORDING TO JASMIN. IT was big Rs that took you to dinner. And yet here we were, at dinner.

So far this was the most pleasant meal I'd had in years. And, if it turned out to be merely Ryan's way of getting between the sheets with me again, I was game for another round of little r.

It wasn't like I planned to stay in Boston for much longer anyway, and my previous night with him had been magical.

Beyond the excellent food, tonight with Ryan was refreshing. In his presence, I'd been reborn as Natalie Spencer. He seemed to be the only person in all of greater Boston who hadn't heard of my ex, and didn't care.

It had been a long time since someone had been interested in *me*——Natalie, not me, Mrs. Winterbourne. For the longest time I had been Damien's wife——not Natalie Winterbourne, but Mrs. Damien Winterbourne. Before the arrest, people had been pleasant enough, but talking with me was merely a path to get to Damien. The distinction wasn't lost on me anymore.

"There you are." The voice came from behind me above the gentle murmur of dinner conversations.

I turned to find Agnes, my friend from the bus, wending her way through the tables.

I smiled and waved her over. "Ryan, this is Agnes. She and I met on the trip here."

Ryan stood and offered his hand, which Agnes shook with abandon.

"Ryan, a pleasure." She put a hand on my shoulder. "So you did invite him after all?"

Ryan cocked an eyebrow.

The heat of a blush singed my cheeks. I didn't answer.

"I'll leave you two lovebirds alone," she said, backing away. "And don't forget my suggestion."

After she'd disappeared, Ryan asked, "What suggestion?" He took the final bite of his potatoes.

"She thought you'd like a mud bath and a facial."

He almost choked on his potato.

"Just kidding," I said.

"Good, because those are two things I'm never doing. Not ever."

"I know. I told her you're a manly man, the kind that wrestles grizzlies before breakfast and shaves with cold water and a dull hunting knife."

He laughed. "Better that than a facial." He made a face.

The view out the window toward the harbor was magnificent. We'd lucked into the best table in the house.

"Isn't this just the best view?"

"I like the view from where I'm sitting just fine." He was staring at me, causing another blush to rise.

"I meant the water, silly."

"I know what you meant," he replied.

And my insides heated because I knew what *he* meant as well.

A little later, the dinner plates had been cleared and we were faced with the dessert decision.

"As filling as dinner was, I should probably skip dessert," I told him. The choices were all calorie-overload specials, except maybe the carrot cake. But even that came with a rich sauce and cream cheese frosting.

"I'm liking the lava cake," he said.

It had been the first thing to catch my eye as well, but if I ordered that, I'd end up so full they'd have to roll me out of here.

I settled on a half measure. "I'll split it with you."

"Perfect. It looks a little large for me."

He was full of it. He'd only said that to make me feel better.

We ordered, and it arrived even warmer, more gooey, and more chocolaty than the picture. In other words, it was perfect.

I dipped my spoon in the center. "Why did you really come down here?"

He licked his spoon. "I told you. I thought it was time for dinner." Another non-answer.

"No, really," I insisted.

He looked up from attacking the cake with a creased brow and dark eyes. "Why do you ask me things when you're determined not to believe my answers?"

I cringed. I had insulted him without meaning to. I was too jaded and beaten down by the Damien-haters.

He checked his watch and waved the waitress over. "Time to go."

The man was impossible. I'd said one thing to upset him and he was calling an end to dinner?

"Could we get the check, please?" he asked the waitress. She had the folder with the bill in her pocket and handed it to Ryan.

I cut off another piece of the scrumptious cake. "I'm not done yet."

He glanced inside the folder, took two one-hundred dollar bills from his wallet and dropped them on the table.

I was still licking chocolate off my spoon when he rose and offered me his hand.

"We're late," he said.

He stood there, hand out, demanding that I leave the decadent dessert.

I surrendered and put my spoon down. "Late for what?"

"Your appointment."

Like hell. I wasn't scheduled for anything until ladies yoga in the morning.

I took his arm, and he hurried us out. I tripped on the carpet, but he caught me, and I avoided face-planting.

He slowed enough for me to avoid repeating my near-fall in these tall heels.

I let go of his arm and stopped in the hallway.

He turned back with a surprised look.

I'd had enough of being treated like a mushroom. "I'm not moving unless you tell me where we're going."

His eyes narrowed.

I crossed my arms and stood my ground. An older couple passed by. They gave us a wide berth.

Ryan smiled and approached. He leaned close. "You have two options, Nat."

My resolve nearly melted when he uttered my nickname, but not quite. The man's voice was smoother than the dessert I'd just abandoned.

His eyes were steely. "Option one, you walk with me like a lady, or...option two, I pick you up and carry you over my shoulder like a child." He offered his arm again. "Please, Nat."

I huffed, took the arm he offered, and started walking, slowly this time. My dress was short, and I had no desire to have my ass out in the breeze if he followed through on his threat to carry me.

"Only because you asked nicely."

We reached the front door of the building, and he held it open for me, a rare treat these days.

"Your carriage awaits." He pointed to a beautiful horse-drawn carriage out front.

I gasped and pulled on his arm. "For us?"

"Only for you."

The driver climbed down when we reached the white carriage and offered me a hand up into it.

"This is beautiful," I told the driver.

"Thank you, ma'am."

The carriage was white with gold trim, red velvet seating, and bright red blankets to keep us warm.

Ryan stepped up after I did, and the driver urged the horse forward with a clucking sound. Ryan took off his jacket and draped it over my shoulders before unfolding the blanket for our legs.

I shimmied closer to him. "I didn't know they had horse-drawn carriage rides here."

Ryan snaked his arm behind me and pulled me against his side. "They don't, but Liam knows the guy who runs carriages in Boston. It helps to know people who know people."

"It would have been better if you'd explained. I don't do well with secrets."

He patted my shoulder. "This wasn't a secret, just a surprise. There's a difference."

I rolled my eyes, but couldn't help smiling. I needed to remember that.

We stopped at an intersection and started again. The clomping of the horse's hooves sounded a relaxing cadence in the evening air.

I shivered, not just from the chill, but from anticipation. "So, not just dinner after all?"

"I have something important to talk to you about." He adjusted the blanket. "It's about work."

My anticipation shrank with his mention of work.

"I haven't been able to get my usual amount of work done, and it's hurting the company. We aren't making the progress we should, and it's my fault."

I placed my hand on his thigh, under the blanket. "What's the problem? Maybe I can help."

"You," he said softly. "You're the problem."

I pulled my hand back.

"I can't go on like this," he said. "You are too damned distracting. So I talked to Liam."

I tried to pull away, but he pulled me back.

"He understood the problem," he continued.

I struggled away and crossed to the facing seat. I wrestled the other blanket over my bare legs and schooled my face to be as cold as I felt.

I wasn't going to make this easy for him.

"So I have a question for you," he said with a shit-eating grin.

I stared daggers at him. "The answer is no. I will not quit."

He laughed and pulled something from his pocket, keeping it hidden beneath the blanket.

"For Christ's sake, Nat. Would you stop and listen for once?" He leaned forward. "Natalie Spencer…"

Was it a bad omen that he shifted from the nickname I adored to my full name?

He pulled a box out from under the blanket. "Will you be my girlfriend?"

I gasped. I recognized the red and the stylized gold border. It was Cartier. Yet another surprise.

I wasn't handling this one so well either.

He opened the box. Inside was the ruby and diamond necklace I'd gone crazy for that first day he'd been shopping for his sister. A gorgeous, blood red, heart-shaped ruby and a stunning diamond.

I gasped at the sight, speechless.

"You have to answer the question, dammit. That's one of the rules."

I jumped across the carriage, straddled him, and clamped my lips to his for the kiss we hadn't had since that fateful day the FBI had dragged me away. I didn't care that my dress rode up and my ass was cold.

His arms pulled me tight, one hand keeping my ass cheek warm.

He bit lightly on my lower lip, and his tongue soothed it.

The cadence of the horse's hooves on the pavement melted away as the blood rushing in my ears overwhelmed the sounds.

His hand found its way to my breast, and his thumb circled my nipple slowly, hardening it to stone.

I speared my hands through his hair, holding my mouth to his, our lips and tongues intertwining. My heart beat faster in the arms of the man who wanted me as his special someone, his woman ——*his* alone.

He pulled me down, and I ground against the undeniable hardness of his arousal, his desire for me.

I really was a new woman. My own woman. I breathed in the pine scent of his hair, and it smelled like renewal, a fresh chance at life.

The carriage went over a bump. I lifted up and came down on him again, eliciting a moan of pleasure.

He broke the kiss, too soon for my taste, and pulled the blanket around behind me, protecting my bum.

"Thanks. It's cold out."

He smoothed a finger across my bottom lip.

"It's lovely," I added, pulling the pendant from the box. This was all moving so fast. "You never said why."

He touched his forehead to mine. "Why what?"

"Why me? Why this?"

He chuckled. "Is your mirror broken or something?"

I giggled, rolling my eyes.

He pulled back. "And I used to think you were brilliant. Now give me that back. You're not worth the trouble if you can't answer a simple question."

I leaned back. "The answer is yes. I'll be your girlfriend, but I still want to know why. Why now? A few weeks ago you told me you couldn't."

I snaked the chain behind my neck to fasten the clasp.

"Because I'm crazy about…" He touched a finger to my nose. "*You…* And because I want to try it this way. I'm done denying myself. I want it to be normal for us to have lunch together. I want it to be normal for us to run together in the morning. I want it to be normal to wake up next to each other. And, I want everybody to know you're mine."

His caveman-style possessiveness was cute.

"But the distraction problem?" I asked.

"This is my solution."

"Just like that?"

"Dammit, woman. Stop being the lawyer for a moment, and stop deconstructing everything. Do you want to do this or not?"

I re-initiated the kiss, and gave it my all.

His hands roamed my body, and I pulled him close with equal ferocity.

We were still exploring each other when the carriage came to a stop back in front of Land's End.

CHAPTER 24

RYAN

THE CARRIAGE PULLED UP AT THE SPA BUILDING, AND WE disentangled ourselves.

I tipped the driver and looped my arm around my lady.

Like giddy teenagers, we stumbled through the main door with our hips welded together and hands all over each other.

Inside we quickly found the elevator to the second floor and joined another couple in the car. The woman smirked and shook her head, apparently disapproving of our public display of affection——or it could have been the obvious tent in my pants.

They went left, and Natalie urged me to the right after the doors opened.

She found her cardkey and let us inside. "I thought——" she started.

I spun her around, put a finger to her lips, backed her against the door, and pinned her in place with an arm on either side. "Shhh."

The shock on her face morphed into a smile.

I flicked off the light she had turned on. Tonight was going to be the braille method. I brought a hand to her chin and guided my lips to hers. I gently traced them with my tongue.

She opened for me, but I traced her lips again, then moved to her ear. Gentle kisses down to her neck and collarbone brought soft moans of pleasure. Her hands smoothed over my chest and sides, leaving sparks in their wake.

I pulled her away from the door and slipped my coat off her shoulders and onto the floor. I ran my hands up and down her sides and traced the undersides of her breasts with my thumbs as she pulled at the buttons of my shirt.

She undid my cufflinks with speed I couldn't match in the dark, and wrestled the shirt off my shoulders to join the jacket.

I urged her to turn around and located the zipper on her dress. A slow pull, and then the whole thing fell loosely around her feet. I located and unhooked her bra strap before turning her to face me.

She kicked her shoes off and was instantly shorter.

My fingers found her face and traced the smile she wore.

I shuffled us in the direction I thought the bed was, and we fell onto it.

She giggled, but didn't speak. She lay beside me and worked on my belt as I traced her body with my fingertips from her hips to her shoulders and down the center of her chest to her bellybutton.

She got the belt loose and pulled down my zipper.

I lifted up, and she pulled my trousers down to my ankles. I kept a grip on my boxer briefs. "Later."

She pulled my shoes off followed by my trousers and socks.

I brought her back to me. "Lie down."

She relaxed into the bed. Her hand made a move for my cock, and I pulled it away. I had imagined having her again dozens of times. As tightly as I was wound tonight, I wouldn't survive her touch for long.

~

NATALIE

HE PULLED MY HAND AWAY WHEN I REACHED FOR THE MEGA-cock.

My hands roamed over his hair, his shoulders, and his arms ——areas he would allow me to touch.

He traced circles around my breasts——under, over, between, but never quite reaching my nipples. His fingers left little paths of heat where they touched my skin, only to lift up and set down an inch away before traveling farther, teasing me with their feathery lightness.

I rolled ever so slightly toward him, and he pushed my shoulder down again.

He urged my legs apart.

Would he finally stroke my wetness? I so needed his touch.

His fingers traced my inner thighs, and I gasped as they stopped at the edge of my panties, then moved down the other thigh.

Teasing was clearly the name of tonight's game.

He kept this up forever, drawing gasps and shivers from me as he almost-but-not-quite touched my nipples or pussy. Each touch felt feather light, just grazing my skin. I was soon covered with the goosebumps of anticipation.

"Please," I murmured.

The magic word resulted in his fingers tracing the damp fabric over my folds several times.

"Please," I repeated.

I got my wish as he pulled on my panties. I lifted up, and he pulled them down to my knees. I worked them off and spread myself again. I pulled at his neck, and he brought his lips to my throat. He kissed a trail from one shoulder to the other while two fingers traced the outside of my folds.

I arched my hips into his hand without success as he moved

away and kept his touch light. My breath hitched with each airy brush. Then a finger parted my folds and circled my entrance. I gasped for air from the shock of it.

"Please," I tried again.

Two fingers parted my folds and traced the length of my slit, either side of my clit, and then back to my opening. He circled again and again, refusing to enter me even a bit. The torture continued with licks and blows of cold air around my hardened nipples as every muscle in my body tensed in anticipation.

With every second I came closer to the edge, and he hadn't even touched me where I really needed it most.

His two fingers again made their slow, torturous journey up my slit to either side of my clit, tauntingly close.

Without warning, his mouth took my nipple and his fingers circled, pressed, and stroked my clit.

My veins burned. "Oh my God," I cried out as my climax exploded and the convulsions took over. I shook, and my fingers clenched his hair and the sheets as pleasure washed me over the cliff.

He kissed my other nipple and held gentle pressure on my clit as the spasms slowed, my bones melted, and I sank into the bed.

"See what happens if you ask nicely?"

Please was my new favorite word. I hadn't known it could be like this, and I hadn't even had him inside me yet.

"Condom?" I asked. I needed him there so badly.

He got up and fumbled around in the dark.

I heard the tear of the package, and he placed the circle in my palm.

He knelt beside me, and when I felt for Mega, I found he'd finally shucked the boxer briefs.

I pulled on his cock and brought my lips to lick his tip, coming away with a drop of salty pre-cum. I couldn't tell in the dark if I had the right side, but I got lucky and the latex rolled down his length little by little. I stroked it down a half inch at a time, receiving a loud groan of pleasure with each pass of my hands. I went as slowly as I could, torturing him the way he had me.

When he was fully sheathed, he pushed me back on the bed and settled between my thighs, the thick weight of Mega sliding against the slick wetness of my desire.

I shuddered with each stroke as his fat tip rubbed over my clit, pushing me back up the mountain of pleasure again.

"Tell me your fantasy," he said. His chest scraped over my nipples.

"I don't have one," I lied. I wasn't ready to share what had immediately come to my mind.

He stilled, depriving me of stimulation. "Tell me."

"I don't have one," I repeated.

He breathed hot air on my neck. "Then tell me something you haven't done."

That was easier. The list of what I *had* done was short.

"Doggy?" I offered weakly. It was a lie, but I had to say something, and I guessed at what he wanted.

He resumed his movement over me, scraping my nipples, kissing the sensitive skin of my neck and sliding his cock over my pussy, teasing me up the hill again.

"Come for me first, baby."

I pulled my knees up to his side and rocked into him for more pressure.

He stroked faster and ground down on me harder. Each pass of him over my little nub brought me closer, until the wave crashed over me suddenly and without warning. I clawed at his back and clamped my legs around him.

Instantly he lifted me up and rolled me over.

Head down on the bed, I lifted my ass up and reached between my legs to guide him in. As wet as I was, he slid in easily.

He went slow, letting me acclimate to his girth before he pushed in farther. His groans told how hard it was for him to hold off like this.

I held his balls and shoved back into him, taking all of him in a quick thrust. The jolt of pain subsided quickly.

He grasped my hips and started thrusting for real, slapping against me with each push.

I rocked back each time he pushed in, and his breathing quickly became labored. His legs tensed. He groaned and shuddered and slammed into me as he snapped and pulled me back hard against him, coming deep inside me.

He thrust some more and added a finger to my clit, and I came unglued for the third time, falling over the cliff into a pool of bliss. I collapsed forward onto the bed, panting, spent, and languid with pleasure.

He settled down, half off to my side, and we lay there, Megacock still impaling me. His throbbing slowly diminished, and my body dissolved into mush, I was so relaxed.

"Cupcake, next time you're going to tell me your fantasy."

I didn't utter a word.

He rolled off and fumbled in the dark until he found the bathroom light.

He came back after disposing of the condom, turned off the light again, and pulled me in to snuggle. "You're mine, Cupcake. All mine."

I pulled his head toward me for a kiss.

My phone rang.

"Don't answer that," he said.

I desperately wanted to ignore it, but I couldn't.

"I have to answer. It's Jasmin."

It was the distinctive ringtone I'd set for my sister. I wiggled off the bed to find the loud, insistent device.

"Are you okay?" she asked breathlessly when I found it.

"Sure." I considered telling her about the necklace but decided it could wait. "How 'bout you?"

"You're not at the apartment then?"

"No, I went to P-town like you said."

She let out an audible breath. "Good. I was worried. I got a call from the police. The apartment was broken into, and it looked to them like there might have been a struggle."

"Broken into?"

I heard Ryan getting up.

"I was afraid one of those crazies had taken you," she said, almost sobbing.

"No. I'm fine. I'm with…uh…Ryan."

"Ooohhhh. That's good news, right?" she asked.

"Uh-huh," was all I said in response.

Ryan turned on the light.

I blinked at the brightness, but the concern on his face was obvious. I finally got Jasmin off the phone after I assured her another half dozen times that I was safe.

CHAPTER 25

R YAN

WE ROARED PAST ANOTHER CAR ON THE WAY BACK TO TOWN.

Natalie sat beside me, looking straight ahead, her body tense. The look on her face seemed something between sullen and scared. She'd been quiet for the last five minutes.

"What's wrong?" I asked.

I only realized how stupid I sounded after the words had left my mouth. Her apartment had been broken into; that would upset anybody.

"It would help if you slowed down."

I slowed down to the speed limit plus five.

"Thank you."

Reading these cues wasn't my strong suit. I hadn't realized I had scared her driving so fast.

"This is a lot nicer than your other car," she said. "Damien had nice cars, but never an Aston-Martin."

"It's Liam's," I told her. "I borrowed it."

"What's wrong with your car?"

"I wanted to impress you," I said. This was the first time I'd been ashamed to drive my old Camry. It was not a car to impress a girl.

I caught a glimpse of her smile in the glare of the oncoming headlights——the smile that warmed me, the smile I always wanted to see on her face, the smile I wanted her to save for me.

"In the carriage, you said...you said I was hurting the company," she said.

I swallowed. "I said *I* was hurting the company by not working as efficiently as I used to."

"And this is really your solution?"

"Yup. I figured it out. I was trying to hide my feelings from you, from myself, from everybody. That was the problem. I don't want to hide how I feel about you anymore."

Even in the dim light, her blush was apparent. "That's sweet."

"And," I added, "I want everyone else at the company to know you're off limits. You're mine."

She fingered the necklace I'd given her and didn't complain.

"And your college girls?" She'd obviously heard my history.

"Haven't been any of those since I met you, and there won't be."

She laughed. "Better not be, or you'll be singing soprano. And no secrets. You have to promise me no secrets. Damien hid things from me, and I can't take that. I just need the truth..."

I removed a hand from the steering wheel to take hers. "I promise. No secrets. I'll tell you exactly how I feel." I squeezed her hand, and she squeezed back.

It wasn't record time, but we reached her street quickly after I convinced her to let me drive just a little faster.

I parked two buildings down.

Three black and white Cambridge PD SUVs were parked outside. Having your apartment broken into by kids was not an uncommon problem in this area of Cambridge, but three cop cars was overkill.

I took her hand as we approached.

She told the cop at the door she lived here, and that got us inside and up to her apartment.

The door hadn't stood a chance. The door jamb was splintered.

Natalie's hands went to her face at the sight inside.

This was not a local-kid burglary. They would have grabbed the expensive items and high-tailed it out of here. The place had been demolished. All the drawers had been emptied. The picture frames had been shattered. All the furniture cushions had been cut open.

"Ralph," Natalie cried. She dove to check under the couch. "Ralph," she yelled again.

A weak meow came from the corner.

Natalie rushed over.

A policewoman handed Natalie the cat carrier. "We found him under the couch and caught him before he got away."

Natalie thanked the lady profusely and fussed over her cat before putting him down in the corner to join me in the bedroom.

That scene was even worse. Clothes were everywhere. The mattress had been cut open. The mirrors had been ripped off the wall in the bathroom. The place was an utter disaster.

A man in a suit with a badge hanging on his belt stood in the bathroom.

"I'm sorry, you can't be in here," he said when he noticed us.

"But this is my place," Natalie responded.

The man consulted his note pad. "Jasmin Spencer?"

"No, I'm her sister. I've been staying here."

"And your name is?"

"Natalie Spencer."

He wrote a note. "And where is your sister now?"

"She's in LA, has been for a while."

"And you've been living here? Anyone else?" His eyes shifted to me.

Natalie swayed a bit. "For a few weeks, yes. And, no. I live alone."

"And where were you tonight around seven?" he asked.

I stepped forward. "She was with me. In Provincetown."

"Provincetown," he said, making another note. "And you would be?"

"Ryan Westerly. Do you have a card, detective?"

He produced a card for me and wrote my name down slowly. "Well, Ms. Spencer. This is pretty unusual. Whoever did this really didn't like you or your sister. Does your sister have any enemies? People that might do something like this? An ex-boyfriend, perhaps?"

Natalie shook her head. "No, she's with her boyfriend in LA."

"Nobody comes to mind that would have it in for her? Or for you?"

Natalie folded her arms and looked at the floor. "Damien Winterbourne is my ex-husband. Some people blame me for their losses," she mumbled.

The detective nodded and wrote a note. "That's a very nice necklace you're wearing." Apparently hearing her previous name was enough explanation for him.

Natalie fingered the ruby and diamond necklace I'd just given her.

"Is it real?" he asked.

I answered for her. "Yes, it's real."

"Did you have other expensive jewelry here in the apartment?"

She shook her head. "No. Nothing."

"Earrings, rings, cash?"

"No," she repeated. "Nothing else."

The detective took another note. "It looks to me like the door won't lock, not until it's been repaired. Do you have a safe place you can stay tonight?"

I put my arm around her. "She can stay with me."

Natalie looked up and smiled.

A really large older man arrived. "Natalie, I came as soon as I heard. Are you okay?"

The guy had to be four hundred pounds easy——and not short and fat, tall and fat.

She turned. Recognition flashed across her face. "Mason. Thank you, I'm fine."

This Mason had to be her husband's attorney, the one who'd forced her to talk to her dirtbag ex-husband in jail.

Mason handed his card to the detective.

I held out my hand and received one as well.

The detective's eyes narrowed as he examined the card. "Attorney. Why would Ms. Spencer need an attorney?"

"Friend of the family," he answered.

The detective nodded, but his face gave it away. He didn't believe Brosnahand.

"You can come stay with me, if you like," Mason offered to Natalie.

I pulled her close. "We've got that covered, thanks."

She didn't need help from any slimy lawyer, especially one associated with her ex-husband.

She was mine to protect.

She was mine, period.

Brosnahand shrugged. "Okay, but the offer is an open one."

"Can I take some of the clothes with me?" Natalie asked the detective.

"Sure. Just be careful of the broken glass." The detective urged Brosnahand out of the room. "One more thing. Before you go, we'll need both your fingerprints. Just for elimination purposes, you understand."

"Sure," I said.

Natalie nodded and reached to pick up a pair of jeans from the floor.

A half hour later, we had her cat and two garbage bags full of clothes, and we were leaving the destruction behind. The lawyer and the detective had gone. Only one crime scene tech remained, dusting for prints.

That and a detective on the scene made it obvious the police knew this wasn't a simple burglary.

"I didn't know they'd found me," Natalie said as we climbed into the car.

I closed my door and started the engine. "Who?"

"The Damien-haters."

The cat meowed.

"He doesn't like car rides," she told me.

I didn't have anything to say to that.

Natalie was lucky she hadn't been home when it happened. There was ample evidence knives had been used. It could have been bad.

It didn't take long to reach my building just north of the MIT campus.

I carried the bags into the elevator after Natalie. "Twenty-three," I told her.

She pushed the button, and we were whisked from the garage to my floor. In a snootier building, the button for my floor would have been marked with a P.

When the doors opened, I motioned my head to the right, out of the elevator. I had the south-facing penthouse apartment. It had been two units, but the previous owners had combined them into one.

"Two-thirty-one," I said. There were still two doors next to each other at the end of the hallway, but I only used the one.

~

NATALIE

HE REMOVED HIS ARM FROM MY SHOULDERS TO UNLOCK THE DOOR.

I instantly missed his warmth. Unnerved by my jittery legs, I leaned against the wall.

He guided me inside with a gentle hand on my back——a strong hand, a hand I needed right now.

A wall of floor-to-ceiling glass graced the far side of the room. "Nice view."

Our house, my house, had been nice, spacious, and upscale even for Brookline. But it didn't have the view Ryan did here. The scene out the wall of windows was stunning. The MIT campus and the town beyond shone like twinkling stars from this height. The cars on Memorial Drive formed moving snakes of red and white light alongside the river.

"Thanks. I don't notice it much anymore."

The room was gargantuan, with a large open kitchen area to the left. It hadn't struck me at first, but the space was as large to the right as it was to the left, and I noticed the second door from the hallway also opened into this great room.

"Two front doors?" I asked.

He swept his arm to the right. "That side used to be another unit."

The furniture was almost all situated on the right side. A lone dilapidated sofa faced the television mounted on the wall to the left.

Ryan noticed my stare. "I bought it right after the units were merged. The previous owners on that side left their furniture." He pointed to the lone couch. "That I brought with me." He hadn't even bothered to rearrange the pieces.

"How long did you say you've lived here?"

"Two years."

Two years and he'd added maybe one piece of furniture? There was nothing on the walls save the television. Even a minimalist college student would have done more with the space.

Ralph shifted in his carrier, and I put him down. "Is it okay if I let him out?"

"Sure. *Mi casa es su casa.*"

I unzipped the door to his carrier and Ralph ran out, heading straight for the lone couch to the left and disappearing underneath.

"We'll need to set up something for a cat box unless you want presents on the rug."

"Got ya covered. The Merrits had a cat. Left the box."

"Merrits?" I asked.

"The people who left their furniture."

Sure, who doesn't leave a cat box to make a furnished condo complete? And who buys a place and leaves the cat box lying around?

I started for the couch. "We'll need to catch him to show him where it is."

"Come here, Ralph," Ryan called. He was clueless.

"Cats don't come when you call them," I told him. I walked over to the couch.

Ryan went down on a knee and clucked three times.

Ralph ran out from under the couch and over to him, proving me wrong.

Traitor.

Ryan scratched my cat's back and then picked him up. "Let me show you something, Ralph." He walked him to the other side of the room and disappeared down the hall.

I searched out the bathroom and returned to join Ryan on the couch when I was done.

He put his arm around me and I leaned into him. I was still trembling.

"Do you have something to drink?"

He stood, removing my source of warmth. "Wine, or stronger?"

"Stronger. I can't stop shaking."

He returned with two glasses. "Grand Marnier okay?" He knew it was.

I nodded and pulled down half the glass in a series of gulps. The warmth of it soothed me.

He sat, sipped the cognac, and pulled me close again.

I snuggled in, drawing comfort from his embrace.

"I'm sorry about your apartment," he said, stroking my shoulder and arm.

My tears threatened again. "It's so unfair."

"I've got you, Cupcake. You're safe with me. Tell me everything."

I believed him. His warmth, his voice, everything about him comforted me.

"It started with Damien's arrest. It came out of nowhere."

~

*R*YAN

NATALIE SPENT HOURS DETAILING THE DIFFICULTY OF HER LIFE with Damien, and the horror that followed his arrest.

I soothed her as best I knew how.

She needed to tell her story and be listened to more than anything. My Cupcake needed support, and I was here for her.

There weren't any concrete steps to take beyond what she had already started by getting her name changed——except maybe some protection. My mind was already turning on that.

My heart constricted when she mentioned for the third time that she needed to leave town to fix the problem. I kept my opinion that running wasn't the answer to myself. That discussion could come later. Tonight was for listening.

She was convinced people who hated her for her association with her ex-husband had destroyed the apartment.

I wasn't so sure. The destruction had been methodical. It made more sense that they'd been searching for the ledger the FBI goons had hauled her in to discuss. The mere thought of what could have happened if she had been home scared me all over again.

"And then…" Her words trailed off and didn't start again.

She had fallen asleep in my arms, shortly after demanding another glass of orange cognac.

I waited a few minutes before I lifted her and carried her into the bedroom.

She woke in my arms, confused.

"Time for sleep," I told her as I laid her down and started to unzip her dress.

She mumbled unintelligibly.

I pulled the dress off her with little difficulty and pulled the covers over her. I joined her after flicking off the light and shedding my clothes.

She needed rest and my support.

I would see to it that she got both. And protection. Definitely that.

She was mine, and I protected what was mine.

CHAPTER 26

Natalie

THE SOUND OF THE SHOWER PENETRATED MY SLEEP-DEPRIVED FOG.
It felt like the middle of the night, but the light peeking past the
edges of the curtains said morning. The memory I dredged up of
our time at the spa brought a slight tingle between my legs and a
much larger smile to my lips. I hadn't had an evening like that
since...since never.

As my eyes started working, the high ceiling came into focus. I
shifted, and my brain registered the luxurious feel of ultra-soft
sheets beneath me. And...I had my bra and panties on. I slept in
the nude, or with a nightshirt if it was cold.

I fingered the necklace around my neck. Ryan had put me to
bed after listening to me all night. The memory was fuzzy, but
comforting.

I was in Ryan's room, and the nauseating reason came back to
me. The scene at Jasmin's had been beyond description. I had no
idea how I'd ever get the apartment back to a livable condition.

The sound of the shower stopped, and I heard the glass door

swing open. I closed my eyes to retreat back into the safety of unconsciousness. He would go to work, and I could sleep.

"I saw that." It was Ryan's voice from the bathroom.

I held my eyes closed, feigning sleep, but couldn't control my mouth well enough to avoid the hint of a smile.

"Up and at 'em, Cupcake. No rest for the wicked today," he said.

I ignored him and stayed as still as possible.

He whipped the covers down, and the chill hit me.

"Hey," I complained. "I'm not wicked, so I'm sleeping in." I reached for the covers, but he held them firmly.

"You are too wicked. Wicked beautiful, wicked smart, and wicked late."

Defeated, I swung my legs over the edge and sat up. "Where do you get sheets like this? These are decadent. I need some."

"No idea. They were a present from Alyssa." He leaned over, took my face in his hands, and planted a kiss on my lips——way too quick. "Off to the shower with you."

I ambled that direction. If I couldn't sleep, a hot shower sounded like the next best thing.

"Why the hurry?"

He didn't answer my question. "Ham, egg, and cheese, or sausage, egg, and cheese for breakfast?" he asked as he opened the door to leave the bedroom.

I smiled at his offer. "Scrambled eggs, and I like sausage better than ham. And a smoothie would be great if you have fresh fruit. I like strawberries best."

A man that cooked me breakfast… I could get used to that.

The door closed behind him.

His shower was the size of Jasmin's kitchen, even bigger than what we'd had in Brookline. A full-length bench seat ran along one side, and there were opposing shower heads for two people, overhead rain heads, and jets from the walls. It took me three tries using the various handles to get it set the way I wanted, but after that? Steamy, wet nirvana.

Just as I was getting relaxed enough to melt, he came back in. I was soaping myself, and his eyes went straight to my breasts. "Hurry up. Breakfast is ready." He picked up my underwear and disappeared again.

I dressed quickly with a mixture of clothes from the bags I had brought: yoga pants, a long-sleeve shirt, and running shoes. After last night, I decided to go without makeup. I wasn't hiding anything from Ryan.

The aroma of fried sausage and coffee greeted me as I exited the bedroom.

"Time to go. We're burning daylight," he said as he held out a paper towel bundle for me.

It was hot. I unwrapped it to find a breakfast sandwich.

"Jimmy Dean's best," he announced.

I deposited the monstrosity on the counter. "I don't eat microwaved breakfast."

"Suit yourself." He handed me my sweatshirt and phone. "It's cold outside."

I put on the sweatshirt. "All the more reason to stay in."

He pulled me toward the doorway.

"Where are we going? And, and, you promised me breakfast."

He handed me a travel mug. "Coffee." He wouldn't let me stop. At the door he handed me a paper bag. "Carry this."

He pulled a suitcase, grabbed his silly fanny pack, and opened the door, hurrying me outside. The man was on a mission, and apparently I wasn't allowed to slow him down.

Once inside the elevator, I peeked in the bag and found my clothes from last night——purse, shoes, dress, and underwear. "Where are we going?"

"You'll see."

The elevator doors opened to the garage level.

I stayed planted in the corner of the car. "No, you can tell me now."

He held the door-open button and waited for me to exit. "Once we're in the car."

I didn't budge.

The aggravatingly curt, prickly Ryan had returned. "Cupcake, you have the same two choices as last night. Under your own power, or over my shoulder."

I sneered at him and walked out.

We packed the things in the trunk of the Aston Martin, and he held open the door for me. He handed me his fanny pack to put at my feet before closing it.

The gentleman had returned.

Ryan pushed the metallic key fob into a slot in the dash, and the engine rumbled to life.

We pulled out onto the street, and I waited for my promised data-dump.

"I'm taking you back to your spa, so you can finish the weekend you were *so* looking forward to, and I'm coming along to keep you safe."

My mouth dropped open. "Thank you." I tried to process what he'd said. "But I don't need to go back, and I don't need a babysitter."

He glanced my direction, then punched the throttle, and the acceleration slammed me back into my seat.

"Don't argue. We're going back, and I'm keeping you safe until we get some professional help."

"You can let me out if you're going to be bossy like this." If I could have stomped my foot, I would have.

"I'm not letting you out of my sight. It's not safe."

"Don't be ridiculous."

He pulled the car swiftly to a stop at the curb. The words came out slowly and forcefully, "Now. Listen. Carefully." His eyes were fiercely determined. "It wasn't kids that broke into your place yesterday. And it wasn't some crazy person who hates your ex-husband."

I laughed him off. "Of course it was."

"No fucking way. I called that detective and that asshole lawyer this morning first thing. I've seen plenty of petty burglaries. That's not what that was. Your place was tossed to find something, and there's only two groups that want something from you: the FBI and the Mexicali Cartel——that tidbit came from Brosnahand. The FBI would have barged in with a warrant, so that means the cartel did your apartment, and they're done fooling around. They want that ledger, and they want it now, and they have the crazy idea that you have it or know where it is."

I shrank in my seat, shivering. "But I don't know a thing."

"A lot of good that does you. If they get their hands on you, they'll torture you until they finally believe what you're telling them. Then it'll be over."

The car was suddenly ice cold. By *over* he clearly meant dead.

"Look in the fanny pack," he said.

I pulled it from the floor and wrestled the zipper open. Inside, the large, ugly, metal shape of a gun revealed itself.

"A gun?"

He pulled away from the curb and joined traffic again. "Yes, a gun. Those turkeys won't be carrying water pistols."

"But I don't know anything about guns."

"Lucky for you, I do."

I had to ask. "Did you just put this in here, or have you been running with it every morning?"

He stared straight ahead. "About a year ago I got some threats, and I started carrying that."

Ryan was in the business of saving lives. I couldn't imagine why a biotech developer would get threats to his life.

I stayed quiet and contemplated what he had just said. Damien had robbed me of years of my life and my respectability. Now people wanted to torture and kill me because of him? I almost threw up at the thought; luckily my stomach was empty.

Ryan drove onto the freeway leading south. "What was on your schedule for today?" he asked.

When my memory failed me, I pulled it up on my phone. "Yoga, mud bath, massage, and a facial," I told him.

"What time is the first one?"

"Ten."

He sped up and passed a truck.

He was carrying a gun and spiriting me out of town. He had to really be worried, but it didn't add up. Why would I be in any more danger now than any other time since Damien's arrest?

I vacillated between being shit-in-my-pants scared and fatalistically nonchalant. I mean, what else could they do to me? Unfortunately, Ryan had answered that for me.

The scenery whizzed past in a blur as Ryan passed car after car in this super-expensive warp-drive machine. The eyes of the other drivers followed us as we passed.

I swore I could almost see them salivating at the sight of this silver chariot rocketing by. Even the sound of the engine was musical. The throaty lions under the hood roared when Ryan stepped on the gas, not at all like the choked whimpering of the pussy cats powering the sedan I'd been driving. This car oozed testosterone and screamed money, all wrapped in style——a rocket ship on wheels. We were riding in another dimension, separate from the mere mortals driving Chevys and Fords.

Ryan jammed on the brakes to bring us down from warp speed as a truck pulled out from the right-hand lane.

The fanny pack slid from my lap, and the heavy gun landed on my foot, bringing me back to reality. Somebody out there wanted me, and right now the only thing between me and them was Ryan, and his gun.

I put my hand on his forearm to feel the warmth, the strength, the conviction.

He looked quickly my direction and smiled. "I know you're scared, Cupcake, but it'll be okay. I promise."

"I'm going to hold you to that," I said.

The corners of his mouth turned up. "I know something else you can hold."

I punched him in the shoulder. "Really? Somebody out there wants to filet me like a fish, and you ask me to hold your dick?"

He shifted his hand to my side of the center console. "I meant my hand."

I shrank a few inches and took his hand. "Sorry."

His grip was warm, firm, and reassuring, like the rest of him ——a man I could count on in every way.

I held his hand with both of mine, unwilling to let go of my anchor. "I thought..."

"I know what you thought. That's what I like about you. You come up with better ideas than me." He laughed.

I let go with one hand and punched him in the shoulder again, harder. It still had no effect. I returned to holding on to my anchor.

A half hour later, I took a deep breath and released his hand. I had to be strong enough to stand by myself as well. I could do this. I started counting the cars we passed to take my mind off our conversation.

Everything changed when we reached the cape and the freeway eventually turned into a two-lane road. Ryan whipped around to pass other cars, and I trembled as we zoomed by a truck.

∾

*R*YAN

I IGNORED THE CAR COMING THE OTHER WAY, PUNCHED THE GAS, and flew around another minivan on Route Six.

"I'd like to arrive in one piece. I don't need to make the first class, really," Natalie said.

I swerved back into our lane. "I don't like to be late."

"Then we should have left earlier."

I pointed out the obvious. "I wasn't the one who got up late."

She put a warm hand on my arm. "I'm sorry about that, but this weekend is supposed to be about relaxing, not stressing. A fashionably late start is fine... Please."

I let off the gas and slowed. I'd forgotten how speed scared her. I looked over and shot her a smile. "Late it is, then."

"Thank you."

The two simple words soothed me. All I needed to make my day complete was for her to be happy and safe. It was now my job to ensure both.

She turned on the radio and tuned it to a satellite station. Frank Sinatra's "That's Life" started playing. We both sang along.

I took her hand. She knew the words. We had something in common: Sinatra.

Many Sinatra songs later, we pulled up to the Land's End Spa for a retry on her weekend.

I snapped on my fanny pack and then grabbed the suitcase and her paper bag of clothes. "Your room number?"

She started toward the building. "Two-forty-two."

"I'll follow you."

She checked her phone. "I'm just a little late. I'll go straight to class and catch up with you later."

I hustled along with her. "No way. I'm not leaving you alone."

"So you want to join ladies yoga?"

"I'll wait outside."

She stopped and bit her lower lip. "You're serious, aren't you?"

"Do I look like I'm kidding?"

She shook her head and marched off.

I followed with the luggage.

Inside, instead of heading for the elevator to her room, she went down the left hallway and into the room labeled Yoga #1.

I parked the suitcase outside and followed her inside to get the lay of the land.

The stares of a dozen concerned women positioned on blue mats made it abundantly clear that this was a Y-chromosome-free room.

I retreated and parked my butt in a chair in the hallway outside.

Soft instrumental music wafted through the door, with the occasional muffled sounds of instruction.

I pulled out my phone to dial for help. I couldn't handle this alone.

Liam answered on the second ring.

"I need some help," I told him.

"Sure. What can I do?"

"I remember you said you had to provide security for your sister-in-law a while back."

"Yeah," he answered.

"Well, I need that for Natalie."

He sighed. "Ryan, I know you're armed, so tell me what the problem is that you can't handle."

I started at the beginning. "She was staying at her sister's place near Central Square, and yesterday it was broken into and completely trashed. They tore the place apart looking for a book, a ledger."

"How can you know that for sure?"

I paused while two ladies walked past me down the hall. "I had an interesting chat with the cops. Did you know that in addition to ripping off half the town, her slimeball ex was laundering money for the Mexicali Cartel?"

"No. I hadn't heard that," he said.

"Well, apparently he kept a ledger. The prosecutor has been after Natalie for it, and now the cartel thinks Natalie knows where it is."

He was silent for a second. "Then she should turn it over——"

"She doesn't have it, and she doesn't know anything about it. That's the problem. I'm afraid they're going to come after her next. So I need protection for her, and I need the best."

"In this town, I wouldn't know who to trust. Vincent Benson might have a name, but I'd prefer to fly my uncle Garth's people out from LA. That way nobody will recognize them, and that could be an advantage."

"That's why I called," I told him.

"Let me make the call, and I'll have people here tomorrow."

"Thanks."

"Until then, you can bring her over here, if you want."

I couldn't accept that. "We're out of town for the weekend. We'll be fine until tomorrow." I'd promised her a weekend at the cape, and I intended to deliver.

"Okay, expect a team from the Hanson firm at your place tomorrow."

We hung up after more than one hearty thank you from me.

Half an hour later, my butt was going to sleep on the hard chair. The door swung open, and the yoga group filed out. I caught more than one sideways glance, along with a few mumbled comments I didn't quite hear.

Natalie was near the end of the line.

"Fun?" I asked as I stood.

"Hard."

"I thought you girls liked it hard."

She laughed. "Can't you come up with a better line than that?"

"Not on no sleep. And they need better chairs here." I rubbed my sore ass.

We took the elevator to her room, deposited the bags, and decided we had time for lunch down by the harbor. She said her friend Agnes had recommended a place.

CHAPTER 27

NATALIE

THE NEXT MORNING, RYAN STARTED THE MONSTER ENGINE OF THE silver time machine as I tightened my seatbelt, a necessary precaution with the way he drove. Now it was back to reality, back to the cleanup of my sister's destroyed apartment and to dealing with whoever it was Ryan thought he had to protect me from.

"Ready?" he asked as he backed out of the parking space.

"Not really."

The weekend had been relaxing, but most of all magical being here with Ryan, having him all to myself——no running off to the lab or the hospital, no hurried conversation before getting to the next project or prior to checking on the next experiment. I could use more weekends like this. The spa trip was a gift from Jasmin, but it was Ryan's gift of his time and uninterrupted attention that had made it special.

He checked his watch. "Maybe we can do this again when the weather improves."

It had been chilly, but even walking on the sand by the beach, I hadn't been cold——not once. Ryan had been here to snuggle up to, the ultimate portable body warmer. And it wasn't just my skin he warmed, but my soul.

We'd climbed to the top of Pilgrim Monument, the tallest all-granite structure in the country. It was definitely a place I wanted to return to.

"That would be great. How 'bout Memorial Day?" I asked.

He hesitated. "I'm not sure. We'll have to see what my schedule looks like."

I shouldn't have pushed. Being his *Cupcake* was totally unlike any previous experience I'd had with a man. Even when he was bossy, he was adorable, and underneath it all, I knew he had my best interests at heart. I'd finally found a man I could trust.

He looked over. "But I'd love to. It was fun." Those words helped my attitude as we joined the highway back to civilization. After ladies yoga, he'd even been game to join me in my activities.

I'd liked the couples massage the best, lying next to him with just a few feet separating us while they tortured our muscles with kneading and hitting, followed by the soothing heat of the hot stones. The masseuse told us the black stones had special proper-ties, and afterward I felt so relaxed I was willing to believe her, even though Ryan told me it made no scientific sense.

Our group meditation session had been boring, but I had to give it to Ryan. He had gone the extra mile. Although he'd sworn to never ever do such things, he had joined me in the mud bath, and even the facial. It was all way beyond what I would have expected. His continual complaints had only made the experiences more special.

Back on the divided highway, Ryan kept our speed down to match the flow of traffic, and I was able to contemplate the weekend without having to brace myself and hope we arrived home safely.

The meals with him had been surreal. Hot dogs and fries by the harbor or an elegant meal overlooking the water at night——it hadn't mattered. He kept the focus on me and made me feel appreciated with the smallest gestures. Everything from his smirks when I caught him checking out my cleavage, to the gentle touches of his hand at my back going through a door, or the strong pull of his arm around my shoulders——it all felt real, yet also magical. Surprisingly, he hadn't called work, or mentioned it a single time.

I sighed. "This is going to suck."

"What?"

Damien still controlled my life. "Damien's the criminal, and now I have to be locked up."

"It won't be that bad. With protection, you can go out and do whatever you want…within reason."

I huffed. "Right."

The within-reason qualifier meant anything I contemplated doing had to be analyzed for safety. Even something as simple as going to lunch would mean taking an entourage with me——I knew Ryan wouldn't remain my sole bodyguard for long. He'd talked to Liam about getting some professionals, and I doubted they'd let me go to the bathroom by myself.

"We don't have a choice," he said. "I'm not taking the risk."

I liked his caring, but it didn't make the situation any more pleasant. "What are they like? My bodyguards?"

"I haven't met them, but Liam assures me they're the best. One is ex-FBI and the other is ex-Secret Service."

That didn't answer my question.

∽

BACK FROM THE CAPE, I LOOKED OUT OVER MIT FROM THE vantage point of Ryan's condo. It was nice here, a lot more than nice, twenty-three floors up.

While Ryan was in the bathroom, his phone on the counter dinged with an incoming text.

BRIANA: See you at the hospital

I returned to the window, unsure what to make of that.

A minute later he joined me by the window and offered a glass of chardonnay.

"Who's Briana?"

He cocked his head momentarily. "She's a nurse, why?"

I flicked my head toward the kitchen. "You got a text."

"Later," he replied.

"Why this place?" I asked sweeping my arm around.

"What? Don't you like it?"

It was incongruous, considering everything else about Ryan was casual, even studiously cheap. His worn jeans, his old car, his Timex watch. He only owned the one suit. Everything except this place screamed "guy just out of college and barely scraping by."

I shook my head. "What's not to like? It's marvelous. You spend millions on a place like this, but you won't even spend a few bucks on new shoes, new jeans, or a car that's not a rust bucket. I don't get it."

"My car is fine. I've had it since I learned to drive."

"Right. Fine——if you like rust and mold," I shot back. "You forget, I've seen your car."

"It runs. It's a good car." In Ryan-speak, that equated to shut up and don't bug me any more.

I took the hint, sipped my wine, and dropped the line of questioning.

"My dad bought me that car," he offered after a moment. "He taught me to drive in it."

I put my arm around him. "I'm sorry. I get it."

"Liam made me buy this place," he continued. "My old apartment was next to the train tracks, and I had trouble sleeping. Liam said he needed me well rested. He picked this place out and said I couldn't come back to work until I bought it. I closed the transaction the next day."

It was clear that Liam had figured out work was the biggest motivator in Ryan's life.

I looked up at him. "Well, I approve. I'll thank Liam."

His face crinkled in disapproval. "Him rushing me cost me at least twenty grand."

"You can afford it."

"That's not the point."

I pulled away and fixed my eyes on him. "How much did you net when you sold Luxxamin?" I had already researched the answer and was ready if he fudged.

"One point one billion." He had decided not to fudge it.

"And what percentage of that is twenty K?" I asked. I knew he would have the answer instantly; the man was a human calculator.

"That's not the point."

I wasn't letting this go. "Answer the question, Dr. Westerly."

"A little less than two one-thousandths of a percent."

I had him. "And it saved you days away from work, and left you some untold number of hours more rested. How can that not be worth it?"

He shifted his weight and fidgeted with his wine glass. "Why do you have to be so damned logical?"

"It's what makes me good at patents."

He reached for me with his free hand and pulled my chest to his. "That's just one of the things I love about you, Cupcake." He kissed my forehead.

The words turned my brain to mush.

He whispered into my ear. "We haven't tried the kitchen counter yet."

I pulled myself closer, up against the hardening bulge in his pants. The offer was tempting.

There was a knock at the door.

Fuck.

"Somebody's timing sucks," he said as he released me and went to check the door.

I finger-combed my hair and straightened my shirt, willing my blush to go down.

Ryan opened the door

"Dr. Westerly, we're from Hanson Security," the man said.

"Call me Ryan, please, and please come in."

Ryan admitted them, and I was introduced to Winston Evers, the big man who'd spoken first, and his petite companion, Constance Collier. Ryan referred to me as the *protectee*.

Constance's handshake was firm and her eyes steely, probably par for the course for a successful woman in the male-dominated field she had chosen. It had to be hard for a woman her size to command the respect of all these big, physical guys.

"Miss Spencer——" Winston started.

"Natalie," I cut him off before he could get any further. "Please."

I was not going to be either the protectee or Miss Spencer.

Winston winced. "Sorry, Natalie. We are here to keep you safe, but to do it in the least-obtrusive way possible. In general, I'll be on duty here in the unit at night." He waved around our condo. "And Constance will be available to accompany you anywhere you want to go during the day. If she deems the location too vulnerable, she'll ask me to join you as well."

I nodded, following along.

"And don't be put off by her size," Winston said.

Constance shot him a sneer.

"She was previously with the Secret Service, on the First Lady's detail. She's more capable than any two men I know."

Constance smiled and suddenly didn't look so short to me anymore. If she was good enough for the President's wife, she was good enough for me.

Winston turned his attention to Ryan. "I'm told you are also carrying a weapon, is that correct?"

"Yes," Ryan replied, going to fetch his fanny pack. He pulled out the big gun and handed it to Winston.

The ex-FBI agent ejected the clip, reinserted it, and handed it back. "Do you know how to use it?"

"I was fifth in the Olympic trials for fifty-meter pistol," Ryan said, surprising me with another fact I didn't know about him. Fifth place in the Olympic trials for anything had to be damned good.

Winston's eyes widened. "Impressive, but accuracy won't count if you can't get your gun out. This fanny bag won't do. The bad guy will be on you before you can unzip it. You'll need a shoulder holster or something equivalent."

Ryan nodded. "I'll think about it."

The orientation went on as they explained what to expect. It sounded thorough and well thought out, but still incredibly confining. Ryan and these two would keep me safe, but Damien had won. He had canceled my pass to roam the city freely, the asshole, another way he had made living here hell for me.

He was in jail, but I was under house arrest.

CHAPTER 28

(TEN DAYS LATER)

NATALIE

WE HAD JUST FINISHED DINNER.

"Hold on, where are you going?" Ryan called.

Constance was in the bathroom, and I had almost made it out the door. "Out. I can't stay cooped up in here forever."

Since Jasmin's place had been trashed, we'd stayed at his place, run with them in the morning, come in to work with them, and left work with them. It was nonstop Ryan and Constance. She even insisted on checking the bathroom stalls before I went in.

He grabbed his shoulder holster and leather jacket. "Then I'm coming along."

I closed the door behind me and raced for the elevator. I banged on the down button. This had gone too far. I realized I should have taken the stairs, as Ryan emerged before the elevator arrived.

"You know the rules."

I knew his rules all right: no going unless it was necessary, and never alone, ever.

"I can't just stay inside. I need some fresh air. I just want to go for an evening stroll on the Common."

"Sounds like a good idea. I'd love that too."

The elevator car arrived, and we headed down to street level.

I hated being trapped into living like this. I couldn't escape the Damien curse. All I lacked was an ankle monitor.

It had been ten days——ten wonderful days spent with Ryan, but also ten regimented days of not being allowed to go anywhere without consulting Constance. She tried to be accommodating, but the entire situation was untenable. It made me hate Boston, and Damien, even more.

We walked out of the lobby downstairs and turned toward the bridge.

"You know we still have alternatives," Ryan said before we'd gone a block.

Constance ran up behind us and took position a few paces back.

I knew the alternatives well. Stay locked down like this, trading out Winston and Constance for perhaps a half dozen permanent security people, or go talk to Damien.

Ryan took my hand. "When he hears how much danger you're in, he might give you what you need."

That was the option I found least acceptable. "You don't know him. I don't want to see him ever again, and he'll use this as leverage to get me to keep visiting him. That's giving him what he wants."

We turned left toward the bridge over the Charles.

Constance followed.

"Try one meeting and see if you get anything. You might be surprised."

Ryan was the eternal optimist, but being optimistic with Damien was always naïve.

"I'll meet with him then," Ryan offered.

I stopped instantly and turned. "No. I'll call Brosnahand and set up a meeting. Just me, not you."

I couldn't let Damien get his hooks into Ryan. No way would that turn out well. Damien corrupted everything he touched. The demands would start, and they wouldn't stop.

~

R YAN

THE NEXT MORNING, NOT LONG AFTER I ARRIVED AT WORK, LIAM called me into his office. Dillard, our attorney for the court case with Valestum, was already seated in the office.

I closed the door behind me and took a seat.

Dillard passed me a printout.

"When did this come?" I asked him.

"It was posted yesterday."

Part of Dillard's job was to keep up to date on what Valestum was putting into the patent office, to see if we could detect any more activity from our mole.

"Is it one of ours?" Liam asked.

I quickly read through the abstract. It was exactly like one of ours. I flipped to the claims section at the back. My blood began to boil as I read the exact wording Natalie and I had agreed to change for one of our claims only a few days ago.

"Those fuckers. This is ours, all right. Natalie and I have been working on this for about a week."

"You're sure?" Dillard asked.

"Of course I'm sure. The first four claims here are identical in wording to what we came up with a few days ago. And that's not a coincidence. Claims three and four have the intentional mistakes we inserted a few days ago."

Liam exhaled loudly. "This was leaked recently then?"

"Three days ago max," I told him.

"You're sure?" Liam asked.

I was certain, given the incorrect wording Natalie and I had chosen for two of the claims. "Absolutely."

Liam sat back. "That rules out Molnar then."

Sandor Molnar had left the company two weeks ago, and Liam had him on his short list of suspects.

Liam thought for a moment. "Thank you both," he said, calling an end to our short meeting

Dillard picked up his briefcase and made a hasty retreat.

Liam spoke before I reached the door. "Ryan, if you could stay a moment."

The door closed behind Dillard.

Liam steepled his hands. "I'm going to call in the FBI on this. Extra security measures are clearly not enough."

I nodded. I had opposed getting law enforcement involved earlier, but no longer.

"No one outside of you and me will know about this," he said.

I asked the obvious question. "Not even security?"

"No. Not even security."

I still had a looming problem. "I need to tell Natalie."

Liam's eyes narrowed momentarily. "That's not a good idea."

I couldn't keep this secret from her. "Don't you trust her?"

"Yes, but——"

"So do I. And she needs to know."

"Then you need to make her understand that nobody else, and I mean *nobody*, can even get a hint that we've called in the FBI for help."

"Of course."

I left Liam's office with a rock in the pit of my stomach. Valestum had now snatched three of our recipes, and that could have disastrous consequences for the patients in need.

∼

NATALIE

BACK FROM LUNCH, I LEFT MY OFFICE DOOR OPEN.

Not five minutes later, Rick walked past for the third time today, at least that I had noticed.

I ignored him and went back to work on the patent file I was putting together. So far, each one of Ryan's stacks had led to what I considered quite a good patent application, with a solid set of claims. I had yet to find one that had a serious problem with prior art in any of my searches——and Dad had taught me how to search, both deep and broad.

Ryan was clearly breaking new ground, no doubt about that. If the treatments worked, they would be truly innovative.

My phone jingled with the distinctive ring tone I had assigned to my sister. As I answered, I got up to close my office door.

"How's life with Mr. Incredible?" Jasmin asked.

"Ryan and I are doing...fine," I answered.

"I can hear that everything's-not-fine tone in your voice," she said.

"It's all good. It's just that this house arrest sucks."

"Too protective, huh?"

I debated cutting off the conversation here. "I can't figure out if he's being paranoid, or I'm rebelling against the confinement. I mean, he wears a gun every time we go out."

"Armed and dangerous, I like that."

I did as well. It was comforting to know how concerned he was.

"Me too, for the first few days, but how do I live like this going forward? I'm trapped. I can't go out of the condo without him and/or Constance. I feel like the only thing missing is the ankle bracelet."

Another incoming call beeped. I checked the screen and

ignored it. Kirk Willey didn't rate interrupting my conversation with Jasmin.

"What if you go up to Gramps's place for a few days? Is that far enough away?" she asked.

I had forgotten about Gramps's place in Vermont.

"I'm not even sure joining you in LA would be far enough. But thanks for the suggestion."

The longer I thought about it, the more perfect a getaway to Vermont seemed.

"On the bright side, I get my paycheck in a few days, and I can start to replace your things," I told her.

I was feeling incredibly guilty about everything that had been destroyed by those assholes. I had gotten the door fixed, but it would take more than one paycheck and several shopping trips to get her place back to normal. Ryan had offered to help, but I'd refused. It was my responsibility.

"No hurry on that. Since Imogene is out for her honeymoon, I can't get away for a few weeks at least."

She complained for a few minutes about her boss's unwilling-ness to add more multilingual staff to the crew. They seemed to be perpetually understaffed in that department. At first Jasmin had enjoyed the extra money from the additional hours, but now that she wanted more free time to be with Corbin, the job didn't fit as well as it once had.

After hanging up with her, I made a quick trip to refill my coffee.

Back at my computer, I resumed where I'd left off, constructing claims with the help of a little diagram Ryan had drawn for me.

Ten minutes later, Rick slowly sauntered by my doorway again, this time with another of the IT guys, Mike somebody.

I avoided eye contact again.

I constructed another three claims before my phone resumed ringing.

Mason Brosnahand, the screen said.

I paused, deciding between the red and green buttons. I hit the green one and took the call. No doubt he was calling back to tell me when I was scheduled to meet with Damien.

"Natalie, glad I caught you. I wanted to give you the good news, and the bad, before you saw it on TV."

More bad news was not what I needed, especially Damien-related news bad enough to rate television coverage. There had already been hours too much of that.

"I was hoping the mania would die down at some point," I said wearily.

"It's not what you think," he said without elaborating.

I waited for the punch line, probably along the lines of *it's even worse than that.*

"The FBI has recovered your husband's ledger, and the most recent shipment of twenty million dollars he had been laundering for the Mexicali Cartel."

"I told them I didn't have it!"

He continued. "The FBI has also arrested Carlos Mendoza and eight other members of his organization." I couldn't tell from his voice if that was good news or bad.

Ryan appeared at the door, and I waved him in.

"Close the door," I mouthed.

He did and took a seat.

I set the phone down, putting it on speaker. "That's good, right?" I put my finger to my lips for Ryan to stay quiet.

"For them, not so much," Mason continued. "For you, absolutely. Since the ledger and the money were what those criminals had been after when they tore up your apartment, it means you no longer need to worry. They now know you don't have, and never had, what they wanted, not to mention that several of them are now in jail anyway. You don't have to be afraid anymore. You won't need protection; they aren't a threat any longer."

I sighed in relief. "That's great." I dreaded asking about the bad news.

Ryan smiled and gave me a thumbs up.

"The story will be on this evening's news, and I wanted to give you a heads up," Mason said.

"Thanks. You have no idea what a relief that is."

House arrest had ended. We could let Constance and Winston go back to their normal lives.

"The bad news..."

I braced myself.

Ryan frowned.

"...is that since the discovery came from a deal your husband brokered by himself with the prosecutor, I don't have any leverage with this to get your house or your money back."

That sucked, but it was still a win.

"So, once again, Damien screwed me."

"Yes and no," he said. "I told him you wanted to meet. He'd heard about the apartment incident and the danger to you. He told me he did this for your safety. If he had only let me handle it, we might have served both goals."

I didn't want to think about whether it was true that Damien had done this for me, or to bargain for a better deal for himself.

"Thank you for the news, Mason. I appreciate it. You're sure the danger has passed, right?"

"Absolutely. Given what's happened, they have a beef with your husband, not you."

"Ex-husband," I noted.

"Of course," he said. "Natalie, you can get on with your life now. The original reason for your meeting is moot, but I still think you should meet with Damien again to try to convince him to tell you something about the remaining missing money. That could still be leverage to get your house back."

"I'll think about it." I wasn't going to commit to more than that today.

We hung up, and I fist pumped the air. *Free again.*

Ryan came around the desk to give me a big hug. "We should go out and celebrate. That's terrific news."

"Yeah, you can stop toting that ugly gun everywhere."

"You know, that was a good gesture on his part."

"Who?" I asked.

"Your ex-husband."

I huffed. "I'm not sure I believe that."

"Doesn't matter. The fact is you're no longer in danger due to something he did, and you should thank him."

"You want me to meet with him again?"

He shook his head. "I said thank him. It's the right thing to do, so write him a note if you don't want to talk to him. But do the right thing. Don't let his lack of morals rub off on you."

I relented. "Okay."

Ryan's words made more sense after I let them sink in for a moment. A note I could handle.

He pointed a finger at me. "Now that you're off lockdown, I'll make reservations for dinner, and you can join me at the hospital this evening."

I smiled. "Sure."

I had asked to join him on other hospital visits, but since they wouldn't let Winston or Constance go in armed, it had been ruled out during my confinement. But I loved being part of Ryan's work. Those visits seemed like something we could schedule to do together.

CHAPTER 29

RYAN

"AND THAT'S HOW WE BAIT THE HOOK," LIAM SAID.

Natalie looked at me and shrugged. "I guess it could work."

"It'll work if the honey is sweet enough," Liam said.

And he should know; he had experience with this kind of sting.

I took a breath. "But I don't have results yet on CTX-41."

"That's fine, but you have to sell it as if you do," he said.

My next question was harder. "And...how do I do that?"

He laughed. "Start by looking happier than you do right now. You've had a breakthrough, and you need to tell everybody you would normally tell. Don't leave anybody out. It would be great news if it worked, wouldn't it?"

"Of course," I answered.

"Then act like it has and you believe it. Let the grapevine do the rest," Liam added.

Natalie stood. "That's it then. Monday is the day, right?"

"They set up on Sunday night, and next Monday we're a go," Liam replied.

I didn't like the idea. I waited until Natalie left and then closed the door.

"Liam, there has to be another way——like a search warrant for Valestum. We know they stole it."

He shook his head. "We've been through this. We can't meet the threshold for a search warrant, and since a paper you and Natalie had scribbled on was the last thing they stole, we can't count on finding an electronic footprint. Most likely the thief took the paper out of your office and either copied it or photographed it with his phone. That means he got access to your office somehow, and we need him to repeat the process."

He got up——my cue to leave.

I left his office to locate Natalie for lunch.

We walked to the sandwich shop down the block. She ordered a BLT, and I chose the French dip sandwich.

We took a table by the window and waited.

"Do you think this will work?" she asked.

I surveyed the room again to be sure there weren't any other Chameleon people present. "It has to; this is just too important. Dozens of lives hang in the balance with each of these leaks."

"We could announce to everyone that we've placed a trap for the mole," she offered.

I sipped my water. "That would defeat the purpose."

"It would freeze whoever it is in their tracks, and give us time to work on filing the rest of the patents."

"How long do you figure that would take?"

"Three to six months," she answered.

"The guy probably wouldn't stay scared for that long."

"I guess not."

They called our number, and I retrieved our orders.

"It was just an idea," she said.

As I took a bite of my sandwich, her phone rang.

She checked the screen. "That asshole Willey again."

"If you keep avoiding him, he'll just send his goons after you," I told her.

She sighed and answered the phone.

After a moment she said, "Say that again." Her face fell. "When... How could that happen?" Her shoulders slumped. "Why would they?... Thank you for letting me know." She ended the call with a solemn face.

"What did he want?" I asked.

"Damien is dead," she said.

I put down my sandwich, not sure I'd heard her properly. "What?"

"He was killed in prison this morning. The prisoners that did it are linked to the Mexicali Cartel. Willey said it was probably payback for cooperating."

"He should have been in protective custody."

"He was."

There wasn't any more to say.

We'd both lost our appetite, and after a while, we gave up on lunch and went back to work.

~

NATALIE

THE NEXT DAY, THE DOORBELL SURPRISED ME.

I checked my watch; it was too early for Ryan to be home.

Peering through the peephole revealed sheriff's deputies in the hallway. Walking away and letting them cool their heels was what I felt like, but I bit the bullet and unlocked the door.

"Mrs. Natalie Winterbourne?" the taller of the two asked. They carried cardboard boxes in their arms.

"It's Ms. Spencer now," I told them.

When would they ever get it right?

"We have your husband's effects," the short one offered.

"Ex-husband," I spat. "And I don't want any of his things."

Even from beyond the grave, Damien was reaching out to me.

The short one looked to the taller one and shrugged. "Ma'am, you're listed as the next of kin——"

I interrupted him. "Not anymore. Ex-husband, I told you."

The tall one rolled his eyes.

"Ma'am, the regulations are clear. We have to give you his effects," the short one told me.

I stood my ground and didn't answer.

The taller one offered his box to me.

I shook my head. I could be as stubborn as the next person.

The short one moved a step closer. "Ma'am, we don't have a choice."

I relented and moved aside, motioning them inside. "In the fire-place will be fine."

The tall one laughed. But they ignored me and placed the two boxes on the table.

The short one took a clipboard off the top of his box and brought it to me. "We need a signature." He offered me a pen. "Please."

I took the board and signed my name, my *real* name, Natalie Spencer, above the line with the hated Winterbourne name. I handed it back to the short one.

"Thank you, ma'am," he said.

I let them out and closed the door.

~

AN HOUR LATER, RYAN WALTZED IN AND PULLED ME UP OFF THE ground in one of the hug-twirls he'd taken to giving me. He never arrived with a mere *hello, how are you*? The man knew how to show a girl he thought of her all the time. Every trip up and around was like the first had been: exhilarating. My heart beat faster after he set me down.

I wrapped my arms around him for our I-missed-you kiss. How do you spell romantic? R-Y-A-N, that's how.

"What are those?" he asked when he spied the two cardboard boxes on the table with Suffolk County Sheriff's Department stamped on them in bold lettering.

"For the fireplace," I told him.

His brow creased. "Come again?"

"Damien's belongings from the jail."

Ryan walked to the table. "What's in them?"

"Nothing I want, that's for sure."

He lifted the lid on the first box, pulled out a suit coat, and unfolded it. "Brooks Brothers…nice," he said.

I shook my head. "It won't fit you. Like I said, bonfire material."

"I think Goodwill would be better," he said, pulling the matching slacks out of the box and checking them over.

I hadn't thought of donating them. "You think some homeless person wants a Brooks Brothers suit?"

He shot me a glare. "Homeless? Really? That's who you think goes to Goodwill stores? I've shopped there."

I cringed. "Sorry. I didn't mean…" I decided to shut up before I dug an even deeper hole. I opened the second box.

Ryan picked Damien's red boxers out of the box and held them up. "What kind of pansy was this guy?"

That got me laughing. "He just liked silk."

Damien had always worn silk boxers, most often red. He'd said it was a power color, but I didn't get the importance of a power color for underwear nobody saw.

Ryan threw them to the side. "Trash or fireplace material."

We could agree on that.

The box I'd opened contained a series of large, sealed envelopes.

Ryan found shoes, socks, a shirt, an undershirt, and suspenders. "This guy not believe in belts?"

"He said belts were for jeans, and suspenders were for suits."

"Definitely a pansy."

I didn't answer, remembering my father had counseled against speaking ill of the dead. I had never considered Damien effeminate, but he was if you used hundred-octane Ryan for comparison.

I pulled out the first envelope.

"I'll take these to Goodwill tomorrow," Ryan said.

He had made a neat pile of the suit, shirt, and shoes. He considered the undershirt, socks, and definitely the boxers unfit for second-hand ownership.

I opened the envelope I had retrieved from my box. Damien's gold Rolex Yacht Master watch slipped out onto the table. It had been one of his favorites. His collection had taken up two drawers in our closet. Why anyone without a boat needed a yachting watch I never understood.

Ryan picked up the watch and appraised it.

"Want it? It's yours," I told him.

"A pansy and a show-off." He shook his head dismissively. "Not my style. I'm a Timex guy, keeps time just as well."

That was one of the things I'd noticed early on about Ryan. Although he was wealthy——way beyond what Damien and I had ever had——he didn't flaunt it. On the street, you would take him for Joe Everyman, not the billionaire biotech startup founder he was.

"Goodwill?" I asked.

"No, the suit is okay, but better to pawn that watch, or donate it to a charity, if you want." Ryan pulled another envelope from the box. He tore it open and Damien's wallet slid out. He examined it, pulled out the license and credit cards for the trash heap, and added the leather wallet to his Goodwill pile.

The next envelope contained Damien's keyring.

Ryan examined the keys. "Medeco keys. These locks are

expensive. You know it's the kind they use in the White House. He sure took security seriously."

I nodded. "He was borderline paranoid about it. Of course now we know why."

He handed me the keyring.

"I don't want them." I threw them on the to-be-thrown-out pile.

Ryan pulled the ring out of the heap and offered it to me again. "A good luck charm, for when you get your house back."

I accepted them and put them to the side, to go in my purse later.

The last envelope contained the money Damien had on him at the arrest. Three one-hundred dollar bills, a twenty, and three quarters.

"You should keep the money; you earned it," Ryan said.

I certainly had. "Okay."

And the FBI had stolen more than this from me when they'd confiscated my house. My five-hundred-dollar emergency reserve had been in the flour jar, and they hadn't let me go in the house to pull it out.

The money went into my wallet. The watch and keyring joined the jumble in my purse.

CHAPTER 30

R YAN

It was before seven on Wednesday morning. We had been cooped up in this van for two nights running——two boring nights with next to no sleep in uncomfortable positions, while breathing stale air and worse farts. Liam's choice to dine on bean burritos had been a poor one.

The speaker in front of us had been silent all night.

"I need to take a leak," Liam announced.

Agent White passed him a bottle.

"Not like that," Liam said.

"You can't leave the van," White told him, checking his watch. "We've got another half hour before we call it a night, and I'm not letting you blow our cover."

Liam moved the bottle to the floor.

The three of us were on a fishing expedition. We sat in the Cambridge Water Department van the FBI had borrowed for this stakeout, parked around the corner from Chameleon.

The bait had been laid out the day before yesterday, when I'd told Paul before lunch that the latest results on CTX-41 looked like the best ones ever, and then told several others in the afternoon. I'd made a point of smiling broadly all afternoon, hoping I hadn't overdone my acting part.

"I warned you to skip the coffee," I told Liam.

He squirmed in his seat. "Half an hour, and not a minute more."

"It can get worse. One time I had to be on these overnights for over two weeks to catch the guy," White said.

Liam groaned. "Tomorrow night, you two can do this. I'm sleeping in my bed for a change."

"You want an airtight case against this guy? This is the only way. You don't show tomorrow, and I'm calling it off. You two turkeys can catch him on your own. I got a wife and kids, too. The deal is simple. If we devote the resources, you do too."

"There's got to be an easier way," Liam lamented.

"Look, Mr. Bigshot. This isn't rocket science. You catch the guy in the act, or else you don't get a conviction. It's your choice. Personally, I'd rather be chasing bank robbers in the daytime than spending my nights here with you two schmucks. Say the word, and we call it off right now."

Liam gave up. "No. We keep at it. We have to nail this guy."

It had to be hard for Liam to give in to this government employee. He was used to snapping his fingers and getting whatever he wanted, whenever he wanted.

A few minutes later, the sound of a door being unlocked came over the speaker.

"You hear that?" I asked.

"Quiet, this might be it," Agent White told us.

We all strained to hear the amplified sounds from the speaker in front of us.

We only had audio, no video, but that would be good enough. We would know if the mole took the bait.

I held my breath. The faint sound of rustling papers coming out of the speaker got my heart beating faster, and the blood rushed in my ears.

The sound of a door closing, and the lock being reset filled the vacuum of silence inside the van as we waited.

A bang, more like a loud pop, exploded out of the speaker.

"Jackpot. Move in, move in," White said over his radio to the agents inside our building.

The three of us tripped over each other in our escape from the van.

I stumbled the first few steps. My legs were like jelly from the hours of sitting in the cramped space. I ran a few paces behind White. Once inside, Liam swiped us past the locked door in the lobby.

White and I went right toward my office.

Liam bolted left toward the bathrooms.

The two agents that had been stationed inside had converged on our mole, and the person lay face-down on the ground.

"You are under arrest for the federal crime of trade secret theft," Agent McNally said, holding a gun on our suspect as Agent Parsons cuffed her. The FBI had provided both male and female agents for the interior, because we didn't know who was going to take the bait.

Agent Parsons pulled the woman to her feet and patted her down, checking for weapons.

Gwen was covered in blue dye. Her hands, her face, and the whole front of her was a solid blue——a stark contrast with the red of her hair. The wall and carpet a few feet from my door showed the effects of the dye packet explosion as well.

Liam ran up from behind us. "Gwen?"

She didn't meet our eyes, instead sneering at the ground. She ignored us while Agent Parsons read her Miranda rights off a laminated card.

"Do you understand these rights I have explained to you?" Parsons asked.

Gwen nodded wordlessly, and the two agents escorted her away.

Agent White took photographs of the scene before bagging the remains of the bait envelope that had contained the details on CTX-41. The dye bomb and timer had been hidden inside with a motion-activated switch.

"We should have put more time on the timer," I told them. She had barely made it out of my office. Any more time dawdling inside, and my office would have been an uninhabitable mess of indigo blue.

"Couldn't take the chance that she would have time to put it down," White said.

I would have put money on it being someone else, but the dye pack didn't lie.

"It makes sense now. Paul and Gwen had lunch together every week," Liam said. "I just don't get why she would do this to us."

"Money," White said as he finished with his bags of paper scraps. "It almost always comes down to money."

I shook my head and turned for the lab. "I'll be back later." I intended to let Liam explain this blue mess to the rest of the company.

∾

*R*YAN

IT HAD BEEN A LONG DAY. AFTER CATCHING GWEN EARLY THIS morning and then spending hours afterward telling everybody I met that I had no idea why she'd done it, the elevator door finally opened back at my building, and I dragged my tired butt to the condo.

I'd only been able to catch a few catnaps on the couch in Liam's office during our two days trying to trap the leaker, the mole, the traitor. Tonight I couldn't wait to climb into bed with my Cupcake, my beautiful Cupcake.

Natalie pulled open the condo door after my third bungled attempt to find the right key. I literally fell into her arms. At this point in the day, she was just what I needed.

Fragrant cooking aromas wafted through the open doorway. The sound of the kitchen exhaust fan on high greeted me as well.

"Hey there, big guy," she said as I leaned on her a little too heavily in our kiss. "Where's my carousel ride?"

I picked her up in a tight hug and twirled around once. I almost fell, I was so uncoordinated from lack of sleep.

"Better?"

"You look like crap," she said.

"That's better than I feel."

"Anything I can do to help?" she asked, rubbing my crotch.

I shook my head, a rare time I'd turn down an offer like that from her. "No, I need to crash." I kissed her nose.

She poked a finger in my chest. "You rest then; dinner's almost ready." She pecked my lips. "Love you."

I let go of her and trudged in. "The feeling's mutual."

"Love you more," she responded.

"Love you most." That was no joke.

The times we'd spent together since that fateful carriage ride in Provincetown had been the best *and* hardest of my life. The best because I got to spend time with Cupcake, my woman.

It had been hard, though, because although I no longer needed to worry about her safety, it was difficult leaving her every time I had to put in extra hours in the lab or visit the hospital. But the work had to be done. Lives depended on it. Lives depended on me.

She darted to the kitchen and peered through the oven glass.

I fell onto the couch. "What's cooking? It smells divine."

No joke, her everyday dishes were miles better than the best I could manage in the kitchen, and tonight she was clearly not aiming for pedestrian fare.

"Spinach smoothies with bacon bits," she yelled my way.

I groaned for her benefit. She knew how I felt about rabbit-food smoothies, but the aromas wafting my way belied her dire announcement.

"No, really, what?"

"How would you like chicken cordon bleu and chocolate cake?"

"Sounds terrific, Cupcake. Can I start with the cake?" I didn't want to fall asleep before I got my chocolate fix.

The distinctive pop of a champagne bottle resonated behind me. She brought over a glass for each of us. "This is to celebrate victory for both of us."

I took the glass and we clinked them together. "Final victory."

She repeated the toast and took a dainty sip.

I wasn't doing dainty and chugged a lot more than a sip as she went back to chef duty. I swallowed and gulped; she had broken out the good stuff for tonight.

"I don't understand it. Why do you think she did it?" Natalie called over the noise of the fan. She meant Gwen, of course.

"No idea. She's been with us since the beginning."

Gwen was one of the last people I would have suspected to be involved in something like this. She had been eager to join us and had been enthused, actually ecstatic, that orphan diseases would be a focus area for Chameleon. How she could turn around and sabotage that effort confounded me. I'd racked my brain this morning trying to make sense of it, and the longer I thought about it, the less sense it made.

I heard Natalie open the oven behind me and finished the rest of my glass.

"A little help, please?" she called.

I pulled myself up out of my comfortable, coma-inducing seat and helped her serve a delicious-looking dinner onto our plates.

I carried the plates to the table. "You got me with spinach and bacon bits."

She followed with the salad bowls. "I just exaggerated about how cut up they would be." The salad was warm spinach with bacon bits to go along with the chicken and sautéed mushrooms.

She refilled our champagne glasses, and we toasted the end of our joint struggles. Now that Damien was gone, the cartel was no longer after her, and Gwen had been caught, so our problems were behind us.

I dug into the meal and held up a forkful of her chicken dish. "You've outdone yourself, Nat."

"Thank you. How's your spinach?"

"Great," I told her. "You can feed me this anytime you want."

She smirked. "Watch out, I might put the leftovers in a smoothie for breakfast."

I shook my head. "I'll do fruit, but nothing leafy in mine."

"You won't even know there's spinach in it."

I refilled my champagne flute. "Dream on."

∿

NATALIE

I CLEARED THE DISHES AND BROUGHT OVER THE CAKE I'D BOUGHT: the ultimate chocolate concoction from Red Ribbon Decadence.

Ryan poured himself another glass of bubbly, his fourth at least.

When the first forkful reached his mouth, I knew I had a hit on my hands.

He closed his eyes. "Wow. You have to get this one again."

Some people had a sweet tooth, my Ryan had a chocolate tooth.

I lifted a bite, and as soon as it hit my tongue, I had to agree that this one went on the repeat list.

He pointed his fork at me. "Sooner or later, I'm going to get it out of you, ya know."

"What?"

"Your fantasy."

"I don't have one," I lied. Early on it had been too soon to tell him. Now I was waiting for the right time.

He gobbled down more cake. "How can I make you happy and make your dreams come true if you won't tell me?"

"You do, Ryan, every time you come home to me."

He licked his fork. "Love you."

"Love you more."

"Love you most, Cupcake, and I want to do something special for you. So tonight you're going to tell me."

I cut off another bite. "Nothing to tell."

He smiled my direction. "Do you want to be spanked?"

I shook my head.

"Tied up? Blindfolded? Handcuffs? You know they have fur-lined ones? A threesome?"

I kept shaking my head.

"Vibrator? Hot lotions? In a pool? On the beach?"

I kept shaking my head. He wasn't going to guess it, and that last one——it wasn't warm enough this time of year.

"Reverse cowgirl?"

He should know that wasn't it. We'd already done that multiple times.

I shook my head, smiled, and waited for his next guesses.

"Out in public? Or in a hammock?"

That sounded fun, but it wasn't it.

"Anal?"

I scooped some of the frosting on my fork and flung it at him. I got him on the forehead.

He wiped it off with a napkin. "I'll take that as a no."

He had that right.

A wise-ass grin grew across his face. "Nat, we promised no secrets, and now you're violating your own rule."

I couldn't deny that truth. No secrets was my number-one rule.

He had already finished his cake, and he washed it down with his remaining champagne.

I pushed my piece away half eaten. "Okay. I'll clean up here, and you get in bed and get ready."

He trudged off to the bedroom. "And you'll tell me?"

"Maybe."

I cleared our dessert dishes and started on the pans. The mere thought of it was getting me wet. As I started the dishwasher, I shivered with anticipation. Tonight would finally be the night——just the right time for the next step. I wiped off the island, washed my hands, and headed to the bedroom.

I opened the door a crack; the bedroom light was off. I clicked off the hall light and snuck into the bathroom to rinse with mouthwash. I shed my clothes in the walk-in closet and ran my hands up my sides and under my breasts, imagining they were his.

I was ready.

As I slid under the covers, he didn't make a move for me.

He was snoring.

The poor man had been up more than forty-eight hours straight to catch the traitor.

I lay my head on the pillow.

He deserved the rest.

Next time.

CHAPTER 31

NATALIE

THE FAINT SOUND OF HORNS IN THE DISTANCE WOKE ME. SIRENS accompanied the honking. At street level, the sirens and horn of a fire truck could wake the dead. Here, twenty-plus floors up, they were barely perceptible through Ryan's thick, triple-pane windows.

Rubbing my eyes, I focused slowly on the clock on my side of the bed and made out the time. Five-ten in the morning. The alarm would sound before long. Groggily, I did the math; Ryan had been asleep long enough to recharge.

Slipping my head under the covers, I kissed his stomach and made my way down to sleeping Mega-cock.

Ryan's fingers found me and scratched my scalp the way I liked.

His greeting was mumbled. "Morning."

I kissed the tip of him. "You fell asleep on me last night."

"Sorry, I was pretty out of it."

"Four glasses of champagne didn't help."

He shifted a leg. "That too, I guess."

I blew on his tip. "Does Mega want to play?

"No."

His cock's quick growth in my hand revealed the lie.

I pulled on his length and took what I could in my mouth, swirling my tongue around and then pulling away with my lips and my hand.

"Sure about that?"

"Not unless you tell me your fantasy." He pulled on my hair to bring me up to him.

I captured his mouth with mine for the good-morning kiss he deserved, all the while not letting my hand slip from his cock.

He rolled over on his side and ran his hand from my inner thigh, by my heat, up my side, and under my boob and around. He knew he drove me crazy with this. He had perfected the teasing touch, coming just close enough to my nipples and pussy with feathery lightness and skimming over my pubic hair, all the while denying me the most intimate of touches. Close but not quite there, *teasing.*

I stroked his fully awake cock, and moaned with his tempting caresses.

"Okay, in a minute——when I'm ready." I pushed his shoulder over and straddled him.

His hands continued their teasing journeys up my sides and under, around, and over my breasts, lighting my skin on fire, and causing goosebumps.

I leaned forward to offer him a nipple, brushing the stubble of his chin.

His lips captured it, and the kiss, the suck, even the nip were just what I wanted.

I slid my slippery slit over his length, rubbing my clit over Mega-cock's tip.

He arched up, giving me extra pressure, such wonderful pressure.

I continued to slide forward and back, vulva-fucking his cock.

"Can you come like this?" I asked. I knew I could, with just a little work.

"Is that your fantasy?"

I threw my head back and shook it as I continued to slide along the hard bar of his erection. This was good, but not the thing I wanted. Each time my little bud ran over his tip, a jolt went through me.

His breathing grew more rapid, and his hands on my hips forced me down on him as I kept the strokes going. He didn't need to answer my question, I could read it in his face. He wouldn't last long.

The waves of pleasure were building. I was getting too close. I slowed down; this was going too fast.

In the dim light, I could see the broad smile on his face, the way his chin rose up and his stomach tensed every time I slid over the crown. I sat up and reached around to caress his balls.

His hands moved from my hips to my breasts, holding their weight and running his thumbs around and over my erect nipples. When he pulled me down toward him to suck my nipples, I lost my hold of his balls. The shocks from his lips on my nipples ran to my toes.

He pushed me up and reached over to retrieve a condom. He offered me the packet.

I pushed him back down and climbed aboard once more. I'd learned that having me roll the latex down his shaft was a super turn-on for him. I'd perfected an overlapping, two-handed technique that drove him crazy. I took the packet in my hand, and started to slide my wetness over him again.

His hands guided my hips as I did.

I slid one more time to the end of him, gasping and almost coming undone as my clit ran over his tip. "You want to know what my fantasy is?" I asked, grinding into him.

"Cupcake, you know I do."

I closed my eyes and imagined what was about to happen. I put the condom on the bed and leaned forward to whisper in his ear. "I'm on the pill, and I want skin, not latex."

He took my face in his hands. "Baby, why didn't you say so? I'm clean; no need to worry."

I hadn't worried about him, but me. I'd wanted to wait for just the right time.

In a swift motion, he rolled us over and positioned himself between my legs.

I guided the steely hard cock to my entrance and wrapped my legs behind his thighs, pulling us together.

He pushed into my slickness easily, in increments, pulling back out and then moving in again.

The pleasure built rapidly as he filled me, the sensation of skin-to-skin contact better even than I'd dreamed it would be with Mega-cock.

He pushed and rocked, and I arched until every glorious bit of his cock filled me and he began to thrust rhythmically, lighting my nerve endings on fire. He drowned me with kisses between panted breaths before moving to the sensitive skin of my neck.

I could feel him shuddering and tensing, holding back. I rocked into him as my blood sang with each thrust, my heels pulling him in deeply.

A hand gripped my ass, pulling us closer yet.

The pressure inside me built unbearably as I tried to hold off, to make him be the first to come.

His words spilled out uncontrollably. "You feel so fucking good...so fucking tight...so wet...sooooo good...oh fuck." He lifted up on his arms enough to scrape his chest hair against my pebbled nipples, causing shivers I couldn't control.

The intensity of it all rolled through me in building waves as my climax burst over me. My toes curled, and my pussy pulsed around him. I threw my head back into the pillow to keep from screaming. I fought to get my breath back and clawed at his hair to pull his head to mine.

"Fuck me harder, goddammit."

He lifted up on his arms and pounded into me fiercely, losing himself with each push and coming to the end of his rope with a series of groans as he buried himself to the hilt and the throbbing spurts came. Slowly he fought to catch his breath and relaxed his weight on top of me, as spent and satisfied as I was.

Breathing under his weight was difficult, but still felt perfect. My man inside and on top of me, our hearts beating together, connected by flesh and feeling. I stroked and scratched his back ——my protector, my lover, my perfect man——with nothing separating us.

He rolled to the side, and after a few minutes of snuggling, I got up to clean off.

Barely a minute later, the alarm clock buzzed, and Ryan joined me in the bathroom.

"Do you want to know my fantasy?" he asked.

"Not if it's anal."

He laughed and pulled me to him, my swollen breasts up against his chest and a half-hard cock against my stomach. "You shaved," he whispered into my ear. "Completely."

I pushed away. "Get outta here. Not unless I get to shave your balls."

He grimaced. That was apparently not in the cards.

I trimmed, but I'd never shaved it all off. "Don't you have to run this morning?"

Freshman year at Brown, Amy had tried it and told me it itched like the devil growing back.

"You coming along?" he asked.

I briefly considered it. "Nah, you go ahead. I need to get into work early."

He dressed for his run while I started the shower and brushed my teeth.

When I heard the front door close after him. I climbed into the steamy shower with a fresh razor.

Bit by bit, the curly hair began to collect by the drain.

～

Ryan

I FINISHED CHECKING THE CTX-39 SLIDES WHILE PAUL WAITED patiently for my verdict. "Paul, I have to say, you've done exceptional work here."

He beamed. He should be proud, and both he and I knew it. He had thought to try an approach I had set aside as a longshot, and it had worked.

"I'm glad you didn't follow my lead on this."

He nodded, leaving the words unsaid as he always did.

I had forgotten to turn off my cell when I entered the lab, and it buzzed with an incoming text. I checked it. Liam wanted to see me. I nodded and left for his office. The lab was in good hands.

Sydney Roundhouse was leaving Liam's office when I arrived. I poked my head in. "I'll come back when you're free."

"No. I was just waiting for you."

Waiting didn't sound good. I closed the door after me and took the visitor's chair. It felt like being called into the principal's office in middle school. But Liam was the boss I appreciated having almost every day. Today was probably going to be one of those *almost* days.

I braced, but decided good offense was the best defense. "I know I'm behind schedule, but I should be able to catch up in a few weeks."

He laughed. "Is that what you think this is about?"

I shrugged. I didn't have anything else.

"Ryan, I can see the hours you're putting in."

I had to get ahead of this. "I can do better."

"Stop right there. Sometimes I think you're so smart you're stupid. You can't see what's right in front of you."

I didn't know what I'd missed, so I waited to be educated.

"Ryan, you're a biochemistry whiz, but you don't know squat about physics."

"That's because physics has nothing to do with what we do here."

He smiled and leaned back in his chair. "Are you familiar with the concept of leverage?"

I missed the trick in the question. "Go ahead."

"I've had a few talks with Syd and Paul."

That didn't sound like anything good.

"We're going to reorganize," he continued. "I'm putting Syd Roundhouse underneath you. You'll be running Lab Two as well as number one."

"I don't think that's a very good idea. To put it bluntly, Syd's instincts aren't very polished." I should have put it more diplomatically, but what was said was said.

"You know, that's exactly what Syd told me yesterday. He wants to learn from you, Ryan."

The statement surprised me. Ever since he'd arrived, Syd had wanted to blaze his own trail, and it hadn't gone very well so far.

"I'm not sure he's going to be able to adjust," I replied.

Liam steepled his hands. "Actually, Ryan, he's not the one I'm worried about."

"Paul?" I asked.

He pointed a finger at me. "This is going to require you to change."

I was justifiably proud of what I had done. "My system works just fine, thank you. Look at all we've accomplished."

He leaned forward for effect. "Your system is broken."

"It is not," I shot back.

Liam paused before responding. "You have to step back and

manage, rather than trying to do it all yourself. This is about team-work, not just individual effort."

"The way I do it works, because I don't make mistakes."

He unnerved me by waiting to see what I would add to that, if anything.

I didn't add anything. I didn't make mistakes. I was right, and he knew it.

"We need teamwork, Ryan. You need to learn to teach. You teach them to do it your way. They make a mistake, you teach them how to avoid it the next time. Sure, there will be setbacks, but they're not stupid. They'll learn, and the team will get more done than you ever could alone."

He was partly right. Both men, particularly Paul, were bright and quite capable of learning anything I threw at them, no doubt.

"No," I said bluntly.

Working in the lab was comfortable for me. It was what I did, and I wasn't going to give it up. It was how I contributed; it was how I saved lives.

"Your talents are wasted doing the grunt work. Instead, you come up with the paths to pursue, and let them wield the machetes, slashing through the undergrowth to find out if the trail leads anywhere."

"You know, your jungle analogy sucks big time."

He laughed. "Then you come up with a better one. The fact remains, your time is too valuable to be wasted hunched over lab equipment."

I liked being in the lab. It was where inspiration came to me. "But——"

"I've made up my mind. Now deal with it."

"Yes, boss. Is that all?"

He let out a long breath. "One other thing." He paused. "I may have to be out of the office for a few days next week."

"Okay," I said warily.

He passed me a set of papers. "Can these be faked?" The

papers were Y-DNA test results.

The lab report said the two samples were a complete match on over a hundred STR markers. "Who was tested?"

He didn't answer my question. "I have to ask. Scientifically, is there any way this could be faked?"

"Not that I know of. Y-DNA tests are the gold standard in determining family trees. If you're worried about contamination, you can re-sample and retest with a different lab."

He took the papers back. "My brother Bill sent me these. Those results are between him and one of the twins in England."

"I don't understand. What twins?"

"It looks like Dad had an affair. We have brothers in England."

"And none of you knew?"

He shook his head.

My issues were suddenly nothing next to what he was dealing with.

He rose. "Okay then, figure out how to talk with Syd."

I hoisted my ass out of the chair.

∼

NATALIE

I SAT IN MY OFFICE, WORKING ON THE LATEST OF RYAN'S PILES *WE* were attacking. And I could honestly say *we*. Instead of Ryan fighting me on it, the patent work had become a joint endeavor for us.

Ryan poked his head in. "Got a sec?"

He didn't wait for an answer but came in and closed the door behind him, as he had been doing recently. Closing the door generally allowed him to shed the Mr. Prickly Pear shell he carried around at the office.

"Today I do, but what if I told you *no* one of these times?"

He took a seat. "Then I'd know it was time to take you into a closet and change your mind. Either that or I'd have to take you to the hospital to get you checked for a concussion."

I laughed. "Forget I asked."

"I was thinking about the claim sequence for CTX-19."

I waited for the punch line which didn't come. "And?"

"And, I decided you were right——"

I put my hand to my ear to interrupt him. "Can you say that again?"

He took a deep breath. "Okay, I admit you were right. Making the filtration rate claims the independent ones makes more sense."

It wasn't the first time I had changed his mind on one of these issues, but it felt good just the same. "Why thank you, Dr. Westerly."

He stood and opened the door. "Just thought I'd mention that before I forgot. Lunch at one?"

"If it's Indian this time."

"Do you lawyers have to negotiate everything?"

"It's part of the coursework."

"Indian it is."

The next instant he was gone again.

I didn't get a lot of his time, but he no longer treated the application-writing process as an anchor slowing down the good ship Chameleon and his efforts to develop new treatments.

I had managed to convince Ryan how important the structure and wording of the claims could be to protecting the lab work he and Paul had put in.

He now applied himself to the process of wordsmithing the documents as an important project that required focus and determination.

Rick walked by, but didn't look into my office the way he used to.

I fingered the ruby and diamond necklace Ryan had given me. It seemed to be heavy-duty Rick-repellant.

CHAPTER 32

(TWO WEEKS LATER)

NATALIE

I WAS ALONE IN RYAN'S KITCHEN, WHICH, I SUPPOSE, WAS ALSO MY kitchen. Ryan had said he wanted it to feel normal waking up alongside each other, and now it did. Even though I'd recently gotten enough replacement furniture to make Jasmin's place livable again, at Ryan's request, I wasn't planning on going back.

Tonight's dinner plan wasn't fancy, just grilled sausage and garlic mashed cauliflower. I'd found the cauliflower recipe online and thought it sounded like an interesting alternative to mashed potatoes, so I'd chosen the meat to fit. It would be my little surprise. The food processor had been cleaned and put away, and the cauliflower remnants had gone down the disposal. No shred of evidence was out for him to see.

Ryan ate broccoli, but he wouldn't touch cauliflower for some unexplained reason. He "couldn't stand it" was all he'd ever said on the subject. But with a little luck, he wouldn't know the difference tonight, and I wasn't planning on telling him until after he'd finished.

We'd gone out to dinner last night, and I wanted to stay in and enjoy a homecooked meal, with cuddling on the new couch afterward. The couch I'd bought to replace Ryan's ratty one from college had been delivered today.

The delivery guys had been nice enough to move the old one to the corner——its first step toward the garbage heap, if I got my way.

The sound of the deadbolt snapping open was audible over the sizzling of the sausage in the pan. My man was home.

Ryan waltzed through the room and over to me without even a glance in the direction of the couch.

I put down the grease-covered spatula.

He lifted me up. "Hi, gorgeous."

"You sure know how to show a girl a good time." I wrapped my legs around him and kissed him as he spun me around before setting me down. I regretted it as soon as I smelled his hair. "You smell gross."

He released me.

I backed away. "What have you been playing in?"

"Paul was busy, so I had to change some of the blood cultures in the lab. Bad, huh?"

"If you don't shower right now, I'm calling the EPA."

He backed toward the bedroom. "What's for dinner?"

"London night. Bangers and mash." I returned to the stove and turned the sausage. The butcher had assured me this was identical to the Cumberland sausage served in English pubs.

"A touch of London, sounds good."

"A break from Italian," I said. We'd had marinara and alfredo dishes the last three nights.

He disappeared to rinse off the lab stench.

I had detected a faint version of that same smell attached to Paul one day when I'd talked with him in the break room. At the time I'd assumed it came from something rotten in the trash bin.

Ryan returned a few minutes later, hair wet from the shower and wearing his bathrobe.

He went to the fridge. "White or red with this?"

I hefted the plates. "Beer would be a better fit, but cold not warm. I don't want to be that authentic."

He laughed and pulled two Millers from the fridge.

I'd plated the bangers and was adding the peas beside my fake mashed potatoes when Ryan came up behind me and encircled me with his arms. The foul odor was gone.

"Did I ever tell you I love your cooking?"

"Wait till you taste it. You might not agree tonight. You know there's a reason you don't find restaurants around town hawking British food."

I left out the part about the mash being his most-hated vegetable in disguise.

"The Brits don't know the first thing about food," I continued, "so I added garlic to the mash."

He squeezed me tighter and his hand came up to cup my breast ——always playful, my Ryan.

"I'm sure I'll love it. You made it, and that's good enough for me."

I pulled his hand away from my breast, lest we get engaged in something that would leave dinner cold. "Sit down and behave yourself."

He pouted.

I sat at the table and waited.

He uncapped the beer bottles and brought them over without glasses. For him, pouring beer into a glass was sacrilege.

After he took his seat, he hoisted his bottle. "To a London trip. I should take you there."

I clinked bottles with him. "To London, and yes, you should take me there."

His phone rang, and he rose from his seat.

"Don't answer. It can wait," I pleaded.

But he was already up to the counter, phone in hand. I was too late.

"Hello?" Concern soon tinged his brow. "Okay, I'll be right there." He hung up and put the phone down.

I should have been resigned to these calls by now, but I couldn't understand why they had to interrupt us at dinner.

"I have to go to the hospital," he said.

"How about after dinner?"

"I need to go right now."

I sighed. A clear no. He went to dress.

I took a forkful of the mash and tasted it. Not bad, I decided. It was a little thinner than mashed potatoes, but otherwise a close match. Next time I would add a little flour or cornstarch to thicken it up.

I took the plates to the oven and put them in.

His phone on the counter dinged with a text message.

I picked it up and checked.

Briana: Meet you at the hospital

Odd, but maybe this wasn't her normal shift; she'd been called in too.

I put the phone down and turned the oven on low to keep dinner warm for his return.

Ryan reappeared, clothed, but still with damp hair. He put in his earbuds, pocketed the phone, and gave me a quick kiss on his way to the door. "Be back in just a bit for your touch of London."

"Everything okay?"

"Just something they want me to check."

"Want me to come along?"

"Not tonight. You stay here and stay warm." He waved and was gone in a flash.

At first I had questioned why he couldn't pass off the hospital checks to someone else, but after going with him a few times, the answer became obvious. His compassion for these kids and all the other children his medicines had impacted was what drove him to work as hard as he did. I had to love that about him, even when it pulled him away.

∼

*R*YAN

I PUT THE EARBUDS AWAY AFTER LISTENING TO THE VOICEMAIL again, my brother's last words to me: "*She's not picking up again. They should be there by dinner. Tell them I miss them. We should be landing sometime before midnight. See you then, bro. Mom and Dad send their love too.*"

I still had a hard time coming to grips with the fact that they were all gone. This was the only recording I had of my brother's voice, and I listened to it every time I came to the hospital.

"He was asking for you," Briana said as I reached her. She gave me a hug.

I opened the door, and we entered.

"You came," David said.

I lowered the side rail and sat on the edge of the bed. "Of course."

We talked for a few minutes as I asked about his symptoms.

Briana looked on from the other side of the bed. She took his hand.

A few minutes later, David was asleep again. He didn't have the energy to stay awake for very long.

I got off the bed.

David's condition hadn't improved.

I picked up the clipboard and checked for the latest from the doctor. My stomach turned. His note was hard to read, but it said his request to try our latest iteration, CTX-32, had been denied. I shook my head in disbelief.

"What is it?" Briana asked.

"We got turned down for the new drug," I told her.

"Can we ask again?"

I took her by the shoulders. "It won't do any good. They don't reverse these kinds of decisions." She deserved the truth about her son.

"But there must be something we can do."

I took her into a hug and rubbed her back.

There was only one alternative.

I released her. "You go home. There might be one other way."

It was a risk, but I no longer had a choice.

"Will you call me?"

"Sure."

She gave me a long hug, the tight kind she always doled out. "Love you."

"Love you too," I replied.

Then she was off.

I watched David for another minute before heading downstairs.

Upon reaching the street, I zipped up my coat against the cold.

I reached the Chameleon building and swiped in. Inside the lab I unlocked the cabinet that contained the CTX-32 vials. I took one; it was all I would need for a while.

Pocketing the vial, I returned to my office. My phone startled me, ringing in my pocket. It was Natalie.

~

NATALIE

RYAN HAD ONLY LEFT A FEW MINUTES AGO, AND ALREADY BEING alone didn't appeal to me. *I could kill two birds with one stone.*

This just called for a little creative thinking. I could bring dinner to him. He could do his rounds and we could still get some together time.

Two minutes later I had our dinners in Tupperware, two fresh bottles of beer, silverware, and napkins all in the bag, and I was ready to go.

I pulled my lab coat from the closet. He'd gotten it for me for when I joined him in the hospital. The "Nurse Ratched" clip-on badge was something I hadn't noticed until we got back home after the first time. My getup had been a hit with Tommy, one of the patients Ryan looked in on, but I hadn't realized why at the time. Now I knew, and the badge stayed; Tommy would get a kick out of it again.

After adding a leather coat for the cold, I was ready to go. The short walk to the hospital was refreshing, though I zipped my jacket all the way up against the cold New England air.

Once inside, I made my way to the cafeteria on the first floor where I hung my jacket on the coat rack.

All the staff I passed were too busy to give me a second glance in my fake nurse lab coat. Nobody bothered to read the nametag, so the joke went unnoticed. Which also meant nobody threw me out on my ass.

The elevator trip to the seventh floor where Ryan's patients were located seemed to take forever. We stopped on every single floor; the stairs would have been faster.

I turned left toward his patients' rooms.

I started with David, then Renee. No Ryan in either place, so I moved on to the final patient.

I opened the door.

"Nurse Ratched, you're back?" the little boy exclaimed.

Once again, no Ryan.

"Yes. I was looking for Dr. Westerly. Has he been here yet?"

He ignored the question. "Nurse Betty didn't believe me when I told her you visited me. She thought I was making it up. She made me eat green Jell-O three days in a row." He tried to sit up, but the exertion seemed too much for him. He gasped for air.

I rushed over and urged him back down again. "You really should rest." I could see the headlines now. *"Fake nurse causes patient death."* And the follow-up the next day. *"The Winterbourne scourge returns - this time killing young boy in hospital."*

He lay back against the pillow. "Can you talk to Nurse Betty and have her give me orange Jell-O? I really don't like the green kind."

The lab coat hadn't been a good idea after all.

"Sure, I'll have Dr. Westerly talk to her. Have you seen him yet?"

He nodded. "He was here, but he left."

"Thanks, I'll tell them about the Jell-O." I stepped into the hallway and dialed Ryan's cell. "Where are you?"

Ryan hesitated. "I'm at the hospital still. You go ahead and eat. I'll catch up later."

"Everything okay?"

"I need to spend a bit more time with David, but I'm checking in with your friend Tommy first."

I froze. A bald-faced lie. "How's he doing…Tommy?"

"Nurse Ratched wants to know how you're doing?" he said away from the phone. "Tommy says great," Ryan told me.

I looked back through the doorway at Tommy, right there in the room. Another lie.

I managed to escape down the hallway without crying, ducked into an empty room, and closed the door.

CHAPTER 33

R YAN

"How can you say that?" Natalie screeched into the phone. "I was just in Tommy's room. You're outright lying to me. Why would you do that?" she cried.

I cringed. "I'm sorry. You don't understand———"

"You're the one that doesn't understand," she shot back. "You promised me you'd be honest... You promised."

I sat in my chair, searching for a way out of this. There wasn't one———no way at all. I couldn't keep both her and David safe. "It's not what you think."

She sniffed. "You have no idea what I think, and evidently you don't care. I thought you were different. I... I just don't even want to deal with this."

I couldn't fix this over the phone. "I'll be home in a bit. Then I'll explain."

"But———"

"Trust me, Cupcake. I'll explain when I get home, but not over the phone... Wait up for me?"

"Okay." She sniffed.

"I love you," I replied, but she had already hung up. I was likely fucked if I didn't go to her right now, but I didn't have a choice. I needed to take care of David first.

I put my phone away, double-checked my pocket for the vial of medicine, and left my office. I'd have to monitor David for at least an hour for any reaction before I could square things with Natalie.

～

Natalie

WHAT IS WRONG WITH ME? HAD I DONE IT AGAIN?

I finally got my tears under control and stepped out of the empty hospital room. The elevator doors opened, but instead of entering, I stepped back. I couldn't forget my promise to Tommy. Wiping my eyes one more time, I walked back down the hallway toward the nurses' station. I took off my fake nurse coat and rolled it up. It wouldn't be good to talk to them as fake Nurse Ratched.

The young nurse behind the counter looked up. "Yes?"

I took a breath and leaned into the counter. "Tommy in seven-twelve would like to get orange Jell-O instead of green, if that's possible."

She laughed. "Sure. Last week he asked for green instead of red. I'll change it." She typed on her computer. "Done."

I had one more nagging question. "When does Briana work?"

"Pardon?"

"What shift does the nurse named Briana work?"

She shook her head. "Sorry, we don't have anyone by that name on this floor."

My legs weakened, and I braced myself against the counter. Another lie. Gathering my strength, I thanked her, took my dinner bag, and headed back to the condo.

Once outside in the cold, I walked in a daze. It was happening again——the lies, the deception, and now another woman? Why? Was my whole life a mirage all over again?

A few minutes later, back inside the condo, I closed the door and rested against it for a moment. I put the Tupperware containers and beer in the fridge.

I wasn't sticking around to hear his excuses tonight. I stuffed Ryan's backpack with some clothes and prepared to go back to Jasmin's. I looked down as I headed for the living room and realized the necklace dangling around my neck felt like a collar tying me to him. I went back to the bedroom, took it off, and deposited it in the top drawer of my nightstand.

I managed to corral Ralph into his carrier, without a battle this time.

Once on the street, I turned toward Jasmin's apartment and dialed my sister's number. Ralph meowed. It was three hours earlier in LA, and I hoped to God she picked up.

$\sim$

RYAN

Two hours after I had injected the first dose of CTX-32 into David's IV line, I was on my way back home with the vial.

He hadn't shown a negative reaction in the critical first hour, and now I could only hope the drug would help.

With each footfall, I contemplated what could go wrong. I had crossed the line, and there was no way back now. The system considered what I was doing immoral, or at least unethical. I took the view that denying David what we had to offer was the immoral path. Screw the system.

Still, the danger of what I had done hung palpably in the air. If anyone found out about my relationship to the patient, he'd be disqualified from any of our trials, and that would be catastrophic. That outcome had to be avoided at all costs. That's why he'd been admitted as David Doe. His pedigree was opaque to the system, and it had to stay that way.

To protect the company, I'd not even told Liam. And I'd botched my explanation to Natalie when she'd called tonight. But everything hinged on maintaining the secret of what I was doing ——for their safety and mine. Briana and David were depending on me.

I knew I'd need to come clean with Natalie somehow. It wasn't that I didn't trust her, but what I was doing was clearly illegal. Telling her would include her in my conspiracy, and what would that mean for her if Willey discovered it?

Three blocks later, my thoughts had returned to my patient. Being discovered was not the top concern on my list, not even close. Number one was *would it work*? Would it help David or not? That was the most important question. His condition was precarious.

I shivered, and it wasn't from the cold. This was the most vulnerable I'd felt since the day I'd lost my parents and my brother. I hurried my pace. Since the day I'd lost Bob, I hadn't had anyone here I felt comfortable confiding in. Until Natalie, and now I couldn't talk to her either.

Reaching the twenty-third floor, I unlocked and opened the door. The faint scent of the bangers Natalie had cooked hung in the air. The lights were on, but the room was quiet.

That's when I noticed it.

A new couch stood in place of the old one I'd had since college. Sleek black leather. It looked good in the space.

Natalie had threatened for weeks to upgrade the couch. Our verbal jousting over it had been fun, and not meant to dissuade her. She had come through with a good choice, and she'd accomplished something I didn't have the time or inclination to do. Good for her. I wasn't sure when she'd found the time. She worked almost as hard at Chameleon as I did.

The bedroom door was closed. She must have decided against

waiting up for me. I was starving, so I chose to let her rest. In the fridge I found the English pub fare dinner she had cooked. I spooned a portion onto a plate and started the microwave.

I sat down to eat the re-heated meal and found myself impressed by Natalie's capabilities yet again——not to mention wishing she had stayed up to sit across from me right now. She was a godsend in so many ways, and I'd managed to piss her off like the asshole I was.

Dinner alone had been my normal forever, but now that I'd sampled the joys of dinner with her, it seemed completely inadequate. The empty chair across the table taunted me.

I finished off the last of the tasty mashed potatoes and sausage. I could do without as many peas. They had never been a favorite of mine. After rinsing the plate, I turned off all but one of the lights and ventured to the bedroom door. I missed my other half.

The light from the other room was dim as I slid through the doorway. A chill ran through me. The bed hadn't been turned down or slept in. My Cupcake wasn't here.

In a panic, I flicked on the light.

A folded note lay on my nightstand. I opened it.

Ryan-
    Went to Jasmin's.
    I need some time to think.

Think about what? Unease squirmed in my stomach as I typed out a text to her.

ME: Love you – miss you - I wish you'd let me talk to you about this

The message didn't say delivered, no return text came, and no bouncing dots. She had turned off her phone and probably gone to sleep, or at least I hoped that was why she didn't respond. I was thankful to know she was safe at her sister's place.

I called and left a voicemail as well. "Nat, we should talk. This is a complicated situation, but you know I would never do anything to hurt you... Miss you, Cupcake, and love you most." I hung up the phone, still hoping she would pick it up and call.

My sister Alyssa always told me tomorrow would be a better day, and tonight I hoped to hell she was right.

The bed was cold without Natalie. She wanted space, and if this is what space felt like, it sucked. Sleep did not come quickly.

CHAPTER 34

*R*YAN

WHEN I ROLLED OVER THE NEXT MORNING, THE OTHER SIDE OF THE bed was as empty as my heart. For so long, being able to sprawl out in a king bed by myself had seemed luxurious. Getting up without having to worry about waking someone else, or them waking me, had been my normal. Until it wasn't. And now it definitely wasn't.

Natalie had changed all that. Her warmth next to me had changed a lot of things. She was a lens that changed my view of the world. Nothing was as it had been before she showed me the beauty I'd taken for granted every day. And the first beauty I got to behold every morning was her face as I kissed her nose and her smile grew as she awoke. That smile was the vision I couldn't get out of my mind, the vision I no longer wanted to rid myself of. The vision I lived for.

I shuffled to the sink to brush my teeth. In the middle of the night, when sleep wouldn't come, I'd resorted to two glasses of scotch. It had allowed me to nod off, but my mouth this morning felt and tasted like I'd been chewing on moldy carpet.

Later, under the shower, the hot water revived me, but I finished without getting my hair wet. It would have been a bad idea before my run.

I sent Natalie another text.

ME: Join me for run if you can - normal time

She didn't respond.

Halfway through my first lap, I waited five minutes for her at the BU Bridge. When she was a no-show, I continued my run, less happy, but no less determined. Exercise was good, exercise was necessary, exercise was cleansing.

I would see her at work...wouldn't I?

∿

NATALIE

I TOSSED AND TURNED. SLEEP CAME IN LITTLE BITS AND THEN tortured me by leaving again so I could lie helplessly in bed——the new bed I'd bought Jasmin——wondering what had gone wrong.

Eventually the early morning light came in past the shades and announced the end of my attempt to avoid the questions swirling around in my head. I should have drunk the half bottle of vodka in the pantry. That might have done it, but it was too late now.

After struggling out of bed, I turned the shower on hot. The water soothed me. The heat worked to burn away the memory of my humiliation. I had been too stupid to see it, again.

Once dressed, I ventured into the kitchen and turned on my phone. It held a missed call, a voicemail from Ryan, and a text.

I read the text and then deleted it. I wasn't up for the voicemail.

RYAN: Love you – miss you - I wish you'd let me talk to you about this

I'd had enough lies, enough secrets, enough deception to last me two lifetimes. No matter what he said in explanation, he'd still lied to me. That couldn't be erased.

And I had no call back from my sister.

Fuck.

The bread in the refrigerator had mold on it, and I didn't have any better alternatives for breakfast at the apartment.

After dressing and drying my hair, I fed Ralph and headed to the diner down the main drag, the opposite direction of Chameleon. At least there I could get a cooked breakfast of sausage and eggs instead of the microwave shit the coffee shop offered.

My phone dinged in my purse.

RYAN: Join me for run if you can - normal time

I didn't answer. Things were not normal right now. He needed to understand that.

I took a table in the corner and gulped my coffee while I waited. It didn't have chocolate in it, but it was hot and strong, two things I needed this morning. I waved down the waitress for a refill.

I surveyed the clientele of the small restaurant while I waited: normal people with normal lives, on their way to normal work-places, with normal futures. Not one of them looked as despondent as I felt this morning. I'd ended up right back where I always found myself. Deceived. The new life I'd thought I was building had just revealed itself to be not much different than the old one. I had to stop repeating this pattern.

The waitress delivered my breakfast plate. I thanked her, but couldn't manage to match her full-faced smile. Still, the hash browns were hot and crispy as I dug in and contemplated my situation.

Putting down my fork, I composed a text to Liam telling him I wouldn't be in for a few days. I needed time to think. Time away from everything related to Ryan.

Eating my scrambled eggs, I tried to figure how it had all gone so wrong.

Ryan had lied to me. He'd probably been with the Briana bitch when I called. *Fool* was probably tattooed on my forehead in letters only men could read. Ink invisible to me in the mirror, but obvious to the devious men I attracted. They saw me as an easy mark. Naïve, gullible Natalie, that's me.

Those who don't learn from history are doomed to repeat it. I'd certainly tried to learn from my experience with Damien, tried to do things differently——and I had felt different, better, stronger… until this. Now I just felt lost.

If I went back to Ryan, listened to whatever he had to say, how would I ever know for sure it was true? Damien had tricked me for years. I couldn't let it be the same with Ryan. Repeating my mistake was a sin I would not commit.

I sighed. But I wasn't letting this breakfast go to waste. I finished the last of my sausage before checking my phone one more time.

Still no call from Jasmin. She'd told me her schedule. Now I regretted not having written it down. But if her phone hadn't gone toilet-swimming again, I should be hearing from her soon.

I paid the bill, including a generous tip for my smiling waitress, and stood.

As I left, the couple by the door gave me the look——the look I'd seen a hundred times. They recognized me.

As always, I was surrounded by Damien-haters. Another thing that seemed it would never change.

278

~

*R*YAN

I REACHED THE BU BRIDGE ON MY SECOND LAP AND MADE MY decision: Fuck waiting to hear from her. Waiting would only allow her doubts to further poison her mind. Something had her rattled, and we needed to talk this out. I might not know what to say, but it sure as hell couldn't wait——not if there was any chance she was equating me with her dickhead ex.

I ran to the right, toward Central Square and her apartment.

I bounded up the stairs, eager to see her face, even if it didn't start out with a smile on it.

My knock wasn't answered, and neither were the second or the third.

The neighbor's door opened a crack. "Stop banging so loud. She went out. Now git, and give an old lady some peace."

"Sorry," I said, backing away toward the stairs.

Outside, I looked up and spotted Ralph in the window. She had to be somewhere nearby. I parked my butt and waited for his owner to return.

Natalie had brightened my life in so many ways, but today she was complicating it. I had to figure out how to keep everybody safe *and* satisfy her need for total honesty, even though there were things I couldn't tell her…at least not yet.

When David got better, this would be so much easier. The new drug had to work. That was my path to sanity.

CHAPTER 35

*R*YAN

I'D BEEN SITTING OUTSIDE HER BUILDING FOR AT LEAST THIRTY minutes when she walked my way from Mass Ave.

"Get lost?" she asked when she saw me. "I said I needed time to think."

I stood. "We need to talk." I rubbed my sore ass.

"What's to talk about? You're not a fan of sharing the truth; I get it," she spat.

Her attitude hadn't improved overnight.

"Let me start," I said. "I apologize."

She shook her head, not impressed. "You lied to me after promising you wouldn't."

There it was, the ugly truth I had to admit. Whatever my reasons, I had gone about this the wrong way. "Can we go inside? It's cold out here."

"Maybe Briana can warm you up."

I had no clue where that came from, but her implication was clear.

"It's not what you think, and do you really want to air all our laundry out here?"

She shrugged and started up the stairs.

I followed and closed the apartment door behind me.

She took a seat on the couch. "If it's not what I think, then what is it, exactly?"

"You don't need to be worried about her," I said as calmly as I could manage.

"But you lied about being at the hospital when I called, and you also lied and told me Briana was a nurse."

"I did lie about where I was. And I'm sorry——I panicked. But Briana *is* a nurse, just like I told you."

She glared at me and stood.

I blocked her path. "Sit down. We're not done talking yet." If she was going to accuse me of messing around, we were finishing this here and now.

She didn't budge.

"Sit, goddammit," I insisted, at almost a yell.

She plopped back down, but folded her arms and legs. "I checked at the nurses' station. They've never heard of her."

"She is a nurse, just not at that hospital."

"You're going to go with a technicality like that? You've been sneaking out to see her every time you told me you were going to the hospital to see your patients."

"Not sneaking, and she's not the person I'm going to see." It was my turn to cross my arms. "I go to the hospital to see my patients, pure and simple. Her son is one of those patients."

She cocked her head. "And you just met Briana, and there's nothing between you two, right?"

"Of course not. She's David's mother. If you don't believe me, come to the hospital tonight and ask her. Better yet, ask David."

She let out a large breath.

"Trust me. I'm not cheating on you. Please don't ever think

that. But David is not in good shape. She's concerned, as any mother would be, so she's with him almost every time I go by."

Natalie stood and took my hand. "Then why did you lie to me about being with Tommy at the hospital?"

I looked away. "I can't tell you right now. That's where things get complicated." I couldn't risk revealing that——not yet.

She pulled back. "Ryan, I can't operate like that. You know I can't handle secrets."

"It's for the best right now. I know you don't want to, but you'll have to trust me." I backed toward the door. "I have to get in to work. See you there?"

"Not today," she said with a defeated tone.

"I promise you, it's nothing sinister."

"How about we run away to the cape for a long weekend, just you and me?" she asked with a twinkle in her eye.

I hated to disappoint her, but I couldn't leave David now. "I can't. I'm at a point where——"

She stopped me with a raised hand. "I understand." The twinkle in her eye had disappeared, the victim of my letdown.

"Maybe later…" It was the best I had to offer right now.

"Sure, later. You go to work."

I moved forward and pulled her into a hug she didn't fight. Her warmth was soothing. It was one thing I would never get enough of. "I'll do what I can to get away as soon as possible."

She buried her face against me. "I know. I just need time to figure everything out."

I pulled her head back to place a kiss on her forehead. "You can take the time you need, promise. But know that we need you at Chameleon when you're ready to come back. I need you." I released her and moved to the door. "Love you, Cupcake."

"Love you more." She sighed.

"Love you most," I said before leaving.

I started up a jog back home. *Had I told her enough? Had I fixed this?* She'd thought I was seeing Briana. That was a surprise.

If she knew the whole truth, she'd realize how absurd that was. I hoped we could hold on until that became a possibility.

Though my heart stayed with Natalie, my thoughts returned to David.

∽

NATALIE

I LEANED BACK INTO THE COUCH. AT LEAST HE WASN'T BANGING another woman on the side. It had been an absurd thought to begin with, but after his lie and finding out she wasn't a nurse at the hospital, what was I supposed to think?

With Damien, I had excused every coincidence in his favor, and I'd turned out to be wrong. Now, with Ryan, I had reversed the process and thought the worst of him at the first opportunity. That wasn't working so well either. There had to be some way to get this right, but I couldn't see it. I had to protect myself.

I got up to go for a walk. Ryan had told me he ran in the morning to clear his head. I had always done my best thinking while on a walk, so that was this morning's agenda.

Once on the street, I turned toward the river to walk the loop Ryan and I had run almost every morning.

After one slow loop, I had decided I had to take a chance on Ryan and believe there was a reason he couldn't level with me about something. He'd given me ample evidence that he was a good man who loved me over the past several weeks. I couldn't let my paranoia about past mistakes throw all that away.

He could be working on a secret research program, or moonlighting for the CIA. That made me giggle a little, but I knew there could be some other equally good reason he couldn't confide in me. Hell, Corbin couldn't tell Jasmin some of the things he was working on.

I would have to control my reflexive distrust of secrets for a while. I just wished I knew how long. Maybe Ryan could tell me that much. But if he did, maybe I'd only be more frustrated. I had to will myself to calm down. At least he had apologized.

My phone rang, and I pulled it out of the armband to answer. It was Jasmin. Finally.

"I missed your message last night," she said when I answered. "I hope I'm not interrupting anything important at work."

"I'm not at work today. I'm walking by the Charles."

"Uh-oh, what went wrong? You missing work to walk is like a Defcon-three emergency. What did he do? I'll kick his ass."

I laughed. Jasmin's heart was in the right place, but her kicking Ryan's ass was like the mouse biting the elephant's toe.

"I fucked things up last night. Well, we both did, sort of."

"Tell me all the juicy details, Nat. I'm here for ya."

She was always there for me.

"He's keeping something from me, and I sorta went off the deep end and thought it might be another woman."

"And it's not? Right?" she asked.

I moved right to avoid a skateboarder. "There's this woman who's been at the hospital a lot when he goes over. Anyway, it was a big mistake. It turns out she's the mother of one of the sick kids."

"So you were wrong?"

"Totally," I admitted. "But he lied to me about it, and there was no reason for that. Or at least no reason he'll tell me. There's still something else going on. I asked him to be honest, and he wasn't. That's what makes me feel like I'm on the merry-go-round with Damien again. Maybe they're all like that."

"My Corbin's not. He's a work in progress, but he's a good man."

"Okay, all but one."

"Your friend Amy's husband isn't," she retorted.

"Okay, so I just picked two bad apples in a row."

"Get off the Damien comparison for just a second. Last week he was a great guy, right?"

"Yeah, but——"

"No buts. You accused him of cheating on you, and you were wrong?"

I was guilty as charged. "Uh-huh."

"I would say that's a pretty big fuck-up on your part. So, apologize and go jump his bones. Whenever Corbin and I have a fight, the make-up sex is, like, the best."

I laughed. "Only you would come up with something like that."

"No, it's true. It's a documented fact. It's endorphins and crap. But that can't be the whole story, or you wouldn't be on one of your I-have-to-figure-out-the-world walks."

She hit that nail on the head.

I dodged a pair of bicyclists. "I just don't know if it's going to work out between us."

She laughed in my ear. "I should have recorded our call after your weekend in P-town with the guy, and again last week. Nat, you've never sounded happier."

"Yeah, it was good," I admitted.

She was right. I'd called extolling his virtues, and I had never felt happier than I had with Ryan that weekend. That was what I needed more of——more time with him. More us-time. I loved being part of his work as well, but evidently my access there only took me so far.

"Look, Nat, come out here and see me for a couple of weeks. Down a few pitchers of Pedro's margaritas, and then you'll know."

"How's that work?"

"I'll get you straightened out. Then I get you so drunk you don't remember what I said, and when you wake up, either you'll miss the hell out of him, or you won't. Simple as that."

"Sort of absence makes the heart grow fonder?"

"Yeah," she answered. "But you can't leave out the margaritas."

"Maybe later," I told her.

Going to see her had a lot of appeal, but I had a job and responsibilities in Boston. Plus, Natalie Spencer needed to face her problems——not run from them——and my problem was also here. Ryan had been helping me see that. I explained as much to my sister.

She sighed, but grudgingly agreed.

"Don't say I didn't offer," she added.

We finally hung up after a few more of her urgings to come see her soon.

CHAPTER 36

NATALIE

THE NEXT MORNING I EXITED THE LOCAL DINER AFTER MY SECOND delicious breakfast in as many days. All was well until a block later I glanced left, and Selfie Man was paralleling my course on the sidewalk across the street.

I quickly averted my gaze and lengthened my stride. Home was two blocks away.

As I'd counted my miseries at breakfast, I had omitted a big one: I was still living in a town that hated my guts.

I needed to get back to my original focus: leaving this place and its horrible memories behind. Getting out of town had been my goal, until I'd met Ryan and started working at Chameleon. After that I'd lost my way. With Ryan's support, I'd believed I could still be happy here.

But now all my feelings about Boston were only adding to my confusion about my life. If I was ever going to make sense of this, I needed to be somewhere else. The entire area had become my personal hell. As Selfie Man was making clear this morning, I couldn't walk down the street without being annoyed——or worse.

I turned right down my street after a quick peek in his direction. He hadn't noticed my turn yet, so I sprinted down the sidewalk to my building and up the steps.

My heart raced as I locked the door behind me.

Jasmin's suggestion to join her suddenly looked a lot better than it had yesterday. If I could make it to LA, I could crash with her and Corbin until I figured everything out. Nobody there knew me. My name wouldn't carry the stigma it did here. Los Angeles had to be my goal. I didn't have a credit card or a car, but I did have some cash.

I considered calling Liam to tell him I was leaving——I did hate to leave the project I'd started——but I rejected that. He knew I'd taken a few days off, and that would have to suffice for now. If his wife heard about it, Amy would try to talk me into staying. She and I didn't see eye to eye, and she didn't have the smarts to avoid a fight, but I did.

Ryan was a different problem. He and I had talked last night, and I'd shared Jasmin's suggestion. I could tell from his reaction that if I told him before I left, he'd be here in a heartbeat to talk me out of it.

I wouldn't be able to call him until I was out of town.

Flying was out of the question. My temporary driver's license said *not good for ID* all over it, and a check on the internet weeks ago had told me it wouldn't get me through security at the airport. My call the RMV to find out when I could expect it hadn't gotten me an answer. That jerk Willey was probably pulling strings to fuck with me.

Without that simple plastic card, I was stranded. I couldn't even ask Jasmin to get me a ticket.

The bus looked like it would be my only way out. Three days on the bus with Ralph, what a joy.

I grabbed my jacket and added some more clothes to the duffel

Jasmin had in her closet. I looked around. The apartment was now presentable——not as nice as before the attack, but I'd spent my earnings repaying Brosnahand and replacing most of the destroyed items with what I could afford. I'd pay my sister back later for the rest.

With a smile on my face for the first time this morning, I locked the door to Jasmin's apartment. I was weighed down by a backpack, Ralph's fabric cat carrier, and a duffel, but still I felt light on my feet. I was headed toward a clearer headspace. I had to be——or I would be after the promised margaritas wore off.

My neighbor's door opened a crack.

"Bye, Mrs. Hatfield."

The door closed. The busybody didn't answer.

～

I set Ralph down as I looked over the large, open space of South Station.

Spying the counter across the way, I hefted him back up and got in line to buy my bus ticket.

The person ahead of me finished, and I stepped up to the window. "One adult to Los Angeles, please." I put Ralph's carrier down, and he squealed when the person behind me kicked him. I turned and yelled, "Hey, easy on the cat. How would you like it if I kicked you?"

The man backed off.

I turned back to the counter.

The agent's face had soured. "No animals on the bus."

"But they let pigs and birds fly on the airlines," I countered.

I'd once had to sit next to a lady who'd brought her pot-bellied piglet as an emotional support animal. It hadn't been too bad until the little monster decided to shit on my shoes. Pig shit was the worst. At least the airline had given me a voucher for another flight.

"Then you can go to Logan and fly. No animals on the bus. Unless, that is, you've got a seeing-eye dog. Those we take."

I tried turning on the tears and pleading my case. It didn't do any good.

When I turned to leave, the cat-kicker I had yelled at was smiling at my misfortune. I felt like kicking him, but my mother had raised me better than that.

I unzipped the side pocket of my purse to stash my money away, and that's when I saw it: my ticket out of here, the way to get myself to LA.

Damien's watch.

It was worth a lot——enough to get me a car and some spending money. I could get to California and away from this wretched city. Ralph and I had a new plan.

A pawn shop, a used car dealer, then California here I come.

~

NATALIE

AFTER LOADING UP MY NEW LITTLE GRAY CAR, I STARTED OUT FOR California. Holding some money in reserve, this shit bucket had been the only one I could afford. The guy behind the counter with the eyebrow piercings had not been generous when I went in to pawn Damien's Rolex.

The gray smoke coming out of the tailpipe in my rearview mirror when I got on the turnpike was not a good sign. We still had most of three thousand miles to go.

Two hours later, I pulled into a gas station in Springfield. I didn't need a hell of a lot of gas, but I needed some help. I didn't like the smoke trailing behind me the last hundred miles. After pumping my own unleaded, I ventured into the little mini-mart to pay.

With a tribal tattoo on his neck and gauges in his ear lobes, Tribal Guy looked up to the task. After I paid, he offered to help me check the oil.

I knew nothing about engines and oil dipsticks. To me, a dipstick had always been a dumb guy with a useless penis.

"You can't let it get this low," he told me after examining a long piece of metal he pulled from the engine.

"I didn't know. I just got this car."

"You're at least two quarts low," he said, showing me the stick.

I nodded, without any idea what I was looking at. "Thatbad?"

"Lady, you run it like this and it might seize up on you, and then where would you be?" The answer was obvious: a million miles from anywhere and up a creek named shit.

"Can you put some in?"

He looked inside and sighed. "Give me a few minutes to take care of the other customers."

"Thanks. I really could use the help."

Fifteen minutes later, with several jugs of oil in the car, he had me start it up again.

Tribal Guy waved me out of the driver's seat to listen to the engine.

"Hear that rattle?"

I shook my head. "No." It sounded like any old engine to me.

"That sound is not good. You might have already ruined a bearing or two." His tone was disgusted, as if I was old enough to know better than to mistreat this wonderful machine. "You need to get it looked at before you go very far."

"Can it wait 'till I get to California?"

He laughed. "You won't make it half that far the way this sounds."

Now I had spent more than half my money, and gotten a car that wouldn't get me to Jasmin's. This day was quickly turning as shitty as the few before it.

After buying another half dozen plastic jugs of oil from Tribal Guy and thanking him, I sat behind the wheel.

I'm fucked, that's what I am.

Ralph meowed, and I made an executive decision. Gramps's cabin in Vermont was the new plan. With a little luck and a few quarts of oil, I would make it before sundown.

∼

R YAN

THAT EVENING I HOVERED OVER DAVID'S BED, READING THE charts.

He had fallen asleep a minute ago.

"Well?" Briana asked.

"It's only been two days," I told her. "We won't know anything for a while, but I'd say it's encouraging so far. No adverse signs, and that's good."

"How long before we know more?"

With any other parent I would have been completely noncommittal, but I had to level with Briana. I had always given her my best guess.

"One to two weeks, perhaps three."

Her face fell; she'd obviously hoped for a quicker response to the medication. She managed a slight smile. "Thanks for coming by, Ryan. It means a lot to him."

I had been checking in three to four times a week, but after adding in the new med, I wanted to check him every day for a while.

When the hallway was clear of any hospital staff, I administered another dose and disposed of the syringe in the bright red sharps box.

My phone rang. It was Natalie, so I stepped outside.

"I've gone to Gramps's cabin in Vermont for a little while," she announced when I answered.

Her words knocked the wind out of me. "How long is a little while?"

She didn't answer for a few seconds. "I don't know. I'll call tomorrow. I just needed to get out of Boston and away from the haters."

"I understand," I said. I knew I probably *never* would understand how it felt for her to continue living here. I just wanted her to try. "Love you."

"Love you more," she responded.

"Love you most."

It was out of my hands now. I would have to wait for the next call.

CHAPTER 37

(TWO DAYS LATER)

RYAN

UNABLE TO SLEEP, I WAS UP EARLY, SO I'D DECIDED TO MAKE AN unusual morning visit to the hospital to see if David's progress was continuing. Though I was eager to find out, Tommy would be my first visit as usual. I removed my earbuds just before entering his room.

His condition had continued to improve with the therapy, and his ABI measurements were good. I wrote a note to his doctor suggesting he continue the treatment for now.

Renee was next, and as usual, she seemed to be doing the best of these kids. She would be able to go home soon.

I always saved David for last, so I could spend as much time as I wanted with him.

He was smiling as I opened the door———at least smiling as much as he could while sucking on a nebulizer.

Briana was with him. She rushed around to give me a tight squeeze. "Ryan, he's doing better on the new———"

"Shush," I told her softly, pulling my fingers across my lips like a zipper.

Shame clouded her countenance. "Sorry." She knew what could happen if we were found out.

"Hey, slugger," I said to David.

He gave me a thumbs up.

I pulled up the charts and went over the most recent data. The improvement we'd seen the last few days was continuing in the right direction. It was beyond a fluke reading.

"He is improving," I told Briana.

Relief washed over her face. "Thank you so much."

I nodded and took out my vial of CTX-26. I pulled a dose into a syringe, introduced it into David's IV, and quickly disposed of the incriminating needle, re-pocketing the vial.

"I have to go," I told them.

"Can't you stay a while?" Briana begged. She always wanted me to stay longer.

"He's doing better. I'll be back the day after tomorrow."

She nodded, resigning herself to the situation.

It had been four days now without Natalie at the condo. Four days with hardly any sleep. Four days with hardly any experimental progress at work. Four days of inhaling coffee after coffee during the day to stay awake. I'd been checking my phone every third minute to make sure I hadn't muted it, and I hadn't missed a call or text from Natalie since the one telling me she'd gone to Vermont.

The sleeping pills hadn't worked either. Sure, I fell asleep, but two hours later I woke up again, groggy but unable to descend beyond that into sleep. I'd seen a paper once that said continued lack of REM sleep could lead to insanity. Was that where I was headed?

I'd given her the space she asked for. I hadn't bugged her, but I had no idea what was on her mind, what she was up to in Vermont.

I hated feeling helpless waiting for the next message or next call, but I had promised to give her the time she wanted. It was a promise I regretted.

∿

NATALIE

I WALKED THE PATH ALONG THE RIVER. I MISSED RYAN, BUT I wondered if that was really healthy. Damien had built a wall of lies to keep us apart, but would it be any better with Ryan if his schedule and devotion to his work kept us equally apart?

If he couldn't manage another weekend's worth of time for us, how important was I to him?

Damien's deception had grown from a dark heart and evil motives. I knew deep down that Ryan was nothing like Damien. He was committed to his work, unselfish to a fault, and filled with noble intentions. Yet somehow I still couldn't get him to trust me with his secret, to let me all the way into his life.

Around the sharp corner, I stumbled over a branch that had fallen on the trail. It was a real trip hazard the way it appeared out of nowhere.

The branch was too heavy for me to move. I'd noted it before at this turn, but I'd forgotten to be careful this morning in my trance-like state.

Shortly I would reach the end of the path, where the large tributary with the dairy on the other side came into the river. I would turn around and head back before starting all over again. The walking was my therapy——better than sitting around the cold cabin.

The heat wasn't working, and I kept having to get firewood from our neighbor's pile.

Mr. Tidd hadn't come to open his cabin for the summer yet. If he had, I would have stopped by to say hello. He had always been a pleasant sort.

The Tidds' wood pile was where we always got wood when we needed it. Carrying the split logs all the way from his cabin to ours was a pain, but it beat freezing to death.

My phone rang. I checked the screen before answering. I really didn't want to talk to anybody but my sister, or the guy fixing my poor car.

It was Jasmin. "Nat, how you doing?" she said when I answered.

Not the question I wanted to answer again. She had called each day to check on me.

The attention made me feel good, but it was no substitute for having her here. "Peachy."

"No, really," she said.

"I miss him, but I can't figure out if we can make it work," I lamented. "I don't want to make the same mistakes again." It bugged me constantly, like a dull headache that wouldn't go away.

"Get real, Nat. A week ago you told me you were the happiest you've ever been. Now you want to throw all of that away? Without really trying?"

I hated it when she used my own words against me.

"I don't know if he'll ever learn to balance his work enough to give our relationship what it needs."

"And what does he think about that?"

I stopped walking. "We haven't talked about it since I left."

"And you think you're going to figure it out on your own traipsing through the woods?"

"That's how I think."

She let out a sigh. "No. It's how you avoid. You're making a mistake by not talking this out with Ryan. You have no idea what he has to say about any of this."

The problem was I did. "He'll say his work is too important to the patients."

"You don't know that. And that doesn't mean you can't come to some agreement that will work for everyone. You're both smart. There must be a solution you can figure out. You can move his lab to a cruise ship and sail the world."

Jasmin had a definite knack for thinking outside the box.

"Okay, I give."

"You said you miss him?"

"Yeah," I admitted. I hadn't *stopped* missing him.

"Have you drunk an entire pitcher of margaritas yet? It doesn't work unless you do."

"Get outta here."

"Honest to God, I read it in *Psychology Today*."

She could always make me laugh. "This from a girl who called the Miss Cleo hotline to decide if she should go to the prom with Joey Clopper?"

"You're just jealous because his brother didn't ask you."

"Am not. His brother had wandering hands."

"They both did. That's what made it so good."

I ended up laughing so hard it hurt.

"I'll think about it, okay?" I told her when I'd recovered.

"I guess that's as good as I'm gonna get today. Look, I'll be out there soon," she said. "We can drive that heap of yours cross-country together. That should be fun."

We hung up after she made me promise to think about calling Ryan. The part about driving to LA with her was what made me the happiest. I needed my sister.

I checked the time on my phone before returning it to my jacket pocket. I had time for two more circuits of my riverside walk before lunch.

~

RYAN

I didn't make it past Liam's door without getting called in.

"Close the door," he said as I stepped inside.

I did, and took the seat he pointed to.

"You look like shit this week."

"Thanks, that's just what I need."

"Seriously, what happened between you and Natalie?" he asked.

"What do you mean?"

"Ryan. Look, I didn't intrude earlier, but she hasn't been to work, and she won't take Amy's calls. We're worried, so what's the story?"

I didn't have any choice now. "We had an argument."

"And?" he asked.

"She needs some time to sort things out."

"So go over and talk to her. Work it out. Whatever it is, I can guarantee you were wrong, and you need to grovel enough to fix it."

I *had* screwed up. "I can't."

"Yes, you can."

"No, I can't. She left."

He shook his head. "You two looked really great together the night you were over for dinner. And what about all the patent work you were accomplishing together? Are you willing to let her go, just like that?"

"Of course not," I shot back.

"Then go get her, and don't take no for an answer. The worst thing you can do is let time pass without going after her. A woman's brain works in mysterious ways, but one thing is for sure. No matter what she says, she doesn't want to be left alone. It's genetic. Men chase women, and women expect to be chased. If you don't go after her, how does she know you care? So get out of here and go get her."

I looked down. "I know she went to her grandfather's old cabin in Vermont, but I don't know where it is."

He stood. "Let me work on that. I have some people that can help. In the meantime, get yourself a pair of kneepads for groveling."

CHAPTER 38

NATALIE

THE OLD WOOD OF THE BACK STEPS CREAKED AS I ASCENDED THEM. I stepped over the bad top one and pulled out my keys to unlock the door. I stopped to listen first. The birds were eerily quiet. I looked around, but didn't see anything out of place.

The birds resumed their chatter, and I unlocked the back door to the kitchen.

Inside, the sun shone through the windows, casting streaks of light across the kitchen, highlighting the old gas stove on the wall. It brought back memories of Mom baking apple pie the last time we'd been here as a family. Jasmin and I had been in college, and it was before Dad's heart attack——a simpler, happier time.

Ralph appeared and checked his food bowl.

I went to the deep porcelain sink to wash my hands from the fall I'd taken earlier. I assembled bread, peanut butter, and strawberry jam to make myself a cabin-style lunch. Simple tastes for a simple place.

I was cleaning up from lunch when my phone rang. It was Mason Brosnahand.

""I was worried about you. You haven't been answering your phone," he said.

"Sorry, I left town and the reception's not good here," I lied. He didn't need to know anything about why I'd left. He had been Damien's lawyer, and perhaps mine, but that was all.

"Where are you?"

I chose to be non-specific. "A place in the woods I visited when I was young."

"Must be pretty this time of year."

I hadn't considered that. Instead I had merely focused on it being not Boston. Looking out the window, I smiled. "It is, and peaceful."

"I was calling to see if there was anything I could do. And to suggest that we get together to brainstorm some more on where Damien may have hidden things."

I had no interest in spending any more time talking about Damien, but after forking over a ton of money to the local mechanic to get him to start work on my car, and replacing the glass I'd broken to get into the cabin, I didn't have much in my wallet.

"I hate to ask; you've been so nice, Mason. But, could you loan me a few more dollars?"

I hoped for a yes, given that I'd already paid back the first loan.

"Sure, no problem," he said.

I sighed. He'd been a big help twice now.

"Give me your address there, and I'll have five hundred overnighted to you, or would a thousand be better?"

Relieved, I told him the larger number would be better and gave him the address. I thanked him profusely prior to hanging up.

Ralph rubbed against my leg.

"It's going to be okay, Ralph." I leaned down to scratch behind his neck again. "We're going to be okay."

~

Ryan

THERE WAS A SINGLE KNOCK AT MY OFFICE DOOR, AND LIAM entered.

I sucked down a swig of my coffee.

He stood behind the chair. "Ryan, I've got an address."

I jerked up straight in my seat. My heart pounded almost audibly. "Where?"

Predictably, he made me wait. "She's in Vermont near Brattleboro."

"Great. That was quick."

"This is from my brother's investigators. They located her phone." He grinned.

"You can do that?"

"You don't want to know."

I knew not to ask any more.

He rounded the chair and slid a single piece of paper across to me.

I memorized it before I stuck it in my pocket. "Thanks. I'm outta here now." I grabbed my jacket from the back of my chair.

She wasn't getting away from me again.

"Good luck."

I reached the door in a few quick steps.

"Flowers. Start with flowers," I heard him say as I left.

Brattleboro was only a few hours away. I ran the distance from work back home, grabbed a few things upstairs, threw them into a carry-on case, and locked up.

That's when I remembered the necklace she'd left behind and went back to retrieve the box with the ruby and diamond pendant. I was going to put that around her neck again and not take no for an answer. I also took a can of Ralph's favorite cat food from the pantry.

Minutes later, my trusty old car was westbound on Route Two toward the Berkshires and the Massachusetts-Vermont border. Siri told me I was two and a half hours away. Two and a half long hours before I would see my Cupcake again. Getting her back was the only possible outcome. Nothing else would do.

I was going all-in. I intended to tell her the unvarnished truth. She deserved to know——not just what I had done, but why, and for whom.

I wasn't on the right side of the law with David, but I had to tell her anyway.

I didn't know how this was going to go. All I knew was she had become my future, my only future. There had to be a way forward that would work for both of us.

By the time Siri guided me to Brattleboro, I was no closer to having a good opening line. Once off the exit, I pulled to the side of the road. Liam's words echoed in my ears. *Flowers*. I needed flowers.

After locating a flower shop, it didn't take me long to decide. Red roses were the only way to go. They packaged a dozen in a box for me, and I was off again to find my Cupcake.

Siri took me north and east toward the edge of the river separating Vermont and New Hampshire. Several miles out of town, she finally told me my destination was on the right.

The only thing I saw in that direction was a muddy dirt road leading off the pavement toward the trees. One of the two numbers tacked to the fence matched the address I was looking for. Natalie was somewhere at the end of this path.

A hundred yards down the narrow road, it got even worse. I bounced and sloshed through the potholes, and after a short turn to the right reached a large tree growing in the middle of the road. The road split around the tree and re-converged on the other side. I took the right-hand fork.

Mistake number one: Thinking I needed to keep to the right when nobody else was on the road. The left-hand fork had obviously been drier. Mistake number two: Hitting the gas when the car sunk into a deep pothole and the wheels spun. I managed to sling a lot of mud but made no progress with the car.

Putting it into reverse and drive again, trying to rock my way out, didn't work either. This was now a job for a tow truck, or a friendly farmer with a tractor and a chain.

I shut the engine off, grabbed my box of flowers and the can of cat food, and locked the car as I headed down the muddy path toward the house that held my Natalie.

Butterflies the size of seagulls fluttered in my stomach as I approached.

CHAPTER 39

Natalie

I OPENED THE DOOR.

Ryan.

The sight of him shocked me. "How did you…"

"Never mind that." He held out a can of cat food, his other hand behind his back. "I brought Ralph his favorite food."

I hesitated, but accepted the food. "That's nice."

He produced a bouquet of roses from behind him. "And these are for you. May I come in? We need to talk."

"I don't know that that's a good idea."

I didn't take the flowers from him. I didn't respond in any way. I tried not to show the tingling I felt inside me from his presence. He had an effect on me I had to fight. I had to stay focused. He was like a quart of triple chocolate ice cream: irresistible, but bad for me, very bad for me right now. Make that more like a gallon of triple chocolate. If I let him settle in, I'd end up in too deep without a lifeline.

"I'll probably freeze to death if you don't let me in," he said.

I didn't see a car in the drive.

"I'm not leaving without a talk," he added. "And if you don't let me in, I'll freeze to death out here, but don't worry, I'll write a note to the police telling them it wasn't really your fault."

I couldn't stop my smile. "That's so nice of you." I opened the door wider and stepped aside.

He stepped inside. "Nat, please take these."

I accepted the flowers. I was a sucker for a man who said please.

The brush of his hand against mine had the same distracting electric feel as before. I was going to have trouble keeping this under control.

He stepped back. "We need to talk."

"I'm not ready yet," I shot back.

"See? You can do it. We're talking, the house is still standing, your hair didn't catch on fire. Trust me, you can do it."

I couldn't contain my grin. He had been the only one to make me laugh in months. "Give me a minute to put these in water."

He stayed in the front room while I went to the kitchen and located a tall Mason jar that looked like it might do the trick. After adding water, I brought the flowers back and put them on the mantle over the fireplace.

He took a seat in the old wingback chair.

Ralph wandered out from his hiding spot and rubbed up against Ryan's leg.

Traitor.

Ryan scratched Ralph's back.

I chose the couch. Close enough to hear him, but not close enough to touch. He looked at me expectantly, but I wasn't the one requesting a conversation.

Ralph jumped up in Ryan's lap for more scratching.

I folded my hands in my lap. "I'm listening." I was also watching, and just the sight of him warmed me.

The chair squeaked across the floor as he pulled it closer. "As

I've mentioned, there were certain things I couldn't tell you," he said calmly. "I may not have done it the right way, but I was trying to do what was best for you."

Ralph took umbrage at no longer being the center of attention and leapt down.

I laughed. "Like you're keeping me safe from terrorists or you're a spy or something?"

"Not exactly, but the situation is a bit of a mess." The legs of the chair scraped the floor again as he pulled a bit closer. "I didn't tell you everything about Briana."

My heart stopped.

"She's my sister-in-law."

I blinked, as if that would help me understand what he had just said. "What?"

He reached for my hand. "David Doe is my nephew. He's my brother Bob's son. Briana is his widow."

I slowly put things together. I knew he had lost his brother and parents in a plane crash, but he'd never mentioned his brother being married or having children.

"Why didn't you tell me that before?"

"I couldn't." He squeezed my hand. "Nobody can know David's relationship to me. The FDA wouldn't allow him to be in the trial, and that would be a death sentence for him."

I gasped. "That's not right."

"Family members aren't allowed in. It's just the rules." He paused. "The other thing is, after the FDA's latest decision, I could get in big trouble for treating him with our compounds. But our treatments are his only chance, so I'm administering an unap-proved drug anyway. That's what I did for the first time the night I went to the hospital during dinner. I'd just made the decision to move forward when you called, and I was at work getting the drug for David. I made a poor choice in lying to you. But Natalie, nobody knows about this part of it——not the hospital, not work, not Liam, or you, until now."

"But you *should* have told me. If I'm part of your life, I need to be part of all of it——not just the things you choose to share. You can trust me."

He pulled out his phone, punched on it a second, and set it down in speaker mode. He tapped play.

"*She's not picking up again. They should be there by dinner. Keep them safe and tell them I miss them. We should be landing sometime before midnight. See you then, bro. Mom and Dad send their love too.*" The recording stopped.

He picked up the phone. "That was my brother, Bob——his last words to me the day of the plane crash. He couldn't reach Briana that day because her battery had gone dead. I'm honoring his memory by keeping them safe the way he asked me to in that message, and I *will* not let him down. I can't."

I sniffed. "You could have trusted me. We agreed to be honest."

He looked me in the eye and nodded. "I'm telling you now because you *do* have a right to know everything about me. What I'm doing could be construed as criminal. If I'd told you sooner and Willey found out, he would have used it against you. I couldn't risk that."

"I was upset because I don't deal well with secrets. You knew that."

"What should I have said? Natalie, I want to tell you something because it would really help me to have someone to share it with, but if I do it will make you a criminal and might give Willey a reason to lock you up. Do you want to hear it?"

Even I thought that sounded stupid. "I don't know. Maybe."

He stood. "What say we talk the rest of this out over dinner?"

It was more a pronouncement than a question.

"There's more?" I asked.

"Yes, Cupcake, but over dinner."

I nodded. I already had a lot to process, but until he'd said it again, I hadn't realized how much I liked being his Cupcake.

"It's freezing in here. Don't you have a heater?" he asked.

~

R YAN

"IT MUST BE BROKEN. IT WORKED THE LAST TIME WE WERE HERE," Natalie told me.

I located the thermostat and adjusted it upward. Nothing happened, absolutely nothing——no click, no lights, no noise, and certainly no heat. The register on the floor had cobwebs.

"I'll take a look at this tomorrow. Maybe there's something I can do."

"You're not staying the night," she informed me.

I didn't answer that. "What are you doing to stay warm?"

"I've been using the fireplace and the stove." She pointed to the potbelly stove in the corner of the kitchen. "This was always meant to be a summer place for the family. We never came here in the winter."

I opened the back door. "Where's the wood?"

Natalie rushed to stop me. "Don't go that way. The top step to the stairs probably won't hold you. Best go out the front." She pointed out the window to the north. "See the house over there?"

I looked through the window in the direction she pointed. I could barely make out a light blue house through the trees a few hundred yards off. "Yeah?"

"The wood's under the back steps over there."

"Seriously?"

"Mr. Tidd offered to cut down a couple trees on our property if we let him have the wood. We just take what we need the few times we're up here."

She lifted a large spool of twine off the counter. "Take this. A couple wraps around the wood and you'll have a handle to carry it. That's what I do."

I moved to kiss my girl, but she backed away. "You're even smarter than you look," I told her.

She punched me in the shoulder. "Make yourself useful so we can heat this place up and eat so you can get on your way."

Once out the front door, I couldn't see the house to the north in the failing light. But I turned to the right and headed through the woods toward where the house should be.

After about a hundred yards, the house appeared through the trees, a little closer to the river than the path I'd taken. I adjusted course and made my way to the back of the house. No lights were on, and the drive out front was empty. They hadn't arrived to open it up yet.

The split wood was under the steps, as Natalie had said. I crafted two bundles of four logs each and tied them with a half dozen wraps of the twine, then added some more for good measure. I figured eight in one trip should do us for the evening.

I didn't relish making the trip again. My running shoes were already soaked from trudging through the undergrowth, and the cold was rapidly seeping in. It was too dark under the tree canopy to see exactly the path I had come, so I guesstimated the direction back to Natalie's house.

Carrying the wood was a chore. I kept getting caught by the saplings between the larger trees. More than once, I clipped my forehead on a low-hanging branch.

I came out of the woods almost even with the front door of the house. A faded red Jeep Wrangler had parked out front. We had a visitor.

CHAPTER 40

NATALIE

I HEARD A KNOCK ON THE DOOR. RYAN WAS BACK WITH THE WOOD a lot quicker than I'd expected.

"You don't have to knock, just come on in," I yelled as I pulled a box of mac and cheese out of the pantry.

I was looking forward to getting Mason's money tomorrow so I could start cooking real food.

I heard the door open.

"Natalie?"

As if I'd conjured him with my mind, it was Mason Brosna-hand. I left the pantry.

He filled the doorway as he walked in and closed the door behind him, reminding me how big he was.

"Natalie, I'm glad you're all right." He stayed by the door.

"You didn't need to come all the way out here, Mason. Sending the money tomorrow would have been fine."

"Is anybody else here with you?" he asked.

I walked forward. My personal life wasn't any of his concern. "Just Ralph. It's the two of us."

His brow creased. "Ralph?"

"My cat. I had to bring him."

"Oh," he said, sounding relieved. "Your cat. We need to talk."

"About?"

"Damien, and where he hid things."

"No, thanks. I'm all talked out when it comes to him." Mason should know better than anyone that I had nothing to add at this point.

"We really need to have this talk."

I put my hands on my hips. "No, we don't. He was a jerk. He was a criminal. He was a habitual liar, and he didn't tell me a thing. There's nothing more to say."

Brosnahand pulled a gun from his coat pocket.

I gasped and backed up.

He cocked the gun and pointed it at me. "I'm afraid I'm going to have to insist."

My heart pounded a million beats a minute. He was supposed to be here to help me, not threaten me. I glanced at the front door. He'd closed it, but he hadn't latched the deadbolt. Yet.

"Now sit," he said angrily. He motioned to Gramps's beat up old Queen Anne armchair with the gun.

My mouth was suddenly too dry to swallow. "What?"

"Sit," he insisted, starting in my direction.

I half walked and half fell into the chair. My eyes darted to the window before sitting, hoping I would catch a glimpse of Ryan. I willed him not to walk in on this and get shot.

"Mason——"

"Shut up," he shouted, cutting me off.

I sunk back and kept quiet. Arguing with a man carrying a gun was not a smart plan. The closer he got, the bigger the gun looked. The blackness in the end of the barrel was threateningly dark. He pulled out a zip-tie and grabbed my arm.

I kicked at him and earned a fist to my cheek.

My head jerked back, the taste of blood filled my mouth, and my face stung.

After he'd secured one wrist to the chair, no matter how hard I tried, I couldn't keep him from tying the other down as well.

He waved the gun in my face. "I'm going to tie your feet to the chair. If you try to kick me, I'll put a bullet through your foot. You hear me?"

I nodded.

After finishing with my legs, he pulled up another chair, which creaked under his weight as he sat.

"Damien told me about the money," he began.

"What money?"

He still didn't get that I really hadn't been told a thing by my lying fucker of an ex-husband. Willey had given me a chance to get my house back if I told him where the money was. I would have taken that deal in an instant if I could have. Mason knew that. Or I'd thought he did.

"The money he hid. Where is it?" He waved the gun. "The money that was going to pay me. He wouldn't tell me where it was. All he said was that you would know. When he gave the cartel money to the feds, my clients got really pissed, and they want me to make them whole…or else."

"Clients?" I knew he was a criminal defense attorney, and not just white-collar crime like Damien's, but nobody had told me he worked for the cartel that had employed Damien.

I tried to slide my hands back; the zip-ties were cutting into my wrists.

"The people your husband was laundering money for, and they don't play games. They think it's my fault Damien told the FBI where to find that last shipment. Now where is the rest of the money? What did he tell you?"

"If Damien told you I knew something, he lied. Just like he lied to me about everything." I didn't have a clue, and I had already told him that. I'd told everybody who asked me the same thing: the truth. I had no idea.

"Why do you think I took this case?" Mason scoffed. "The public-defender rate for taking him on is not my usual fee. I want the money he hid."

I could guess his usual fee was pretty high if he represented mobsters and the like.

"So you and I are going to have a nice, long chat," he said again.

"But I don't know anything."

"When your fucking husband gave the feds that ledger and the money, it made my people very unhappy. I need the money he hid to pay them back or I'm a dead man."

I didn't smile, but right now I liked that idea just fine. "But... But if I knew where Damien hid money, why would I need you to send me any?"

He laughed. "I'm not falling for that anymore. You know, and you're just waiting for Willey to lose interest. Then you'll pull it out from wherever it's stashed and waltz off. That's what I'd do if I were you. But that's not the plan anymore..." He waved the gun back and forth. "...Mrs. Winterbourne," he added with a smirk. He knew how much I hated that name.

I looked him in the eye. "This is going to be a really long night, because I don't have anything to tell you."

"Who said anything about only one night? You're not gonna like this one bit. If you don't tell me where it is right now, you're going to wish it was only one night."

~

*R*YAN

. . .

"THE MONEY HE HID. WHERE IS IT?" I HEARD AN ANGRY voice say.

I was almost to the house. I put the wood down and started to run.

That's when I saw him through the window and stopped dead in my tracks. I crouched down.

It was fucking Brosnahand, and he was waving a gun.

I reached behind me for the gun in my fanny pack.

No fanny pack, no gun. I had left it at home like an idiot.

I reached in my pocket for my phone. Nothing. I had left it in the car. Going back to the car to call 9-1-1 was not an option; we might not have that much time.

With where he was standing, facing the front door, there was no way I could come in the front and get to him. Any idiot could nail me coming in that door. So I crouched down and scooted to the back of the house. If I could get into the kitchen, I might be able to come up behind him.

I started up the stairs and caught myself just before I stepped on the top step. I pulled back and braced my fall with my hands. Almost no sound. I stepped over the rotten step and up to the back door.

A gentle turn of the knob.

Locked.

Goddammit, Natalie, couldn't you have forgotten for once?

There was no way to get in silently from this direction.

The twine.

I stepped back over the bad step and raced to my wood bundles.

The yelling continued unabated.

"Where is the money?"

"I don't know," Natalie kept repeating.

I brought the wood to the back and untied the bundles. I set up a stack on the corner of the back deck and tied one end of the twine to the bottom log. One good yank, and it would all tumble down. Hopefully the noise would be loud enough to be heard inside.

I let out the rest of the twine as I scurried to the front and scrambled under the window to the front corner where I could see the door leading back to the kitchen.

I waited for the right pause in the yelling.

"You have to believe me. I have no fucking idea," I heard Natalie tell him.

I yanked hard on my twine, and the pile came down with a resounding crash.

"Ryan, run. Run!" Natalie yelled.

Good girl.

～

NATALIE

"I CAN'T TELL YOU WHAT I DON'T KNOW."

He stood up, waving the gun in my face some more. "Where is the damned money?" he yelled again.

"You have to believe me. I have no fucking idea," I told him again.

A loud sound came from the back porch.

Mason jerked toward it.

Then there was another sound from out back. Ryan was setting down the firewood.

"Ryan, run. Run!" I yelled as loud as I could.

Mason slapped me. Hard.

I struggled in vain against the zip-ties holding me to the chair. All I accomplished was making my wrists hurt more. I shook my head to clear my eyes.

Mason stopped momentarily to look at me before deciding to continue to the back of the house.

I heard the back door open, then a moment later, the crash of breaking wood followed by a scream. Mason must have put his weight on the bad step and fallen through.

Karma strikes, asshole.

If I got lucky, he would bleed to death.

The screaming stopped, and two shots rang out. Then, one more.

My heart stopped.

Ryan?

CHAPTER 41

RYAN

FINALLY BROSNAHAND TOOK THE BAIT AND WENT THROUGH THE door to the kitchen.

I silently turned the knob to open the front door.

I heard a crash and a yell.

As an added bonus, the asshole had hit the bad step. I was behind Natalie. She couldn't see me.

Two shots sounded from the back, followed by another.

Natalie gasped and started to sob.

I came around in front of her, my finger to my lips and my Swiss Army knife in my other hand. This all depended on her being quiet.

She jerked with a start when she saw me and started to say something.

I clamped my hand over her mouth. "Quiet," I whispered.

She nodded. She had made me waste valuable time.

I might only have seconds to get her out before he came back. I cut her wrists loose first, followed by her ankles. I urged her out through the front door and closed it silently behind us.

We crouched by the front corner of the house and waited. I put a finger to her lips again. She had to be quiet.

Brosnahand groaned, and I could hear him on the back deck, limping back and forth.

I heard the creak of the back door opening.

That was my cue.

I pulled Natalie along the side of the house to the back.

The back door closed, and I could hear the kitchen floor creak under his weight.

I peeked in the lower corner of the kitchen window and saw Brosnahand go into the front room. I grabbed Natalie's arm and yanked her with me. "Run," I said softly.

She pointed to the left toward what looked like a path.

I had planned on just getting lost in the woods, but she knew the area better than I did. I went with her.

Just as we reached the edge of the woods, the back door burst open.

"Come back here, you bitch," Brosnahand yelled.

A shot rang out.

My heart stopped for a beat as Natalie stumbled.

She caught herself. "Pick up your feet," she said. "It's easy to trip out here."

Neither of us was hit. We kept running down the path in the dim light.

"This way," Natalie told me.

We kept going.

I could hear Brosnahand behind us.

He moved slower than us with all his extra weight and his injury, but we hadn't lost him. He yelled every now and then. It wasn't smart, but it was scary as hell.

"Where does this lead?" I asked Natalie.

She stopped me just before a sharp left around a stand of

poplars. "Careful of the fallen branch right around the corner." She panted heavily.

I stepped over the branch. "Where does this go?"

"It ends up ahead at another creek. There's a dairy on the other side."

Great, she had taken us down a dead-end trail.

I grabbed her arm. "You go ahead to the end. Hide in the bushes and wait for me," I said quietly but firmly.

"No, I'm staying with you."

"The hell you are. Now go." I turned her and gave her a shove. Reluctantly, she ran ahead.

I opened my Swiss Army knife and crouched by the base of the poplar trees, waiting for Brosnahand to come around the corner. The short blade of my knife was not much of a weapon against a bear of a man protected by six inches of blubber. I picked up a stout piece of wood and began carving a point at the end.

I had learned in a bar tussle once that big and fat didn't mean weak. A guy with his weight had to be strong just to get all of himself out of a chair and walk around.

The noise of his footfalls became louder.

My pulse quickened, and my mouth dried. I tensed up as I heard him approach the turn.

He came around the corner in the dim light and tripped over the branch with a grunt and a splat in the mud.

I pounced and jabbed the tiny knife into his side, and my sharpened stick as well.

He screamed, then rolled and shoved me with his foot and arm back toward the tree.

I hit the tree along my spine, and a sharp pain shot up my back.

He struggled to his feet, and I ran at him again.

The gun went off just as I hit him.

My side stung with a pain like I'd never felt before. I fell back against the tree, and my head hit hard.

The world went black.

～

NATALIE

AFTER RYAN SHOVED ME FORWARD, I JOGGED AHEAD TOWARD THE end of the trail, but I stopped before I reached the river. Searching around, I found a branch on the ground suitable for a club. I broke off the excess length and started running back to where I'd left Ryan.

We stood a better chance with two against one. This was my fight, not his. Brosnahand wanted a piece of me, and I was about to give it to him. I had played plenty of softball and could swing a mean bat. Home runs had been my specialty, and I intended to swing and connect when I ran into him. His head was going over the fence.

The sound of a primal scream reverberated through the woods. It had been Mason's voice. Ryan had gotten him. Then I heard the grunts of scuffling.

A gunshot.

"Ryan," I cried as I neared the spot.

I passed the bush and skidded to a stop.

Mason held his side with one hand, and the other had his gun pointed at me.

"It's just you and me now, bitch," he hissed.

I froze, not near enough to hit him with my bat, nor far enough to be safe. I had no direction to go.

In a blur, Ryan emerged from the shadows and swung a branch down hard on Mason's gun hand.

The branch broke, the gun dropped, and Mason cried out in pain.

I moved forward to take my home run swing at his head.

Before I could, Ryan plowed into him with a groan and shoved Mason, screaming, over the edge and down the embankment.

Ryan collapsed on the muddy ground.

I dropped my bat and rushed to him.

A loud splash confirmed that Mason had ended up in the river. His screaming stopped, and it was silent, save for our panting.

My heart pounded. "I thought he shot you." I was jittery with adrenaline.

Ryan groaned as he got to his knees, holding his side.

Even in the fading light I could see the blood seeping past his hand. "My God, he did."

Ryan attempted a weak laugh. "Like they say in the movies, it's just a flesh wound." He grimaced as I helped him to his feet.

"We gotta get you to a hospital."

"Get the gun," he told me.

I located the dark hunk of metal and picked it up. They looked lighter on TV. I started to put it in my waistband.

"Stop. Is the safety on?"

I had no idea what a safety was. "I dunno."

He stretched out his hand, so I handed it to him.

After a metallic click, he handed it back. "You don't want to shoot yourself." He was breathing hard, and he winced in obvious pain.

It wouldn't fit anywhere but in my waistband at the small of my back.

He stepped over the trip-hazard branch. "We have to get to a phone and call the cops."

"We have a phone at the cabin."

Gramps hadn't believed in cell phones. I moved to Ryan's hurt side and lifted his arm to rest on my shoulder. He needed all the help he could get. If we didn't make it back to the cabin, we were in big trouble. There was no way I could carry him.

We hobbled our way back in the encroaching darkness.

A sudden noise behind us caused me to turn. I saw a blurry shadow on the trail behind us.

Ryan leaned against a tree.

Pulling out the gun, I aimed, closed my eyes, and pulled on the trigger, but nothing happened.

"Safety. Thumb switch," Ryan said.

I flicked the thumb switch and pulled the trigger.

The sound of the gun startled me, and the recoil almost put me on my ass.

I saw the shadow move again and fired another time. The stench of the gunpowder was strong, and my hand was sore from the kick of the gun. Waiting a few seconds, I didn't see any more movement, so I turned and caught back up to Ryan.

"Did you get him?"

"I think so." I really had no idea if I'd hit him or not, but I didn't want Ryan to worry.

It was almost totally dark when we emerged from the trees at the back of the cabin.

We ascended the back steps of the cabin slowly, stepping over the one Mason had broken through.

I flicked on the light after we got through the door.

Ryan slumped into a chair in the kitchen. "Thanks...phone." The blood had seeped down his shirt into the top of his pants. The sight was sickening.

I rushed to the sink and grabbed two dishtowels to staunch the bleeding. "Hold it tight."

I ran to the front room and dialed 9-1-1.

They told me an ambulance and the police were on the way and to stay on the line.

"I can't." The phone was a corded model that wouldn't reach into the kitchen. I put it down to rush back to Ryan.

Ryan's face was pale, and sweat beaded on his forehead. "I love you, Cupcake." He was barely pressing on the wound. The blood had soaked down his leg.

I knelt and pressed firmly on the towels. "Hang on. They're on the way."

He groaned at the increased pain, and his eyes rolled back in his head. His head lolled to the side, and I could feel his hand going limp.

"Don't give up on me, dammit." I slapped his face.

His eyes opened. "Is that any way to treat your fiancé?" he asked. Then his eyes closed again, and he fell forward in the chair.

Fiancé?

I grappled to get him to the floor without hitting his head. I rolled him onto his back and pressed hard on the wound.

"Don't you leave me, dammit."

His chest barely moved, his breaths were so shallow.

I pressed even harder on the wound. My tears fell on his shirt. I couldn't lose him.

CHAPTER 42

Natalie

THE FRONT DOOR SLAMMED OPEN. THEN I HEARD "HANDS WHERE I can see them" from a male voice behind me.

"I can't. I have to control the bleeding." I was not releasing the pressure on the wound after Ryan had already lost consciousness.

"Freeze. Don't move," the same voice said.

I didn't look back. I kept as much pressure on the wound as I could.

The gun in my waistband at the small of my back was pulled away and thrown to the side. "Tom, you take the wound," the voice said.

Tom knelt on the other side of Ryan, holstered his gun, and put his hands over mine, pressing down hard.

Then someone yanked me away and to my feet. They pulled my hands behind me and cuffed one wrist and then the other.

The sound of another approaching siren became louder. Then the sound of tires skidding to a stop on the gravel outside came in through the open front door.

"Pete, you got the perp?" Tom asked.

Now I was the perp?

The cop named Pete pulled me back away from Ryan and Tom and spun me around. "Why'd you shoot him?" he demanded.

"I didn't."

He pushed me against the wall. "Stand there."

I now saw they were deputies from the Windham County Sheriff's office.

He knelt down beside Brosnahand's gun and sniffed the barrel. "This gun's been fired."

Newsflash.

"Of course, but I didn't shoot him. It wasn't me."

"Name?" Pete demanded.

"Natalie Spencer."

"And his?"

"Ryan Westerly."

EMTs rushed in and took over for Tom, who went to the sink to wash his hands of Ryan's blood.

Within a minute they had Ryan lifted onto a rolling stretcher, still applying pressure to the wound and hooking up an intravenous line to his arm.

"Male GSW to the midsection, BP eighty over forty, unconscious on the way in," one of the EMTs spoke into his radio.

"Ryan Westerly," Pete called out as they rolled the stretcher to the front door and were gone.

I moved to follow them. I could only hope they were in time.

Deputy Pete grabbed me and pulled me back.

"I need to go with him," I pleaded.

"Not yet," he said sternly.

"But, I need to go with him."

Pete glared at me with cold eyes. "Not until we get your statement." The words were as icy as his expression.

"Sit down," he commanded as he pulled me toward one of the kitchen chairs.

I sat uncomfortably. I shifted forward on the seat, my hands coated in blood and cuffed behind me. "Mason Brosnahand attacked me and shot Ryan. That's my statement. Now, can I go?"

Pete laughed. "Not so fast."

Deputy Tom pulled on blue gloves one by one. He removed a pouch from his pocket and ripped it open.

"Stand up, please," he said.

I did.

He went behind me and rubbed the pad on my arms and wrists. "You can sit back down now."

The seat wasn't any more comfortable than before.

Tom placed the pad in the pouch and shook it with some liquid. He removed the pad, examined it, and showed it to his partner, who nodded. Tom then picked up the gun, got on his radio, and read a series of numbers into it as he walked into the other room.

"I need a trace on this now," I heard him say.

"You want to tell me now why you shot him?" Pete asked again.

"For the second time, I did not shoot him," I said slowly and firmly.

The disbelief in Pete's face was obvious. "Let's do this one more time. The man's been shot. You have a gun. The gun's been fired. The GSR field test shows you recently fired a gun. Now, would you like to try that again?"

It wasn't a question, but a rather clear accusation.

Deputy Tom removed his gloves and took out his gun.

I shook my head. They unlocked the cuffs and let me wash my hands. The questioning went on for almost an hour.

"Let's start at the top again," Deputy Pete said. "You broke into the house, but you say the house is yours?"

I'd already been through this a half dozen times, just like the FBI interrogations about Damien. Repeat, and then repeat, again and again. "Yes, it was passed on to my sister and me by our grandfather."

The deputy looked unconvinced. "If you belong here, why did you have to break in?"

"I told you, I lost my key, so I had to break the glass on the back door to get in when I arrived." I wasn't going into the fact that the key had been in my house when the FBI seized it, and that's how I'd lost it.

"And your lawyer came to the house and attacked you?"

"Yes, his name is Mason Brosnahand."

The second deputy, Tom, took a call in the other room and re-entered with a piece of paper he showed Deputy Pete.

"The search shows the gun you were holding isn't registered to Mr. Brosnahand. Can you explain that?" Deputy Pete asked.

"No."

"It's registered to a Damien Winterbourne," he continued.

My mouth must have dropped halfway to the floor. "That can't be."

"You said you were attacked by Mr. Brosnahand. So who is Damien Winterbourne?"

Even in death I couldn't escape Damien. "My ex-husband."

"And where is he now?"

None of this made any sense. "Dead."

"And you came here from Boston, is that right?" the other deputy asked.

"Yes, I told you that already."

"And is the car out front yours?" Deputy Pete asked.

"No, it's Brosnahand's."

"According to the Boston PD, that car was stolen a few days ago, at the same time you claim to have come to our fine state."

I shook my head; that couldn't be.

Deputy Pete scooted his chair forward. "To summarize, you claim that the man in the hospital, Mr. Westerly, was shot by your lawyer, Mr. Brosnahand, with your gun, after Mr. Brosnahand brought the gun here to assault you in a car he stole at the same time as you left Boston. Is that correct?"

"I don't know how to explain the car, but I didn't shoot Ryan, Brosnahand did."

Deputy Tom's phone rang. "It's the hospital," he said. He went into the other room to answer it.

When he came back in he said, "Time to go. He just came out of surgery."

~

RYAN

THE LIGHT WAS BRIGHT. AS I STRUGGLED TO PRY OPEN MY eyelids, only a blurry image appeared, an angel in white. The beeping nearby was annoying, but somehow familiar. I tried to sit up, but my muscles barely responded.

"Don't," she said. The angel put a firm hand on my shoulder, urging me to lie back down, which I did. "It's best if you don't try to move yet."

I shivered from the cold and tried to quell the nausea I felt rolling over me.

"Are you cold? Would you like another hot blanket?"

I nodded, not sure what *another* meant.

The warm fabric was a welcome relief.

I tried to focus, but the lights were too bright. I brought my hand up to shield my eyes, but it was tied down by strings.

"Stop," she said firmly, pulling my hand back down. "You'll pull out the IVs."

IVs?

I'd been in the kitchen with Natalie. Where was Natalie?

"Natalie?" I cried weakly.

The woman squeezed my hand. "Relax. You need to rest a few minutes. You just came out of surgery. You're in post-op now, and it takes a few minutes to get your bearings. Try to keep your eyes closed and rest until the doctor comes by."

Doctor?

Post-op?

The gunshot wound came back to me. I felt for it and found a big bulge under the blanket, but no pain.

"Stop that." She pulled my hand away. "I'm going to have to strap you down if you keep tugging at the bandage."

I relaxed into the mattress and fought off the nausea.

"Natalie. I need to see Natalie."

"I see we're back in the land of the living," a masculine voice said. "I'm Dr. Livingston, and no, not the one from Africa. How do you feel, Mr. ... Westerly?"

I blinked open my eyes again and was able to focus somewhat while I assembled my list of complaints.

"I'm cold, I'm about to throw up, and I feel like I've been run over by a truck. Other than that, just great."

"I like your attitude, Mr. Westerly. The nausea and chills are common and will pass quickly, as will the general disorientation."

I nodded.

"The operation was successful. You were lucky. The bullet didn't perforate an intestine, which is what we worry about most in these situations, so your recovery should be swift and complete. But only——and I can't stress this enough——only if you take it easy and don't open up the wound again."

"Got it." The fog began to lift as I followed along. Take it easy; got that part.

He held something up. "We found this vial of medicine marked experimental in your pocket. Are you in a program where we need to administer this to you?"

My eyes now focused enough to make out the vial of David's CTX-26. I shook my head. "No. It's for a patient of mine." I regretted the words as soon as I said them.

"You're a doctor?"

That subterfuge wouldn't work here. "Biotech development. It's a drug trial."

"And you carry this with you?"

"I…" I struggled for an explanation. "The call to come out here was sudden," I explained.

"We can courier this to your hospital if the patient needs the medication. Just give me the details, and I'd be happy to take care of it for you."

I shivered, feeling even colder than before. Having the hospital learn what I'd been doing would be disastrous.

I needed him to drop the subject. "My associate can take care of it for me."

"Okay, if you think that's best. Let me know if you change your mind."

I nodded. "Thanks."

With his loss of interest, David was safe for the moment.

A nurse parted the curtain and entered. "You ready for a visitor?"

"Natalie?" I asked.

A man in uniform came around the corner. "Mr. Westerly, I'm Deputy Stebbins of the Windham County Sheriff's Office. Are you up to a few questions?"

"No. I want to see Natalie."

"She's just outside. This will only take a minute. First, I need to ask. Did you see who shot you?"

I nodded. "Yes."

He looked at me expectantly.

"Brosnahand is his name. Mason Brosnahand."

He wrote in his pad. "And why would he want to shoot you."

"Because I was between Natalie and him. That's why."

"Do you know why he was at the house?"

I shook my head. "No. He had her tied up, and he was waving a gun when I got back with the wood."

Natalie came rushing around the corner and up to me with the most welcome smile I had ever seen. She had been crying. She took my hand and leaned over to give me a quick kiss.

"I love you," she said.

"And whose gun was it?" the deputy asked, interrupting our reunion.

"His," I said, taking in Natalie's beauty.

"Can you leave us alone and just go find the asshole that shot him?" Natalie hissed at the deputy.

"I think I have what I need for now. I'll need a more complete statement, but that can wait." He left as abruptly as he had arrived.

I squeezed her hand. "You didn't need to be mean to him. He's just doing his job."

"He's an asshole. He's spent the entire time accusing me of shooting you."

I laughed weakly. "Then you're right. He's an asshole."

My nurse arrived with another blanket. "Are you warm enough?"

"Yes, now that she's here."

Natalie smiled.

The nurse smiled and shook her head. "Wise guy, I see."

I cocked my head. "When can I leave?"

"It's up to the doctor, but not tonight, that's for sure. And trust me, when the pain medication starts to wear off, you won't be in a hurry to go anywhere."

I had never spent a full day in a hospital bed, and I didn't intend to start now. I would be out of here tomorrow no matter what. David needed his next dose tomorrow night, and that couldn't be postponed——doctor or no doctor, pain be damned.

CHAPTER 43

(ONE WEEK LATER)

NATALIE

MASON BROSNAHAND HAD BEEN FOUND SHOT DEAD OUTSIDE HIS house, execution style, a day after his visit to my cabin. The news-people hypothesized that he'd been the victim of an unhappy client.

For once what they'd written seemed fairly accurate. I just knew it had been a disagreement with one client in particular. I had called Willey, the US attorney, to find out what I could when the story broke.

Willey had told me in confidence that they had video, which hadn't been released to the news media, proving the cartel had gotten to him. He warned me to be quiet about this fact, because it would take them a few weeks to track down all the culprits and make an arrest.

We had just gotten back from Vermont after Ryan's week-long stay in their hospital.

Ryan had insisted I drop him off at his hospital, and I had.

He had also asked me to come back to Boston and Chameleon, and I'd agreed to try it.

I hadn't asked about his fiancé comment, afraid he'd said it while hallucinating from the blood loss, and he hadn't brought it up again.

I closed the solid door behind me in Ryan's condo and set two bags of groceries down in the kitchen.

As I suspected, a survey of his fridge showed there wasn't anything worthwhile in it. The ketchup and mustard would work for tonight, but what little else there was had become inedible.

After a quick clean out and restocking from my bags, the end result was semi-respectable, certainly good enough for a day or two.

I checked my watch and sent the first text.

ME: Dinner at six - don't be late

I didn't get the little bouncing dots of a reply being typed. That was to be expected; his phone was probably on silent.

I pulled the food processor out of the cabinet, followed by a cutting board, and a chef's knife from the block. I moved plates to the table and double checked that I had all the ingredients on my list.

My phone beeped from the counter.

RYAN: Can't make six how about seven

I typed out my reply and waited.

ME: Don't be late

The dots heralded a speedier reply this time. I looked out the window. From up here, the city looked serene, even inviting. Down

there, among the Damien-haters, it was a totally different story
——unpredictable and scary.

RYAN: Where?

ME: Your place

The messages kept coming.

RYAN: Seven - I have an experiment I need to finish

ME: Six - don't be late

He didn't answer, so I couldn't be sure exactly where we stood.
I had a call to make.
Briana picked up right away. "Hey, Natalie. How are you?"
I had met Briana the day after Ryan was shot. I had driven
David's medicine to her, along with Ryan's instructions. It had
been the only way to keep Ryan from breaking out of the hospital.
David had been his first priority. He'd failed to appreciate how he
couldn't help David if he disobeyed the doctor and got himself in
worse shape by leaving the hospital early.
Briana had turned out to be very sweet, and we had talked
several times since then.
"How's David doing?" I asked.
"Better every day. The new…er…approach is helping a lot."
From the background sounds, I could tell she was at the hospital, and Ryan had cautioned us both to not discuss the new medicine David was getting.

"That's great. Listen, I'm cooking Ryan a special dinner, and I need him here at six. He's not supposed to be pushing himself with long days anyway. And it's Saturday on top of that. Can you help me?"

"Are you back in Boston to stay?"

I hadn't told her, but apparently she knew of my problem with this place.

"Up in the air at the moment."

"Consider it done. He won't be late, trust me."

Briana struck me as someone I could count on.

After I got the water boiling under the steamer, the cauliflower went in, and I set the timer. My plan for dinner tonight was the same as the aborted dinner the night I'd left: grilled sausage and garlic mashed cauliflower. Bangers and mash, as far as Ryan was concerned.

A half hour later, the food processor had been cleaned and put away. All the evidence of cauliflower had been washed down the sink, and the fragrant dish was warming in the oven.

The sausage wouldn't need to be started for over two hours. I still had time to go out for coffee. The hospital coffee had sucked big time.

I leaned against the counter. There was something different about the great room setup.

The old couch.

The old couch had met its maker, and the couch I'd had delivered the day I'd left had taken its place as the sole piece of furniture on the left side of the room.

Ryan had embraced a modicum of change and let go of the musty piece. Perhaps it boded well for the future.

≈

NATALIE

. . .

I STOOD CALMLY IN THE COFFEE SHOP, ENJOYING MY RIGHT TO A freshly prepared mocha.

"Bitch," she yelled, spitting in my direction.

I jumped back, but not quickly enough. She got me on the leggings.

"Winterbourne. She's the Winterbourne bitch that stole my money," she screamed to the rest of the crowd in the Starbucks. She pointed at me and her eyes bugged out. She'd morphed into a vision straight out of a horror flick.

My adrenaline pumped, and my heart instantly shifted into overdrive. This was fight-or-flight response at full throttle.

The crazy lady lunged for me, claws out, with something in her hand. I chose flight.

I dodged sideways and pulled away from her grasp on my arm. I raced out of the coffee shop with the screaming banshee hot behind me.

Her yelling only increased in volume and viciousness as she fell further behind, calling me horrible names and alerting the entire county to my whereabouts.

Two blocks later, I turned the corner and the yelling stopped. A block after that I halted my running and caught my breath, hunched over with my hands on my knees. The shaking wouldn't stop. I was bleeding from a cut on my arm, but it could have been worse. She had only grazed me with the nail file. The next one might be carrying a knife, or worse yet, a gun.

After calming myself enough to walk, I made my way back to Ryan's building. I didn't truly feel safe until I had pressed the button for the twenty-third floor and the elevator doors had closed behind me. I couldn't go out in public, and Ryan couldn't accompany me everywhere with his gun.

Freedom was a commodity underrated by the majority of the public, which had it in abundance.

Once inside his unit, I fell into the couch. This torture would never end. I could never be safe in this town——maybe even the whole commonwealth. I couldn't go out without risking my sanity or possibly my life.

I got up to pour myself a glass of wine. Anything to calm my nerves.

CHAPTER 44

NATALIE

I HEARD THE DOOR OPENING.

I checked my watch. Six o'clock.

Thank you, Briana.

"I have a special question for you, Nat," Ryan called from the entryway.

After my brush with disaster this afternoon, my current feelings didn't match the enthusiasm in his voice.

He carried his work briefcase and a small bag.

His brow knit when he saw the bottle in front of me. "Getting an early start on celebrating, are we?"

One glass hadn't calmed me enough, so I hadn't stopped. And I hadn't been celebrating.

"How many?" he asked.

I held up two fingers.

"I thought we agreed on the truth."

I pulled in a sharp breath. Lying was the worst thing I could be accused of. I extended another finger. It had taken me three glasses to calm down. And an hour after that to come to the realization that I couldn't continue like this.

But I remembered Jasmin's words——there had to be a solution that would work for everyone. And I was prepared to compromise. The lawyer in me just wanted a chance to state my case, the case for us. I had to convince him it would work.

"I can't continue to live like this," I told him.

He stopped mid-stride and stared at me with hurt eyes. "What do you mean?"

He closed the distance between us and sat down beside me on the couch, putting the bag on the floor.

I took his hand, then changed my mind and swung my arm around him, buried my head in his chest, and cried. "I can't stay in this town. I have to leave, at least on the weekends. I feel safe enough at work during the week, but I can't lock myself away every weekend."

He hugged me tight, kissed the top of my head, and stroked my back. "Tell me what happened," he said softly.

My tears fell onto his shirt. "The Winterbourne curse struck again." I showed him my arm. "I just can't take it. Everybody in this town hates me."

He kissed the top of my head. "I'm so sorry this happened, but you know that's not true."

It was true enough. "It's going to drive me insane. Every time I feel like…like I can go out again, another one of them pops up and threatens to kill me."

I shivered in his arms. This wasn't an irrational fear. *Not* being afraid would be the irrational response.

"Stay here with me. I can keep you safe."

"I feel safe with you, Ryan, I do. But that's not good enough. I have to be able to go out on my own and not be attacked. We have to talk."

"I smell garlic. You've been cooking." he said.

"Bangers and mash. The dinner we never got to eat."

He wrapped his arms around me again. "I have a better plan," he whispered into my ear.

No doubt his plan involved instant nakedness, and I would enjoy it, but it would have to wait.

"I spent a lot of time on this. Dinner first." I pushed away only to find he had undone my bra, one of his special talents. "You're incorrigible."

"It's why you find me so irresistible." He had that part right. His playfulness had taken time to show itself, but it was in full force tonight, and it was endearing.

I turned my back on him. "Now fasten me back up and behave yourself. You probably shouldn't be exerting yourself just yet anyway." I reached behind me to tease Mega.

He re-hooked my bra and whispered in my ear. "I'll let you do all the work."

I wiggled away to fix the plates. "My imitation of London," I told him as he held my chair for me.

"Smells great." He pushed my seat in as I sat. "First, I have something to say."

This was hard enough. I couldn't allow him to sidetrack me with another invitation to dine naked, or play strip trivia, or whatever else he had planned.

"Sit," I said. "This is my dinner, and you promised to behave yourself."

With a knitted brow, he took his seat. "Later, then."

I had already brought out the beer, and I lifted mine. "To David's continued progress."

A brilliant smile bloomed on his face as we clinked bottles and toasted. "Thank you. He's responding well so far."

"I know. I talked to Briana again today."

Ryan's eyes brightened. "I wish I had the time to see him more often."

I swallowed some of my mash, hoping to see him try it soon.

Ryan cut a piece of sausage and chewed it with a reassuring smile. "Just like London."

I took another sip of beer to bolster my courage. "I missed you." It had only been part of a day.

He cocked his head, and his smile broadened. "I missed you too, Nat." The look in those deep blue eyes of his and the way he said the words melted me. He truly was the one I could trust. He took a forkful of the mashed cauliflower.

I cut into my banger while watching for a reaction.

He swallowed. "Delicious. Now tell me, why the insistence on an early dinner?"

"I needed the time to get back to Vermont before it got too late——"

His face fell, stopping me in my tracks. "I was hoping you wanted to stay."

"Get back to Vermont if our talk didn't go well," I finished.

"How's it going so far?"

I scooped a pea onto my spoon and flung it at him. "This is serious."

The pea missed.

He swallowed a bite of cauliflower faux-potatoes without a grimace or barfing it up. "I'm listening."

"I want to try."

He didn't look up. "Try what?" He cut another bite of banger. "Us," I said.

He didn't look up; he didn't smile.

My heart pounded, waiting for a response.

"And what are your demands?" he asked, finally looking up at me.

A grin tugged at the corners of his mouth. He was trying his hardest to hold it back, but it was sneaking through.

"Lawyers like you always have demands," he added.

I could tell he was playing with me.

"Conditions," I corrected. "I want time. We need time for us, as a couple."

"Couple time. I have been giving you couple time."

He had been making what, for him, was a valiant effort, but I worried it wouldn't last. Once his recovery was complete, work would inevitably pull him away more and more if he didn't agree to make a change.

"I want to spend weekends at the cabin with you, without you going into the lab and losing track of time until the entire day is gone."

He took another sip of beer and let out a breath. "I'll try, but I can't free up the whole weekend."

This was hard for him. But this was the thing I had spent the most time thinking about, and I had the answer.

"Sure you can."

"I would if I could, but I can't."

"How can you be so stupid and not see it?"

He got up from his chair.

"Please listen," I begged. If he'd just let me get out what I was trying to say.

"Get up," he said firmly.

I pushed back the chair and stood. "What is it?"

He reached around to take my hand and guided me to his side of the table. He put a finger to my lips. "Don't say another word."

I stood still as a statue while he pulled out his phone.

He started some music and put the phone down. It was Frank, our Frank Sinatra.

He pulled me to him, and we started dancing. "I have to have you in a position where you can't throw any more food at me."

"Sorry."

He pulled me close. "And... And I just need to hold you."

I needed the contact as well. "Me too."

"First rule of negotiation," he said after a moment. "It's okay to act crazy, but it's not okay to insult the other side."

"Sorry," I said, swaying with him.

I laid my head against his chest. Moving to the music in his arms was infinitely better than sitting across the table.

"Nat, there are certain things I just can't do."

I looked up into his eyes——caring eyes, loving eyes. "Like eat cauliflower?" I asked.

"Yeah, like eat cauliflower."

"You just did. That was mashed cauliflower, not potatoes."

He laughed. "I thought we promised to not keep secrets?"

"As you once told me, that wasn't a secret, it was a surprise. I told you bangers and mash. You assumed I meant mashed potatoes."

"Are all lawyers as sneaky as you?"

"Just proving you can do things you didn't think you could."

He stroked my back. "Okay, now tell me how I'm so dumb."

"You know the routine you have of reading through all the recently published papers every morning?"

"Yeah," he said, taking a deep breath.

"You could do that just as easily on the weekend at the cabin. We have an internet connection, and that would free up your weekday mornings for the lab."

～

RYAN

FOR A LAWYER, SHE SURE IS SMART.

As we danced and Frank sang, I mulled over her suggestion. It was a good one.

Syd Roundhouse had turned out to be sincerely interested in working under me in Lab Two, and he had a completely competent tech working for him in Terry. She was almost as good as Paul, and if they alternated weekend coverage, Natalie's plan might work.

"Okay, if..." I told her.

She pulled back to look up at me. "Okay if what?"

"I'll have to ask some people at work to rearrange their weekend schedules, and that may not go over well."

Then she surprised me. "Good, we leave for the cabin every Friday night."

Frank started another song as we continued to dance, my woman and me.

"Weather permitting," I countered.

"Every weekend."

"We won't be able to make it in the snow."

"Yes, we will," she said, poking me in the chest. "You just have to get a four-wheel drive. And I don't mean some old junker Jeep. Something nice, like a Lexus."

"I can't. I only have one parking space downstairs."

"You're really going with that excuse?"

The salt on the roads had not been kind to my car, that was true enough. "But I've had that car forever."

"That there is the problem," she countered. "Since then we've invented airplanes, televisions, and even put a man on the moon. It's time to let it go and get a real car."

She was right that my car was old, but I was comfortable with it, and it was reliable. Mostly. And it reminded me of my dad.

I sighed. "I'm not getting rid of my car. I'll rent another space, but I'm not driving anything fancy."

She touched a finger to my nose. "Trust me, we can find something that won't embarrass your sensibilities. You can still drive in jeans, and nobody will suspect you're as rich as you are."

"I just don't want to show off." I'd take jeans and a T-shirt any day over a suit. One thing I particularly liked about Natalie's cabin was the back-to-basics living, as well as the unpretentious country feel of Brattleboro.

"Okay, it's settled then. We leave for Vermont every Friday at five, and we spend a relaxing weekend together."

"Not so fast," I told her.

"Okay, six," she said, guessing at my first condition.

"Not so fast. I have a *few* conditions of my own."

She pulled back and looked up, stunned.

"This only works if Paul and Terry agree to the weekend schedule, and we can't go on a weekend they can't cover."

"So?" she asked.

"So it's your job to convince them it's a good idea."

"But…"

"No buts. You need to convince Paul and Terry it's a good plan."

"But I hardly know them."

"If you can make a compelling case for it, and get them on board, then fine. Otherwise I have to go into the lab on weekends to keep things going at top speed."

"Will you be home for dinner every night?" she asked.

"Not always. But I'll try." I stopped dancing and pulled her chin up with my finger. "Relationships are a team sport. I give some, you give some, and we both get most of what we want. Are you willing to make changes?"

"Have you been talking to Jasmin?"

"Jasmin who? Answer the question."

"I'll try," she said.

"Me too. But first…" I pulled her over to the counter. "Stand there and close your eyes." I let go of her.

At first she rebelled and crossed her arms. Eventually, she gave in and closed her eyes.

I grabbed the phone and changed the song. Frank began singing "I Love You."

"Do you remember what I said the night your buddy Brosnahand came by?"

She opened her eyes. "Sure, you said *run faster*."

"Keep your eyes closed," I said.

She complied.

"And?" I asked.

"And what?"

I pulled the box from the bag on the counter——the box I had stopped off to get at her favorite jewelry store.

"I asked you something."

"You did not."

"It's a little foggy, so I might have gotten the words wrong. Open your eyes."

She did, and her eyes went wide. Her hand jerked to her mouth at the sight of the open box with the ring.

"Natalie Anne Spencer, will you marry me?"

"Are you sure?" she squeaked.

"Damned sure."

She pulled my face close and gave me the kiss I had wanted since I'd walked in tonight——the kiss that might lead to us christening the couch this evening.

She pulled away. "One more condition."

"What is it with you lawyers?" I asked, holding her up with my hand under her ass.

"Will you make me smoothies in the morning?"

"So long as I don't have to drink the ones with spinach or kale."

CHAPTER 45

Ryan

I returned from the Brattleboro market with bacon, eggs, strawberries, and most importantly, cocoa powder for my coffee. Natalie had brought a blender from Boston and insisted on a strawberry smoothie to go with her breakfast. And after all she had been through, she deserved whatever she wanted. The heavenly smell of roasted coffee greeted me upon opening the door.

It was the first of our planned weekend retreats in Vermont. The drive had been comfortable in the new car Natalie had picked out for us. Until now, I hadn't realized how much seating technology had improved in the years since Toyota had slapped my old car together.

I'd fed the potbelly stove before going shopping, and the little thing was now giving off enough heat that she had the window open. The calls of the birds outside wafted in through the screen.

Natalie was at the counter, pouring the steaming coffee out of the percolator and doing a little dance in my T-shirt, her ass cheeks almost, but not quite, showing.

"Did they have strawberries?" she asked.

The glint of sunlight off the ring on her finger warmed me. "I got the last two baskets."

The market had been small, with meager quantities, but a good assortment of fruits and veggies.

"And the spinach?"

"Yes, I got the spinach, but can't we just have a normal smoothie, without the rabbit food?"

"You're my hero. You can have anything you want," she said, planting a wet kiss on my cheek and dancing back to the stove.

I put the bag down and unloaded my haul. "What has you so chipper this morning?"

She opened the can of cocoa powder with a spoon. "For the first time since Damien's arrest, I feel free. The sun's up, I'm here with you, and I have you all to myself for the weekend."

I came up behind and wrapped my arms around her.

"I feel the same way," I whispered in her ear.

She wiggled loose. "Then make yourself useful and make my smoothie while I do the bacon and eggs."

Her message was clear: *smoothie first, dumbshit.* She stirred heaping spoonfuls of the divine chocolate powder into both coffees and handed me one.

I sipped from the cup and almost burned my tongue off. I'd forgotten old-fashioned percolators worked by actually boiling the coffee.

I pulled open the freezer compartment on the old refrigerator. It was crusted over with ice. The two ice cube trays were empty, naturally.

"How old is this thing?"

The machine obviously dated from before frost-free models were available.

"And how am I supposed to make you a smoothie with no ice."

"Daddy liked his appliances old and reliable. He was

convinced the newer ones were meant to break down, so we'd have to buy replacements."

"He might have been right about that." The coffee grinder Natalie had used this morning had been a hand-crank variety. Everything in the kitchen, save the toaster, dated back decades at least.

"There should be some bags of ice in the chest freezer in the shed."

"Shed out back. Got it." I went to the back door.

"You'll need the key; the shed's locked. It's in the pantry." She flicked her head toward the open pantry door.

I located the hook holding a key ring with two keys just inside the door and grabbed them.

The door to the old wooden shed lacked anything as modern as a deadbolt. Instead it sported a rusty padlock on an even rustier hasp. The second key I tried worked the lock, and it clicked open without a fuss.

There was a single small window on the back wall facing the river. A faded peach-colored drapery covered it and only allowed dim light into the space. Various tools were organized on the wall above a workbench to the left, with everything on hooks and several rows of neatly arranged Mason jars holding screws and nails of varying sizes.

It was evident now where Natalie got her organizing skills. Her father had been a methodical man.

I found the chest freezer on the opposite side. A yank on the handle got me nowhere.

In the low light, I'd missed the padlocks securing it. I pulled the key ring out again, and the first lock yielded to the first key I tried, but the second one wouldn't accept either of the keys on the ring.

I trudged back up the stairs to the kitchen, careful to avoid the broken board at the top.

The scent of cooking bacon had me instantly salivating.

"No ice?" Natalie asked, noticing I'd come back empty-handed.

"I didn't get it unlocked yet. Who locks a freezer of ice anyway?"

"Daddy did after a local boy suffocated to death playing hide-and-seek in an old freezer like that."

I understood the danger. That's why modern freezers used magnetic strips to keep themselves closed instead of latches. "I just need the other key."

"Both the keys are on the same ring," she answered, stirring the eggs.

A round-trip to the shed ended in the same result. The second lock would not accept either of the keys on the ring. I tried reversing the keys. No luck.

I pulled out my phone and turned on the flashlight to get a better look.

The lock was marked MEDECO. This was no cheap, hardware-store padlock. This was a serious, high-security lock. You didn't protect mere bags of ice with a Medeco lock.

I took the stairs again quickly, feeling excitement pump through me. Damien's key ring had held Medeco keys.

"Nat, where's Damien's key ring?"

"My purse, why?"

I reached past her to turn off the burners of the stove.

"Hey, I'm not done yet."

I kissed her surprised face. "Get his keys and come with me."

She ambled to the front room and returned with her purse. It took forever for her to find Damien's keys among the ton of junk clogging the bag.

"I don't understand," she said.

I pulled her along, out the door.

"I don't have shoes on," she lamented.

I picked her up. "Cupcake, stop complaining for one minute, okay?"

I carried her to the shed, set her down inside, and took the key ring from her. I located the key that fit the slot, and the lock slid open with an easy turn. I handed Natalie my phone with the flashlight turned on and yanked on the handle of the old freezer.

The lid opened with a squeak.

Natalie gasped.

It wasn't what either of us had expected.

The smell of decomposing flesh filled the room.

I closed the lid to keep from barfing.

CHAPTER 46

NATALIE

LATE THE FOLLOWING FRIDAY AFTERNOON, THE THREE OF US passed through the metal detectors at the federal courthouse near the waterfront. Liam was out of town in London, so Vincent Benson had volunteered to help. He had taken over running the east coast part of Covington Industries for Liam a while back.

I had dreaded my previous trips here to meet with Kirk Willey, AUSA, but this time, I tried to convince myself I felt a little better. Ryan's arm around my shoulders provided some comfort, but I was still apprehensive about this meeting. A lot of things could go wrong. Vincent and Ryan were taking a big chance with this.

Drawing on my two years of law school, I had counted three ways this could blow up in our faces——and that might not be the full list. The people in the US Attorney's office were not a good group to annoy, much less piss off. The federal government had unlimited resources at its disposal to make our lives miserable.

We made our way upstairs and after a brief pause were shown to a meeting room to wait for Willey.

"Don't worry. It will be just fine, Nat." Ryan patted my knee.

As always, his voice and touch were soothing. Ryan had promised to keep me safe, and I had no choice but to trust him.

The door opened, and Willey walked in. "Good afternoon, Mrs. Winterbourne. And you must be Dr. Westerly."

I didn't react to the insult.

"And Vincent Benson," Benson said, introducing himself.

We all stood and shook hands.

"I thought it would just be the two of us, Dr. Westerly."

"Sorry for the misunderstanding. And thank you for taking the time to meet with us, Mr. Kirk," Ryan said.

I detected a glint in his eye. Tit for tat.

"Willey. Kirk Willey," the attorney corrected him.

"Whatever," Ryan said dismissively.

Willey puffed up his chest, but seemed to decide against any direct attack on my fiancé. "If this is about the trade-secret theft at your company, I'm afraid I can't discuss that case with you," he said instead.

Ryan nodded. "I understand. Actually, we're here about Miss Spencer's house and the other assets that have been taken without cause."

Willey pushed back from the table. "There's nothing I can do about that. She and her husband defrauded innocent citizens, and we're doing what we can to maximize the payout to the victims. Simple justice."

But for the calming hand Ryan put on me, I would have jumped across the table when he mentioned me alongside Damien.

"Ex-husband," I corrected him.

Willey glared at me.

"Nothing you can do?" Benson asked.

"Nothing at all," Willey said, smiling.

That was exactly how I'd expected him to answer, the snake.

Benson stood, and the two of us followed his lead.

"Was that all?" Willey asked.

We made our way to the door before Benson responded.

I opened the door and walked into the hallway, followed by Ryan.

Benson turned before exiting. "Then it seems you wouldn't be interested in recovering any more of Winterbourne's ill-gotten gains."

"Wait just a minute," Willey said.

Benson stopped mid-doorway.

"Recovering more money? That gives us something to talk about. Please come back, and let's discuss it."

Benson looked at me.

I shrugged my shoulders, and we went back in and took our seats again.

"Well? What do you know?" Willey asked Benson.

Ryan took a pen and a check out of his pocket. He signed the check and placed it back in his pocket.

Benson waited until Ryan had finished and pointed to him. "Not me, him."

Ryan smiled.

Willey huffed and leaned forward, red faced. "So what is it, Dr. Westerly, that you know?"

Willey looked ready to blow a gasket by the time Ryan finally started to talk. "I don't know anything for certain, but I have a hunch."

"A hunch?" Willey asked, exasperated.

Ryan produced the key that had opened the padlock on the freezer. "This key opens a container that contains gold bars. A lot of bars."

Willey's eyes lit up. "Gold?"

"Gold," Ryan repeated. "Now, it's not mine, and I don't know who owns it, but I'm sure you can figure it out."

Willey held out his hand. "I'll take that key."

"No. It's my key, and I'm keeping it until we have a deal."

Benson sat back with a smirk.

Willey's eyes narrowed. "What kind of deal?"

"You sign over all of Miss Spencer's assets, returning them to her. And I'll let you have the key."

Willey laughed. "Wrong. You give me the key. You tell me where the gold is. And I won't prosecute you as an accessory after the fact."

"That's not the deal," Ryan told him coldly.

Willey dialed his phone. "I'm in conference room three. Get up here right now." He hung up. "I'm going to arrest you as an accessory right now and confiscate that key."

"No, you won't," Benson said.

"Keep out of this," Willey spat.

Benson wouldn't be stopped. "He just signed a fifty-million-dollar check to the political action committee for your opponent. If you arrest him on trumped-up charges just after he signed that check, how will that play in the papers?"

The timing was perfect. Willey had announced just last week that he was launching a campaign to run for Attorney General of the Commonwealth of Massachusetts, and Benson's threat could completely derail that ambition——for good.

Special agents White and McNally burst into the room and looked to Willey for direction.

Ryan pulled the check out of his pocket, just far enough for Willey to see and smiled.

Willey was like a deer in the headlights, frozen in place.

"You wanted us?" White asked.

"You can go. It was a mistake," Willey told them.

White shook his head, and the pair left.

So far so good.

Willey wagged an angry finger at Ryan. "I'm going to haul you in front of the grand jury, and you're going to tell me where it is, and I won't need a damned key."

"Perhaps, but that will be too late," Ryan replied.

We had considered this possibility, which is why we'd scheduled the meeting for late on Friday.

"How so?" Willey asked.

"You see, Brosnahand warned me the night he shot me that the cartel would stop at nothing to get what they thought was their money. So I'm not taking any chances that they'll come after me. I suspect their lawyer will get an anonymous call..." Ryan checked his watch. "...about an hour from now telling them where to look. That should put me in the clear."

"You can't do that," Willey said.

"Not me. I'm not doing anything," Ryan replied.

Willey was out of good options, and his face telegraphed it. "How many bars?"

"A little less than two hundred, would be my guess," Ryan answered.

Willey licked his lips.

Ryan and I knew the number was exactly one hundred and eighty-three, about one hundred million dollars' worth.

"This could be quite a coup for you, Mr. Willey. That is, if you move fast enough," Benson said.

"Okay, we have a deal. Where is it?" Willey asked Ryan.

Ryan checked his watch again. "Not until we have it in writing. So I suggest you get busy. The clock is ticking. Oh, and one more thing: Your office will issue a press release clearing Miss Spencer of any involvement in her ex-husband's crimes."

Willey shook his head, but gave in. He called in his assistant to type up the paperwork.

Half an hour later, I had signed paperwork in my hands that gave me back my house and everything else they had taken.

"The Marshal's Service will have trucks there on Monday with the items they seized. Now, where do we find the gold?" Willey asked, checking his watch.

Ryan pulled out Damien's padlock key and handed it over. "Check Brosnahand's garage."

Willey's jaw dropped open. "He had it all along?"

"It looks that way," Ryan replied.

We had counted the bricks when we'd moved the freezer and the gold to Brosnahand's garage. We hadn't wanted it at either of our properties, and this way, when the FBI announced where they'd found it, the cartel would figure they'd been double crossed by a dead man. Brosnahand was in no condition to complain about being the fall guy.

We'd wiped it down to remove any of our fingerprints, though that hadn't done much to remove the stench of rotten hamburger. Dad had been wrong about old appliances lasting forever. The freezer had stopped working sometime after Damien loaded the gold into it.

Willey called his team and gave them the address, smiling all the while. He hung up and turned to Ryan.

"I don't like being manipulated. You should have asked for immunity as a part of this deal. If your information turns out to be right, I'm going to haul you in front of the grand jury next week, and I'm going to enjoy charging you as an accessory."

The man was truly a mean son-of-a-bitch.

Ryan pulled the check out of his pocket again, his get-out-of-jail-free card. "Are you sure you want to try that?"

Willey shook his head, fumed, and walked off.

Once he'd left the room, Benson and Ryan high-fived each other, and I hugged the hell out of my man.

Ryan had pulled off the impossible. He had outmaneuvered the federal government to get my house back, as well as help Damien's victims recoup some of their losses. Maybe I'd share that with the next Damien-hater to cross me.

As we left the conference room I did a double take passing the second cubicle.

Selfie Man.

I hadn't been paranoid, Willey was having me followed.

We walked out of the building, each of us wearing a well-earned grin.

CHAPTER 47

Ryan

THE MIDDAY SUN SHONE BRIGHTLY THE DAY AFTER THE MARSHAL'S Service delivered the last of Natalie's belongings to her Brookline home. But rather than staying home to organize them, today we were evidently going out to lunch.

"I thought you hated country clubs?" I asked as the heavy wooden doors of the Salem Oaks clubhouse closed behind us.

"Normally I do, but not today," Natalie responded cheerfully. "I've made a reservation for us. It's a special luncheon I know you'll enjoy."

I doubted that. These places were too stuffy for me. She'd even made me change out of jeans.

"Nat, KFC with you is my idea of a good time——a lot better than this." I waved my arm at the ostentatious walnut walls and inlaid marble floor. It was all too much for my taste.

She poked my shoulder. "I'm having lunch here, and so are you, so stop complaining and be on your good behavior."

"I'd rather meet you back at the office."

She turned, stomped her high-heeled foot, and fixed me with a glare. "Ryan Westerly, how often do I ask you for a favor?"

The answer was *seldom to never*, but I didn't mouth it.

"This is important to me, so just zip it and play along. Get it?"

"Got it," I answered.

Getting on the wrong side of her temper was never a good idea, and *play along* likely meant she had something unusual planned.

Around the corner, we literally bumped into Liam and his wife, Amy. This wasn't a quiet luncheon for two after all.

After greetings all around, Liam asked, "Does he know the details?" He cocked his head toward me.

"Nope," was Natalie's simple answer, with a wicked smile.

Liam put a hand on my shoulder. "Don't say a word, and everything will work out. That's an order, by the way."

I gulped and nodded. Liam didn't normally give orders. But he was deadly serious when he did.

Out the floor-to-ceiling windows on the far wall, golfers were preparing to tee off——taking practice swings at empty grass in their long pants and garish sweaters. They could have it, as far as I was concerned. Any sport where you didn't work up a sweat wasn't worthy of the designation. Golf wasn't any more of a sport than billiards in my book.

But figuring the money that went in to building and keeping up a palace such as this, a lot of people with money to burn disagreed with me.

"He's at the corner table," Liam said, pointing in a direction I couldn't see from this angle.

Following Liam and Amy toward the corner, I could make out that we were lunching with two men, one significantly older. The younger was Vincent Benson, and the older…

Fucking Stanley Lipwitz.

I recognized the older of the two as someone I'd learned to hate: the CEO of Valestum, the company that had stolen from us. This was bad. I stopped.

Natalie urged me forward. "Now be good and stay quiet. You'll like this. Trust me."

I'd have to work hard not to upchuck sitting at the same table as that criminal. In the end I might try my hand at knife tossing.

"Here they are," Vincent announced as he stood.

"I thought we were going to discuss an investment," Lipwitz said coldly, clearly as surprised to see us as I was him.

"Yes, of course. Stanley, I would like to introduce my good friend Liam Quigley, his lovely wife, Amy; Ryan Westerly, one of Liam's co-workers; and his bride to be, the beautiful Natalie."

We all shook. I even shook the crook's hand, although I did consider twisting it off for a moment.

"You didn't tell me we were meeting with competitors," Lipwitz said to Vincent.

"We're actually not competitors," Liam offered.

The denial took Lipwitz by surprise.

"We're *all* in the business of healing people is how we like to look at it," Liam finished.

Lipwitz nodded. "Of course."

The waiter arrived, and we ordered a round of drinks. Natalie and I stuck to iced tea.

After the waiter departed, Lipwitz began the conversation. "Vince, you said you had some news and a proposition for me."

"Certainly did." Vincent sipped his water while Lipwitz fidgeted, apparently not used to waiting for an answer. "How important would you say good PR is to firms in your industry?"

Lipwitz stroked his chin, either concocting an answer or looking for the trap in the question.

"Pretty much the same as any company. Public relations work is right up there near the top of the list."

"Do you know Channel Eight here in Boston?" Vincent asked.

The rest of us were quiet. The question had clearly been aimed only at Lipwitz.

I was in the same boat as he was here. I couldn't get a read on where this was headed.

"Sure, everybody does," Lipwitz said.

We were interrupted by the waiter bringing our drinks and asking about appetizers. Vincent suggested calamari and bruschetta. Liam agreed, and the rest of us nodded.

"We just bought it," Vincent announced after the waiter retreated.

Lipwitz raised his wine glass. "Congratulations, Vince. That's quite a coup."

Vincent smiled. "Yes, it comes with quite a lot of brand power in New England."

Lipwitz leaned in. "Any way our PR people can get an inside track?" he asked, ever the weasel.

"My thoughts exactly, Stanley," Vincent said, clinking his glass with Lipwitz.

The sleazy crook looked like he'd just won the lottery, being a friend of the new owner of the biggest television station in the area.

Vincent put down his glass. "First, though, Liam has an offer for you to consider."

"Shoot," the sleazeball said.

Liam leaned forward. "We'd like to buy the rights to Acromax from you."

I knew Acromax was their new tradename for CTX-13, the drug they'd stolen from us.

I couldn't believe what I was hearing.

Natalie put a calming hand on my arm, holding me back.

Lipwitz smiled. "How much?"

"One million," Liam answered.

Lipwitz laughed at him. "That's a joke, right? It's worth fifty times that, at least."

Liam's face remained impassive. "Not if you sell it for thirty dollars a dose."

Lipwitz couldn't control his laughter.

The waiter arrived with our appetizers, but Vincent waved him off.

If it weren't for Natalie's insistent hand clamped on my arm, I would have reached over the table to punch this joker.

"Yes or no, the offer doesn't stay on the table," Liam informed the still-laughing Lipwitz.

Lipwitz got control of himself. "No is the answer. No way. We're pricing it at five hundred a dose to start."

He took a swig of his wine and smiled at Liam.

Liam remained composed, much more under control than I felt.

"Stanley," Vincent said, "I warned Liam you might say that."

Lipwitz lifted his glass, believing he'd been vindicated. "Damned straight. I'm no fool."

He wasn't a *fool* for charging five hundred a dose; in my book he was a murderer, sentencing all the patients who couldn't afford it to death.

I smoldered, ready to beat the crap out of him.

Liam nodded to Natalie.

Natalie looked behind us and waved somebody over.

I turned to see White and McNally from the FBI. They were followed by two others I couldn't get a clear look at. The agents wore dark windbreakers with the bold yellow FBI lettering.

The talking at the other tables became hushed as all attention moved to the feds, who stopped two tables away and waited.

"What the hell is this?" Lipwitz demanded.

He was loud enough that the other diners' attention turned to him.

"Calm down, Stanley. You're drawing attention to yourself," Vincent counseled him softly.

Glancing around, Lipwitz composed himself. He took a sip of water and sat up straighter.

Natalie pulled a folded set of papers from her purse and tossed them in front of Lipwitz. "You should read these first."

The man acted like they were radioactive, refusing to touch them.

The other diners lost interest in our little side show, and the low din of conversation started up again.

"It's from someone you know," Natalie told him. "A Gwen Osterhous, who has named you as her co-conspirator in the theft of trade secrets from Chameleon."

The blood drained from Lipwitz's face.

"Did you know trade-secret theft is a federal offense? I only recently found that out," Natalie told the ashen Lipwitz.

Lipwitz shrunk an inch or two in his chair. He stared behind me in the direction of the FBI agents.

I looked back, and the other two behind the agents were now visible: a news reporter with a microphone and a cameraman with a Channel Eight logo on his camera.

Vincent pointed to the FBI duo. "These two agents are here to ask Liam if he wants to press charges against you. And, I have arranged for a Channel Eight crew to provide the press coverage you were asking for."

"I'll sell you the drug. I was just kidding," Lipwitz told Liam, who smiled, but didn't respond.

"How about I give it to you for free?" Lipwitz added.

"There is another alternative," Vincent told him, putting a hand on his shoulder.

"Alternative?" Lipwitz asked.

I looked back. The agents were still standing two tables away.

Natalie leaned forward. "You agree to sell Acromax for ten dollars a dose to anyone who needs it, and we will keep this piece of paper between us," she said softly.

"Ten? I can't. That's below cost."

Natalie continued, "The bonus is that the news crew is here, so you can tell the world how generous you're being because you care so much about the patients that will benefit from the drug."

She'd thrown him a bone I wouldn't have. The crook didn't deserve it.

Lipwitz perked up and nodded vigorously. "I like that idea. Ten dollars is great."

"Stanley," Vincent said. "If you could excuse us, we'd like to finish our meal, and you can hold your little press conference out front. I know the club manager would rather the other diners not be inconvenienced."

Lipwitz stood and straightened his jacket. "Good idea. Good to see you, Vince." He didn't mention the rest of us.

None of us reciprocated the goodbye.

Lipwitz escorted the news crew outside, and Natalie motioned the agents over.

Now that the commotion had died down, our waiter deemed it safe to bring the appetizers to the table.

The FBI agents approached.

Natalie addressed them as they arrived. "Thank you for waiting, guys. We just had to convince that man to give up his seat for you. Hope you brought appetites."

The duo pulled out chairs and sat. White took the seat next to Natalie. "Thank you, Miss Spencer. It's not often we get to eat at a club like this."

"Like, never," McNally concurred.

"And thank you for wearing the jackets," Natalie added. "It makes us look like big shots here."

They laughed.

Natalie leaned toward me. "I told you you'd like it."

Boy, was she ever right. The patients would get CTX-13 at an even lower price than we had planned, and we had the goods on Valestum that would keep them from ever trying to steal from us again.

For a moment I had wanted Lipwitz to refuse the offer and be carted off to jail, but that wouldn't have helped the patients, even if it would have made me feel better——for at least today.

But I could see now that what Natalie, Liam, and Vincent had cooked up had been far superior.

"You could have told me," I whispered to Natalie.

"Not my decision. Talk to Liam," she responded.

I leaned in to kiss my Cupcake. "I thought we agreed no secrets."

"No secrets doesn't mean no surprises," she answered with a wink.

~

NATALIE

"ARE YOU READY TO DO THIS?" RYAN ASKED.

"Not really," I admitted. I was scared. "What if it doesn't work?"

Ryan's arm around my shoulders pulled me closer. "Don't worry, truth is stronger than hate."

I wasn't so sure of that. He let go of me to open the door, always the gentleman. I missed the warmth of him by my side as we entered the Peet's near my old house.

The staring started immediately, and the background noise of a dozen conversations fell off dramatically.

Ryan urged me forward to the counter.

The barista behind the register was an old timer, from happier days. Her eyes met mine, and her smile drooped to a frown. She left the register silently and turned her back on me. She picked up a coffee jug to wash in the sink behind her.

Nothing had changed. Typhoid Mary would have gotten a warmer welcome.

My ex-neighbor, Mrs. Garnsey, left her seat to stalk up to me. "You have some nerve coming here, Winterbourne." The hatred in her eyes was ten times worse than the tone of her voice.

I stepped back, but Ryan urged me forward with a hand at my back.

"Haven't you taken enough from us?" she yelled as she approached.

I stepped forward into her space, and she stopped. "It's not Winterbourne. My name is Spencer, so stop calling me that," I yelled back. "He took money from you, but he took even more from me. He robbed me of my identity and years of my life, so GIVE ME A BREAK!"

Her mouth dropped open, but no words came out.

"You can hate him all you want, but I didn't do anything to you. He ruined me too. Go visit the cemetery and spit on his grave if you want. That's what I do."

Okay, not really. His uncle had buried him in Ohio, but it *was* how I felt, and it had the desired effect on her.

Mrs. Garnsey backed up a step.

"My name is Spencer, and I'm getting on with my life," I told them all, looking around the room. "You should too."

Garnsey didn't apologize——that would take time——but she returned to her table and the normal morning coffee shop conversations began again.

I turned back to the counter and the barista had returned.

"What would you like, Miss Spencer?" she asked, this time with half a smile.

"A medium caffè mocha," I responded. "And it's Natalie."

"Make it two," Ryan added.

The barista rang us up, and we waited at the end of the counter.

For the first time in a long time, I felt *almost* at ease in here.

After collecting our cups of hot, chocolaty goodness, Ryan held the door for me to exit.

"How does it feel?" he asked once we'd returned to the sidewalk.

"Liberating," I told him.

The morning sun warmed my back as we strolled.

"I told you it would."

I hadn't been so sure, but he had been right about this——he had been right about a lot of things.

I was Natalie damned Spencer, and I was done backing down. I was done running from these crazy people. This was not just Ryan's town, it was mine. They weren't going to run me off. I was here to stay…with weekends in Vermont.

We turned the corner back to my house, the house I had earned. It wasn't as nice as Ryan's place, but it was mine, all mine, and that meant everything.

EPILOGUE

⚜

A HEART THAT LOVES IS ALWAYS YOUNG.
– GREEK PROVERB

NATALIE

THE FOG OF SLEEP SLOWLY LIFTED, AND I REALIZED IT WAS RYAN'S morning wood poking me from behind, as always. After the flight delays, we had gotten in late last night. We were home again, in the palace in the sky. The blackout curtains had done their job, and we had overslept.

We had a party planned at my old house this afternoon, and we needed to get supplies and prepare. After a ten-day honeymoon in the Bahamas, the fridge would need to be restocked, and the house was a mess.

Ryan's hand found my breast, and his fingers circled my nipple. "Good morning, Mrs. Westerly."

The way my new name rolled off his tongue was like magic. It made me feel renewed every time he said it.

I reached behind me to grab Mega-cock. "Good morning, Dr. Westerly." I rolled his direction and kissed him. "You know we have a party to put on this afternoon, and we still have to go over and get the house ready."

He craned his neck to check the clock. "Not that soon."

I tried to get up. "We don't have time."

He pulled me back down. "I can be quick if you can."

I turned toward him, gripped the nape of his neck, and pulled him to me for another kiss. My mouth captured his, and our tongues intertwined.

"You're never quick." Liquid heat pooled in my pussy at the thought of what he was about to do to me.

"Try me."

Ryan didn't understand quick. His idea of quick was to make me come once or twice before I got Mega-cock. Un-quick in his world meant a lot more teasing than that, and we didn't have the time. His arm slid under the covers, and his fingers parted my folds. A finger dipped inside me to bring lubrication forward to my clit. He started to work his masterful fingers, and the sensations flooded over me.

His cock was rock hard this morning. I had tried turning the tables on him by pulling and twisting and squeezing in all the ways Jasmin had shared one drunken evening. I was learning how to drive him crazy, but I wasn't yet good enough to get him to come as quickly as he could drive me over the cliff.

His head went to my chest. Licks, blowing of cold air, and light nips of my nipples sent shocks through me. I never lacked attention in any of my erogenous zones.

I clawed at his hair and pulled him up to me for a kiss. He tasted like passion and desire. I ached with the same.

His thigh came over mine, pushing against the hand working its magic on my clit——with quick side trips to tease my entrance. The circling and teasing increased my yearning for his touch as his other hand took up nipple-circling duty, always taunting me.

I rocked my hips into him, but he only pulled back, still teasing. All the things he did to me while denying me his cock only made me want him more.

I pulled and squeezed on him. I begged him to enter me. And

then… It wasn't record time, but it must have been close. Ryan knew how to push all my buttons, and he forced me over the cliff and my convulsions took over.

"I love you, Cupcake," he breathed, which only made my convulsions stronger.

As soon as I recovered from his sensual torture, I pushed his leg off, rolled over on my stomach, and poked my ass up. I knew this position would get him to come the quickest. I didn't get to watch him, but I got to play with his balls sometimes.

He moved behind me, and the tip of Mega-cock found my entrance. He started to push in slowly, but I wasn't planning on slow.

I thrust back into him, taking his length. He slid in smoothly, filling me to my limit.

"Give it to me, cowboy."

He spanked me and grabbed my hips, thrusting again and again.

I egged him on with repeated calls to "fuck me harder" and "give me more." I'd learned a little dirty talk turned him on, and I wanted to give him back all the pleasure he'd always given me.

I rocked back into him as his tempo increased and his breathing hitched.

He finally pounded out his release, coming down to rest on me as he pushed me forward, flat on the bed.

He kissed my neck and licked my ear. "I love you, Mrs. Westerly," he panted.

"Love you more, Dr. Westerly."

"Love you most, Mrs. Westerly."

I loved that he had given me his name, along with everything I had ever wished for. He showed me each and every day how much I meant to him. It had taken me a second try, but I finally had a husband, and a partner, in the true meaning of the word. And he'd also helped me to know myself better.

I squirmed out from under him. "We have to get going." I headed to the shower.

~

NATALIE

RYAN SWEPT THE PATIO OUT BACK AT MY HOUSE WHILE I STIRRED cilantro into the potato salad. The barbecue fixings were almost ready.

The doorbell rang.

Ralph saw me coming and disappeared under the couch.

Before I could get there, Jasmin had let herself in.

"Don't you look gorgeous? Love the tan," she said as she gave me a big hug. She handed me a FedEx letter envelope. "This was out front."

I set the envelope aside.

Our honeymoon in the Bahamas had been just the ticket. Sun, sand, clear water, lots of rest, and my man. It was exactly what I'd needed to recharge after the wedding.

I looked around now, realizing Jasmin had sauntered in alone. Sensing my consternation, she tugged me toward the kitchen.

"Don't ask." She showed me her hand. The promise ring was gone.

"You broke up?"

She laughed. "Too much work and not enough progress. He never stopped talking——and when it wasn't about sports, it was all about him. Good thing I only took three suitcases out to LA. I dropped 'em all at the apartment on my way over." She twirled around in a circle. "So I'm back."

"I'm sorry."

"You win some, you lose some," she replied. "I'm ready for

my next little r." She checked her watch. "I've been unattached for almost twelve hours. Does Ryan have any good-looking friends?"

"You're terrible," I scolded.

"I'm terrible at being alone," she corrected. "It never hurts to start looking."

Ryan came in from the backyard, and the door slammed behind him. "You need a doorstop or something for that."

Damien had been paranoid it wouldn't shut securely and had installed an extra-strength spring on the closer.

"*We* need," I corrected him.

"Right, Mrs. Westerly... Hi, Jaz. How long you back for?"

I smiled. Hearing him call me that still sent a tingle up my back.

"I'm staying. I'm tired of LA," Jasmin said.

Ryan didn't skip a beat. "You know you're welcome here anytime you want to come over."

"Thanks," she said.

With Jasmin's help, it only took a minute to coax Ralph out from his hiding place and lock him away before somebody else opened the front door and he escaped.

"I need a guy who will listen more than he talks," Jasmin said as we stowed Ralph away.

"So now he has to be good-looking *and* a listener?"

"And smart and rich," she added.

"Anything else on your wish list?"

"No, that's all," she said, smiling.

"Good luck with that."

"Well, you found one."

She hit that nail on the head. I certainly had found one, one in a million.

"I'll keep my eyes peeled for you."

She wandered into the kitchen, humming to herself.

Ryan was at the front table, examining the envelope Jasmin had brought in. "Cupcake, you'll want to open this."

Looking more closely, I saw that the envelope was from the law school at Harvard.

I trembled as I ripped it open and slid the letter inside out onto the table.

The moment of truth had arrived.

Ryan put his arm around me and pulled my hip to his. "I have faith."

I wasn't so sure. I tore at the envelope and pulled out the single sheet of paper.

I read the letter slowly. After they thanked me for applying, I got to the line that said I had been accepted to enroll for next semester. Relief flooded me and tears filled my eyes. I had worked so hard to follow in Dad's footsteps, and now I could.

Ryan had been reading along, and he picked me up. He twirled me around twice and set me back down. "I knew it."

I wiped my eyes and sniffed, overcome by joy. Now I had the opportunity Damien had denied me.

"This calls for champagne," Ryan announced.

After a quick celebratory drink, Ryan insisted on taping my letter to the front door for all to see.

Then Jasmin and I busied ourselves with food preparation, while Ryan went outside to skim the leaves out of the pool.

Damien had insisted on a house with a pool. It made an impressive statement when we had guests over. In the evening, the glow from the lights transformed the backyard into a magical place to entertain.

I put a Post-it note on the front door telling people to let themselves in. We wouldn't be able to hear the doorbell from the back.

Over the course of the next hour, Liam and Amy arrived, along with Ryan's lab assistant Paul, Rick from IT, and half a dozen others from work, including Syd Roundhouse and his assistant, Terry.

I took a moment to thank Terry and Paul personally again.

Their flexibility with weekend schedules had allowed us to make our regular visits to the Vermont cabin.

Jasmin sought me out as I was setting the tables. "What's the deal with the guy in the plaid shirt?" she whispered, tilting her head toward the lab-rat group.

Paul was the only one in plaid.

"His name is Paul. He works in Ryan's lab. Wicked smart, a nice guy."

She leaned close. "Is he a listener or a talker?"

"I don't know if he's a listener, but he's definitely not a talker." Paul rarely spliced as many as four words together.

She wandered in their direction, and I went back to the kitchen.

"Look at that tan. You look beautiful," Briana exclaimed as she came in, followed by David. The Bahamian tan seemed to be my signature achievement of the last few weeks.

"The secret is tons of sunscreen," I told her. I had been scared shitless I would burn and ruin the honeymoon if I didn't constantly slather it on. The system had worked like a charm.

David clamped himself around my legs.

I knelt down for a hug. "How are you, big guy?"

"Mommy said I get to help with the cooking," he said excitedly.

I let go of him. "You'll have to talk to your uncle Ryan about that. He's in charge of the cooking out back."

In a flash he was at the door. "Uncle Ryan! Mommy said I can help you cook," he yelled. The door banged shut after him.

Briana and I joined the crowd in the yard after making a few trips to bring the plates and food outside.

Ryan had David standing on a chair so he could turn the burgers on the grill, and only one ended up on the ground——at least that I saw. I took the errant burger into the kitchen, wrapped it, and put in the fridge for Ralph later.

The doorbell rang again.

I opened the door to find Kirk Willey. "What do you want?"

He was carrying a bag. "I come bearing gifts, Mrs. Westerly."
It was the first time he'd gotten my name right. "I'd like to talk to
you and your husband, if he's around."

"We're having a few people over. He's out back." Reluctantly I
stood aside and let him in.

Ryan was serving up burgers and dogs on a plate when we
found him.

"Kirk," Ryan called out.

He was now on a first-name basis with this creep? I stood back.

"Glad you could make it," Ryan added.

Glad? His arrival wasn't a coincidence?

Willey eyed me cautiously. "You didn't tell her?"

Ryan laughed. "Not yet. I thought you could do the honors.
After we eat, maybe?"

I had no idea what was going on here, and a quick jab to
Ryan's ribs didn't loosen his tongue.

We sat and ate at the tables. Briana and David joined Ryan,
Willey, and me——an odd pairing if ever there was one. We were
sitting in the backyard of the house Willey had personally taken
from me, and Ryan had invited him to our barbecue.

I stepped on my husband's foot. "What is going on?" I
whispered.

He didn't respond except to tell me to wait. He cut his burger
with his ever-present Swiss Army knife.

The suspense was killing me. I finished the last of my meal and
pushed my plate away with a flourish. "I'm done."

Ryan forked the last of his potato salad and motioned to Willey.
"You can tell her now."

"We would like to thank you for your help with the case
against Mr. Brosnahand's associates," Willey began. "The phone
and the notebook proved invaluable in referring charges against
seven high-ranking cartel members who were arrested on Friday."

Except for the arrests, this was old news. I had found Brosnahand's phone on the trail by the tripping branch, where Ryan and

he had fought. We had put it in with the gold and the notebook Damien had left in the freezer when we'd moved everything to Brosnahand's garage. We'd needed the FBI to find it, and the cartel to think Brosnahand had had it all along.

"I'm afraid I don't know what you're talking about," I told him.

"Yes, I understand," he said.

He went over to the grill and retrieved the bag he had carried in.

I waited for further explanation.

He placed the bag on the table with a thud. "Your husband's ——excuse me, ex-husband's records were quite thorough. They prove conclusively that he purchased this prior to your marriage, and prior to any of the activities he was indicted for. So..." He pulled a gleaming gold ingot from the bag. He needed two hands. "This bar belongs to you." He set the gold down on the table.

"Can I hold it?" David cried out.

"If you can lift it," Ryan told him.

David came around the table to try, and he failed, which we could have predicted.

"It's heavy," David complained.

"Maybe when you're older," his mother told him.

Ryan hefted the bar. "I know what to do with this." He walked over, opened the door to the house, and used the bar to prop it in place.

"A door stop, really?" I asked.

"At least it's being useful."

Willey excused himself and said goodbye.

"You know he didn't have to do that," Ryan told me after he'd gone. "They could have kept it, and nobody would have known."

I looked over at my half-million-dollar present. "Maybe he's not that bad after all."

Curiosity got the better of our guests, and they all went over to admire the world's most expensive door stop.

When they returned to the tables, I noticed Paul and Jasmin sitting together, quite close.

Ryan eyed them as well, and he called Jasmin over. He whispered to her off to the side for a second.

She giggled and returned to her table, and Paul.

"What was that about?" I asked when he returned to me.

"I warned her she couldn't make him late for work," he whispered.

I looked their direction again, and gave my sister the thumbs up when she glanced my way.

She smiled and went back to talking to Paul.

I was walking dishes into the kitchen when I bumped into a late arrival.

"Liam told me to come," she said quickly. It was Gwen.

"Sure, come on in," I told her. "Everybody's out back. There's still plenty of food left."

"Thanks." She waited for me to join her before venturing into the backyard.

Liam had talked with Gwen and decided not to press charges. It turned out Ryan and Gwen shared a common bond. They each had relatives with the misfortune to contract one of these orphan diseases Ryan was working so hard to cure.

Nobody at work had known anything about her niece's condition. We'd learned after the arrest that Gwen had stolen the data and sold it to Valestum to afford the treatment for her niece that insurance wouldn't cover.

Once they'd cleared the air, Liam had also insisted she come back to work for Chameleon. Gwen had originally resisted the idea, but she'd agreed to start again next week.

"Hi, Gwen," Ryan called out.

The looks from the other work people weren't as kind as Ryan's greeting.

"It will take some time, but they'll come around," I reassured her softly.

She shrugged, not seeming convinced.

She walked over to Ryan and gave him a hug. "I can't thank you enough, Dr. Westerly."

"Ryan," he corrected her. "How's Ginny doing?"

"Better now," she said.

I left them alone to talk about her niece, Ginny.

Now Ryan was paying for Ginny's treatment himself, a gesture than made me especially proud to call myself Mrs. Westerly. Both of my married names started with a W, but they couldn't have been more opposite in every other way.

Our table was now just me and my husband, as Ryan finished what had to be his sixth or seventh of my chocolate chip cookies.

I looked around and noticed we were one person short. "Wasn't Vincent going to come by?"

"He was, until I told him Willey might be joining us."

I stopped Ryan's hand as he reached for another cookie. "That's enough, don't you think?"

He frowned. "Chocolate is good for you. It's in all the medical journals."

"I'm sure they also include the words *in moderation*," I countered.

"Not that I remember." He used his other hand and snatched another cookie.

This chocolate line was similar to another medical fact he liked to share: Frequent ejaculations were tied to lower prostate cancer risk.

I was certainly happy to be doing my part to keep him safe and healthy.

Ryan finished the cookie, but he didn't make a move for another.

"Hey, David, come over here," Ryan called to his nephew.

The little boy came running. He had been trying once again to lift the gold bar. Not successfully.

Ryan took his Swiss Army knife from his pocket and handed it to him. "My father gave me this when I was about your age. He said to always keep it with me and it would bring me good luck. Do you think you're old enough to handle it?"

David nodded enthusiastically and accepted the gift. "Yeah." His eyes lit up as he turned the knife over and over, inspecting every inch of it. "Thanks, Uncle Ryan." He successfully opened and closed the main blade.

"The luck comes from keeping it in your pocket. Take good care of it now, and be extra careful," Ryan cautioned.

"Good luck charm?" I asked quietly as David walked away.

He pulled me in for a quick kiss. "Lucky enough to bring me you."

The luck had been all mine.

My new husband had the biggest heart in the entire town.

And I was the luckiest girl in Boston, because that heart belonged to me.

THE END

SNEAK PEEK: CAUGHT BY THE BILLIONAIRE

CHAPTER 1

⁂

VINCENT

THE MAN IN THE SUIT HAD FOLLOWED ME ALL THE WAY HERE FROM work this evening. It was the third time I'd noticed him in the last two weeks.

I stepped inside Holmby's Grill and peeked out the tinted window after the door closed. After a few seconds of not seeing the suited man, I found my way to my usual table in the corner. I mentally kicked myself for not getting a picture of him for our security team to check out.

Less than a minute later, *she* walked up on her tall black heels with the self assurance of the runway model she had once been. Her tits jiggled under the loose fabric of her low cut dress——a dress that flaunted her ample cleavage and threatened to open just a bit too far, but unfortunately never quite did.

Half the men in the restaurant stared as she greeted me with a warm hug. No doubt they wished they were me. And rightly so. Staci Baxter and I would be getting hot and heavy between the sheets before the night was out. She had a body to die for, and knew how to work it. A night with Staci never disappointed.

"Vince," she purred as I pulled out her chair.

She liked to tease me by going braless in low-cut dresses, and it was working tonight. A quick peek down her dress before I rounded the table to my seat jolted my cock.

Staci had no doubt gotten a million teenage boys off via her body-paint pictures in the *Sports Illustrated* swimsuit issue. Since retiring from modeling, she had devoted all her time to her new clothing line.

Her jaw showed an uncommon tenseness this evening.

"You okay? I asked.

She glanced down. "I'm little nervous is all. I could use some wine."

I waved our waiter over. "That I can help with."

He arrived quickly.

"A bottle of Opus One Proprietary Red, please," I told him.

She managed a pasted-on smile after he left and sipped her water——a definite off night for her.

I asked about her sister, and that seemed to calm her while our waiter sought out the wine.

When he returned I approved the bottle, and she guzzled down most of a glass.

She fiddled with her silverware. "I'm not sure I'm ready."

"Don't worry, tomorrow's meeting with the bank will go just fine with the presentation you've got."

"Vince, you've been such a help. I just don't know if it's good enough." Her nervousness was understandable; asking for a half-million dollar bank loan would make anybody stressed.

"You've got this."

Our waiter returned, and I ordered the gorgonzola truffle-crusted New York strip steak, and Staci chose the lamb chops.

"Do you want to go over it one last time?" I asked.

She smiled. "Please." She pulled the presentation folder from her oversized purse.

She placed it on the table and began the spiel I'd worked out with her. "Gentlemen..." she started out.

The food arrived just as she finished the presentation.

I topped off our wine glasses and raised mine to her. "Sounded damned good to me. You don't have anything to worry about."

The blush that rose in her cleavage was enticing.

I cut my first piece of steak. "Now, tell me more about how your little sister is getting on in New York."

She perked up and started with how hard it had been for her sister to find a place to live in the city.

An hour later, we had finished dinner and decided against dessert.

We had long since left the topic of her presentation tomorrow, but the undercurrent of nervousness in her demeanor hadn't dissipated.

"Staci, do you want to talk about what's really bothering you?"

She hesitated before retrieving her purse. After a moment of rummaging, she pulled out a piece of folded paper and extended it across the table with a shaky hand.

I opened it.

Stay away from Vincent Benson unless you want to become collateral damage, the note read.

My stomach turned over.

"What is going on, Vince?"

The meaning was clear enough. Someone was messing with me and using her to do it.

"It's probably nothing... I can arrange some security for you, though."

"I live on the safest street in town. The chief of police lives next door. It looks like you should be the one watching out."

I took a picture of the note before grasping it with my napkin and folding it up. "Mind if I take this?"

She nodded.

There was probably nothing worthwhile on it, but I folded it inside the napkin and stuffed it in my pocket nonetheless.

I turned the conversation back to her clothing business while I mulled over who would be messing with me. No faces came to mind.

Sensing our meal had come to a close, I offered, "I've got a really nice bottle of port upstairs."

She wiped her lips with her napkin, but her eyes telegraphed the answer before the words arrived. "Not tonight, Vince. I've been stressing over this presentation all day, and I'm bushed. How 'bout a rain check?"

It wasn't the first time she'd begged off from our after-dinner gymnastics, but it *was* unusual. This was a standing date we had pretty much every Monday night.

No strings attached, just a good time. Neither of us did commitments, so neither of us expected anything more than companionship and physical pleasure. "Casual intimacy with friendship on the side," she had once called it. She seemed to be the only woman in town who didn't want or expect anything more from me——except Barb, of course.

My situation with Barbara was more commercial in nature. Gifts changed hands, but never cash. She was attractive arm candy when I needed it and an enthusiastic bed partner when I wanted some variety, but the side of friendship I had with Staci wasn't the same with Barb.

"I'll call you," Staci said when we made it to the door.

It wasn't a call I expected soon.

I opened the door for her and waited while she hailed a cab. I checked up and down the street for the suited man. All clear, for now.

After she entered the cab, I checked again in the direction of my condo on Tremont Street. Its safety was not far away.

Before starting out, I rubbed the ring I always wore.

~

ASHLEY

"I'M GOING TO BEAT YOU OUT FOR THAT LA PROMOTION," MY opponent, Elizabeth Parsons, said as she stepped sideways on the mat, looking for an opening to attack me.

I slid to my left and dodged her first attempt. "Try all you want, Liz. But a brunette like you will stand out like a sore thumb in the sea of blondes in California."

She lunged at me again.

We tumbled to the ground, and she initially had the upper hand, but I had the leverage and weight advantage and pinned her fifteen seconds later.

She patted out.

"That makes three," I said.

"Best of seven?" she asked.

As the only women in the office, we usually sparred against each other——and Liz hated losing.

I checked the wall clock in the gym. "Out of time today."

We had gone through Quantico together. At the Academy and every day since, she had made up for her lack of stature with competitiveness and pure determination. She was shorter than me, and more buxom, which meant men often underestimated her. More than one bad guy had taken her for a pushover and ended up with a cracked skull thanks to her baton skills.

We grabbed our towels and headed to the showers. There wasn't a lot of time before our eight o'clock bullpen meeting.

~

FORTY MINUTES LATER, FBI BOSTON FIELD OFFICE SPECIAL

Agent in Charge Randy White looked up when we entered the bullpen precisely on time. He checked his watch. "You're late."

Liz started to complain. "But——"

"New rule: no less than three minutes early, understood?"

Anybody else would have accepted our arrival or told us five minutes early. Only SAC White would come up with something asinine like three minutes. He invented another stupid rule every few weeks——something my partner, John McNally, called Caesar moments.

"Yes, sir," Liz and I said in unison.

From across the room, John rolled his eyes just enough for me to see.

White had been promoted six months ago to the SAC position. Before that he'd been one of us in the bullpen, and only a little difficult to get along with. Now he was the boss, and beyond difficult. *Randy* was no longer allowed, either. *Sir* had replaced it. The running joke was that the new budget would have to have a remodeling line item for changing out the doors to ones his ego could fit through.

The special agents had started betting on how long this phase would last. My bet had been six months——that's how long it took SAC Sinella, the previous occupant of that office, to settle down. Sinella's transfer to Nashville had triggered White's promotion to Asshole Behind the Glass.

Liz and I both had to kiss up to him because he would ultimately recommend one of us for the Los Angeles opening.

White motioned for Liz to join him in his office. "Parsons, new assignment."

She followed him and closed the door.

"What the fuck's with this stupid three-minute rule?" I asked John.

He shrugged. "He told us just before you two got here." He shook his head. "I'm changing my bet to nine months. The guy should be over his stupid Caesar routine by now, but he's definitely not."

"I'll call the agency," Liz said as she left White's office a few minutes later. "Sweet undercover assignment," she mumbled as she passed by my desk, trying to get a rise out of me.

The men in the office seemed oblivious, but it was clear to me: White had gotten balls deep into Liz during that ski weekend in New Hampshire last year.

She'd denied it when I confronted her about it, but the shift in her had been easy enough to see. Back when we were all in the bullpen together, she would walk in front of his desk on her way to the coffee room, and although he tried to hide it, his eyes would follow her.

And now, it seemed White had given her the plum assignment.

I wasn't in a mood to make a scene. My last undercover had netted me a month in a cockroach- and bedbug-infested cover apartment that still gave me the shivers when I thought about it. When your cover persona was down and out, the bureau went out of its way to make the entire experience realistic, and the latest budget cut had us going even further down-market in arranging cover locations.

The Bureau didn't reward people who rocked the boat.

Liz opened the folder on her desk. "Jacinda? Do I look like a Jacinda to you?" she mumbled rhetorically. She shook her head and kept reading.

I didn't answer. She didn't expect one.

CHAPTER 2

VINCENT

THE NEXT MORNING STARTED WITH FIREWORKS.

This one had a temper. "Fired? You can't fire me. I quit," she yelled.

The stapler she threw missed me and hit the wall with a bang. Security grabbed her arms and escorted her out.

It took Morgan Parker, my number two, all of a minute to end up in my office and close the door. "What the hell did you do this time?"

"Nothing," I insisted.

Nothing more than I ever did. I insisted on accuracy with my PA, and that didn't suit Marcy what's-her-name very well.

He plopped down in the red chair he always chose. "At this rate, in a year there won't be anybody left in Boston willing to apply."

"Fuck you."

"What's got you in such a piss-poor mood this morning?"

I pulled up the picture of the note Staci had received and

handed my phone to Morgan. "Staci found that on her car yesterday."

He scanned it. "Somebody's messing with you."

"No shit, Sherlock. Now you tell me who."

He handed the phone back. "Fuck anybody's wife lately?"

"Fuck no, and you know that."

I had played the field, but married women were never my style. And after Marilyn last year went full-house psycho on me when I wouldn't call her back, I'd ended up limiting myself to Barbara and Staci: the only two that were certified commitment-phobes, safe dates without emotional expectations, merely material ones.

As long as they were supplied with expensive dinners, shopping trips, and the occasional extravagant gift, those ladies were happy and supplied me with enjoyable interludes in the bedroom. The gifts were most often jewelry, but never, never would they expect a ring.

My mission here in Boston was simple and clear: grow the Eastern division of Covington both in size and profitability to a point my father couldn't ignore.

He hadn't wanted to give me control of Benson Corp. back home in California. He said I wasn't seasoned enough, or experienced enough, and I intended to show him he was wrong, completely wrong.

"Just checking," Morgan responded. "You ought to give it to security."

"Already did."

"At least you have the advantage now."

"How so?"

"They've given up the element of surprise. You know somebody's coming at you."

Morgan left after badgering me for a few more minutes about who I might have pissed off recently.

I called down to Judith in HR.

She was expecting my call. "I'll have another candidate here tomorrow morning, Mr. Benson."

"Not soon enough. After lunch," I said.

"Yes, sir" came the immediate response.

I glanced at the picture of the note another time. The question remained: who was coming after me and why?

The why could only be answered by knowing the who.

I returned to my spreadsheet on the Semaphore acquisition. Getting our hands on them would be my crowning achievement so far, and it was looking good.

An hour later, the numbers were all swimming on the screen in front of me. I needed a break to clear my head.

Once on the treadmill downstairs, the hum of the machine and the pounding of my feet relaxed me. Exercise always cleared the slate mentally and allowed me to return to a problem with renewed focus.

~

AFTER LUNCH, A KNOCK CAME AT MY OFFICE DOOR.

I checked my watch: half-past one. "Yes?"

Judith from HR popped in. "I've got your new PA outside, if you're ready to meet her."

I closed the spreadsheet and rose.

The girl walked in with plenty of hip swivel and offered a firm handshake. Tall red heels, a short blue skirt, and an only partially buttoned pink top were meant to distract——and had the desired effect.

She extended her resume. "Jacinda Wilder."

Judith excused herself.

I accepted the resume and caught myself drawn to the well of her cleavage as she sat——definitely deep enough to get lost in. I glanced down at the resume and asked her about her experience.

She had an impressive list of prior jobs, but none had lasted very long.

"The nature of temporary work," she explained. "I often get called to fill in for maternity leaves or unexpected vacancies."

The way she smirked when she said *unexpected vacancies* made me guess she was the revenge the boss brought in when his wife decided the old assistant had been too good looking.

"This position can be quite demanding," I told her.

She smiled. "I'm available any time of the day or night, as much time as you need, and whatever services you need."

I wasn't interested, but her implication was naughty.

I liked this girl. Her answers were all couched cautiously, not divulging very much information——exactly the kind of discretion we needed here.

~

ASHLEY

LIZ WAS BACK EARLY AFTER HER FIRST DAY UNDERCOVER, AND NOT looking happy from where I could see her through the glass of the boss's office.

I couldn't make out what was being said, but White was gesticulating in a menacing manner.

He opened the door. "Newton, get in here."

I hustled over.

"You fucked up," White said, pointing at Liz. "Getting blown after less than a day? What were you thinking, Parsons?"

Liz wisely didn't answer.

"This is way too important a case for you to screw it up."

"It's not screwed, not yet," Liz argued. "They threw me out, but we can still get Ashley in, and I don't think they made me, actually."

"What do you call getting caught in the subject's office on the first day, and getting walked out?"

"I got them thinking I worked freelance for a tabloid. The guy is a gossip magnet. They'll think I was looking for dirt to publish, not connect me to here. That tabloid identity just has to be fully backstopped, and they'll stop looking. We're not blown yet."

Liz had thought ahead, if she had that already worked out. It sounded plausible enough to me.

White scratched his chin. "Tabloid could work. Get Randy to help you backstop that front."

"In the meantime," Liz continued, "we send Ashley in right away. They have no way to connect the two of us."

White closed his eyes momentarily. "Newton, you're up then." His eyes bored into mine. "And you better do a better job of this than Parsons here."

"Yes, sir," I answered.

Nothing else would have been acceptable.

Still newly promoted, White's reputation would suffer for a long time if he messed up a big case. Translation: I was cannon fodder, and if anything went wrong, it was my fault. I'd fall on the boss's sword for him, or suffer the consequences.

"Newton, a word," he said, indicating it was time for Liz to leave, which she did without argument.

The door closed.

I took a seat.

"Parsons has better evals than you," he said.

I schooled my face to not show the anger I felt. As far as our evaluations under Sinella went, I knew the statement to be a lie. Liz and I had shared once, and our evals were identical. It could only mean that Liz's evals had been helped by her hide-the-salami sessions with our new boss, and that wasn't fair. I wasn't traveling that road.

"This is DOJ's top priority, so I really want to get this guy," he said. "If you close this case quickly and solidly, I'll make sure you beat out Parsons for the LA slot."

"Thank you, sir" was all I said. I had no doubt he could swing it whichever way he wanted it to go.

My new boss was a much bigger pig than I had thought possible yesterday, but I could only deal with the situation presented to me. The only option for escape was to nail this assignment and get the hell out of Dodge.

He tapped the closed folder in front of him. "DOJ has information that this guy is running drugs through his import business. Oxy and fentanyl mostly. The objective here is to cut off the head of the snake, not just the low-level minions. We want the top guy. Wiretap warrants have been turned down, so you're going undercover inside this guy's business so we can nail him."

"In what capacity?"

White opened the folder on his desk. "His secretary."

I nodded. This certainly beat out my last assignment, an executive assistant wouldn't be getting the crap cover motel I'd gotten last time.

"This won't be an easy undercover," he added. "Since Parsons isn't the first one he's fired this month, you have to figure out how to last longer than she did."

"Not a problem, sir."

"Good. I'm counting on you." He handed the folder across the desk.

"Our contact in the personnel agency is listed on the first page, and she'll be expecting your call. Develop a cover and use John for whatever backup you need."

"Is that all, sir?"

He went back to his screen and flicked his hand toward the door, shooing me away as if I were a fly on the desk.

After I closed the door behind me, I gritted my teeth and realized the faint odor in his office wasn't the new carpet. It was the stench of the swine inhabiting it.

Catching the local DOJ's top target was a career-making assignment. Back at my desk, I opened the file. The problem was on the second page: the name of our target.

Turning this down wasn't an option. Randy Turnbull had refused an assignment White gave him last month and was now in the Alaska field office chasing caribou rustlers or something.

Vincent Benson had taken me to our high school prom, and I had just been assigned to nail his hide to the wall.

I am so fucked.

❧

JOIN ERIN'S MAILING LIST AND BE NOTIFIED WHEN THIS BOOK AND others are available.

ALSO BY ERIN SWANN

The Billionaire's Trust - Available on Amazon, also in AUDIOBOOK

(Bill and Lauren's story) He needed to save the company. He needed her. He couldn't have both. The wedding proposal in front of hundreds was like a fairy tale come true—Until she uncovered his darkest secret.

The Youngest Billionaire - Available on Amazon

(Steven and Emma's story) The youngest of the Covington clan, he avoided the family business to become a rarity, an honest lawyer. He didn't suspect that pursuing her could destroy his career. She didn't know what trusting him could cost her.

The Secret Billionaire – Available on Amazon, also in AUDIOBOOK

(Patrick and Elizabeth's story) Women naturally circled the flame of wealth and power, and his is brighter than most. Does she love him? Does she not? There's no way to know. When he stopped to help her, Liz mistook him for a carpenter. Maybe this time he'd know. Everything was perfect. Until the day she left.

The Billionaire's Hope - Available on Amazon

(Nick and Katie's story) They came from different worlds. She hadn't seen him since the day he broke her brother's nose. Her family retaliated by destroying his life. She never suspected where accepting a ride from him today would take her. They said they could do casual. They lied.

Previously titled: Protecting the Billionaire

Picked by the Billionaire – Available on Amazon

(Liam and Amy's story) A night she wouldn't forget. An offer she couldn't refuse. He alone could save her, and she held the key to his survival. If only they could pass the test together.

Caught by the Billionaire – Available on Amazon

(Vincent and Ashley's story) Her undercover assignment was simple enough: nail the crooked billionaire. The surprise came when she opened the folder, and the target was her one-time high school sweetheart. What will happen when an unknown foe makes a move to checkmate?

The Driven Billionaire – Available on Amazon

(Zachary and Brittney's story) Rule number one: hands off your best friend's sister. With nowhere to turn when she returns from upstate, she accepts his offer of a room. Mutual attraction quickly blurs the rules. When she comes under attack, pulling her closer is the only way to keep her safe. But, the truth of why she left town in the first place will threaten to destroy them both.

Join Erin's mailing list and be notified when new books are available.

Printed in Great Britain
by Amazon